THE MEANING OF DESPAIR

The

Meaning of

Despair

PSYCHOANALYTIC CONTRIBUTIONS
TO THE UNDERSTANDING
OF DEPRESSION

Edited by Willard Gaylin, M.D.

George H. Bercaw

Jason Aronson
New York

THE MEANING OF DESPAIR

LIBRARY OF CONGRESS CATALOG CARD NUMBER: 68–17262

Manufactured in the United States of America.

Acknowledgments and Copyright Notices

The editor and the publisher of this work wish to thank the following
authors and publishers for permission to use the materials noted:

HOEBER MEDICAL DIVISION, HARPER & ROW, PUBLISHERS, INCORPORATED;
Psychosomatic Medicine, Journal of the American Psychosomatic Society;
and SANDOR RADO: for "Psychodynamics of Depression from the Etiologic
Point of View," by Sandor Rado, from *Psychosomatic Medicine,* vol. 13,
no. 1 (Jan.–Feb., 1951), p. 51–55.

THE HOGARTH PRESS LTD., London, and the EXECUTORS OF KARL ABRAHAM:
for "Notes on the Psycho-Analytical Investigation and Treatment of
Manic-Depressive Insanity and Allied Conditions," by Karl Abraham,
from *Selected Papers of Karl Abraham,* 1948, pp. 137–156; and BASIC
BOOKS, INC. for the same article appearing as Chapter VI ("Notes on the
Psycho-Analytical Investigation and Treatment of Manic-Depressive In-
sanity and Allied Conditions") in *Selected Papers of Karl Abraham,*
Basic Books, Inc., Publishers, New York, 1953.

THE HOGARTH PRESS LTD., London, and MELANIE KLEIN TRUSTEES: for "A
Contribution to the Psychogenesis of Manic-Depressive States," by Me-
lanie Klein, from *Contributions to Psychoanalysis, 1921–1945,* by Melanie
Klein, pp. 228–310.

International Journal of Psycho-Analysis, London, and JOHN BOWLBY: for
"Process of Mourning," by John Bowlby, in *International Journal of Psycho-
Analysis,* XLII (1961), 317–340.

International Journal of Psycho-Analysis, London, and SANDOR RADO: for
"The Problem of Melancholia," by Sandor Rado, in *International Journal
of Psycho-Analysis,* 9 (1928), 420–438.

INTERNATIONAL UNIVERSITIES PRESS, INC., New York, and the authors named: for "The Mechanism of Depression," by Edward Bibring, in *Affective Disorders*, 1953, pp. 14–47; for "Anaclitic Depression," by René Spitz, in *Psychoanalytic Study of the Child*, edited by Phyllis Greenacre, 1946, II, 313–342; and for "Transference Problems in the Psychoanalytic Treatment of Severely Depressive Patients," by Edith Jacobson, in *Journal of the American Psychoanalytic Association*, 2 (1954), 595–606.

W. W. NORTON & COMPANY, INC., New York: for "Depression and Mania," by Otto Fenichel, reprinted from *The Psychoanalytic Theory of Neurosis*, by Otto Fenichel, M.D. By permission of W. W. Norton & Company, Inc. Copyright 1945 by W. W. Norton & Company, Inc.

The Psychoanalytic Quarterly and SIDNEY LEVIN: for "Some Suggestions for Treating the Depressed Patient," by Sidney Levin, in *The Psychoanalytic Quarterly*, XXXIV (1965), 37–65.

The Psychoanalytic Review and SANDOR LORAND: for "Dynamics and Therapy of Depressive States," by Sandor Lorand, in *The Psychoanalytic Review*, vol. 24, no. 4 (1937), 337–349.

SIGMUND FREUD COPYRIGHTS LTD.; ESTATE OF MR. JAMES STRACHEY; and THE HOGARTH PRESS LTD., London, for "Mourning and Melancholia," by Sigmund Freud, from Volume XIV, Standard Edition of *Complete Psychological Works of Sigmund Freud*, pp. 243–258; and BASIC BOOKS, INC. for the same work appearing as Chapter VIII ("Mourning and Melancholia") in *The Collected Papers of Sigmund Freud*, edited by Ernest Jones, Basic Books, Inc., Publishers, New York, 1959.

Preface

Like it or not, psychoanalysis is here to stay. By that I do not mean the practice of psychoanalysis as it may exist at this particular moment (for the practice is in a constant state of flux)—but the *influence* of psychoanalysis. It is a testament to that influence that even its most militant critics now utilize the concepts of psychoanalysis while attacking it. Just as the most unlettered man speaking English will use the language of Shakespeare, whether he acknowledges it or not, so today the "language" of psychiatry is permeated with Freudian concepts.

In evaluating the worth and validity of psychoanalysis, one must first decide which psychoanalysis is being discussed. The term is used to describe three things: (1) a treatment technique for emotional problems, (2) an investigative and exploratory *method* applicable to history, esthetics, cultural institutions, etc., (3) a body of thought defining human behavior and emotions, i.e. a psychology.

The first—the treatment technique—is admittedly a limited procedure that at best is frightfully expensive, time-consuming, exhaustively demanding on both physician and patient, and applicable to only a small percentage of patients with emotional problems. But, where applicable, it is capable of the most ambitious modifications of personal adjustment. Equally as important, there is not a major psychotherapy today that is not built on modifications of its techniques. It transformed psychiatry from a nosological discipline to a therapy-oriented specialty.

The second—the investigative tool—is both the most infuriating and the most promising. Infuriating because it has so frequently been applied with such glibness and slickness to "illuminate" works of art, cultural institutions, historic figures, etc. In the early days it was, of necessity, experimental. Some of the results seem wild and less than wondrous today—but then so does nineteenth-century pharmacology. That this kind of way-out assay should be made fifty years later is of course inexcusable. It is, unfortunately, the way-out, the unconventional, that attracts attention. For every individual who may be familiar with Ernst Kris's brilliantly measured essays on art, there are dozens who are more familiar with the "psychiatric survey" on Barry Goldwater. In addition, the serious psychoanalyst has usually shunned (not wisely so) the public exposure of radio and television, so that the "pop-offs" have become wrongly identified by lay people as the leaders of psychoanalysis. The typical intellectual would be unfamiliar with at least half the authors in this book.

Still, with all the past abuse, this investigative aspect is the area of greatest potential for psychoanalysis. If its insights and methods can be intelligently applied to social problems and institutions, its service to humanity will multiply well beyond that which it offers as a psychotherapy.

But that is in the future, and it is in its third definition that psychoanalysis has made its great contribution to the present—as a psychology; as a method of interpreting and understanding the modes and mechanisms of human behavior and human feeling, normal and abnormal. It is here, too, that psychoanalysis has been poorly understood, both by lay people *and* by general psychiatrists. Too often there has been a confusion in the minds of the critics as to what is basic and fundamental in psychoanalysis and what is peripheral and elaborative. The basic concepts have been so generally accepted that, ironically, they are no longer credited as being specifically "analytic." The peripheral concepts are most often more speculative and more changeable. In attacking and dismissing them, one is not dismissing the basic field of psychoanalysis.

What then were the basic contributions of Freud upon which most of modern psychology was built? First and foremost, of course, would be a psychological orientation to the etiology of the various mental diseases. It was the great, and at that time shocking, thesis of Breuer and Freud in their *Studies in Hysteria* that the hysteric was essentially suffering from an idea. Later much elaboration would be made on this—the kind of idea, a wish, a sexual wish, an infantile sexual wish, a repressed infantile sexual wish, etc. Basically, however, the importance is the focusing of attention on ideas and feelings.

The second major contribution would be the idea of the unconscious. Again, psychoanalysis is still in the process of defining the unconscious, but there is almost universal acceptance of the basic principle. Man's behavior is influenced by thoughts and feelings of which even he may be unaware.

Freud's third basic contribution would be the psychodynamic principle. This, briefly put, emphasizes that any piece of behavior is the resultant of forces and counterforces.

The behavior can never be understood as a thing in itself, but rather as a compromise among influences. More than any other basic principle, this concept paves the way to a treatment that is psychological—a psychotherapy. If the purpose is to modify behavior, and behavior is only the balance of many forces and counterforces, it may be necessary only to modify some of these forces to effect a change. This, in essence, is the assumption underlying almost any psychotherapy.

Fourth, and following closely on the principle of psychodynamics, is the idea of psychic determinism. Many psychoanalysts have bitterly struggled against what to them personally may seem the objectionable concept of a deterministic philosophy. Nonetheless, it is of the essence of psychoanalysis that a piece of behavior is the logical and inevitable end product of a group and sequence of behavior preceding it. Psychic determinism has driven the psychoanalyst into the patient's past in order to understand the present, and as such has been a major impetus in the development of research in normal development.

Fifth, and perhaps a summary of all four previous items, is the concept of the meaning of symptoms. A psychological symptom is seen not as an accidental or chance phenomenon, but as an expression having meaning to the patient in terms of coping, problem-solving, resolution of conflict, or whatever language one's orientation may prefer. Basically, it goes back to Freud's original idea of a defense neurosis. The symptom therefore is seen not as the problem, but as the attempt to solve the problem.

Obviously, this brief listing of some basic concepts of Freudian psychology does not do justice to the subject. That cannot be the purpose here, and many books are available on basic psychology. The reason that it is emphasized at all here is to suggest the framework on which modern-day psychoanalysis has been built. Oedipus complex, penis envy, castration anxiety, death instinct, psychic energy—all of these are concepts of relative importance, accepted by some and denied by others. But they are all part of the evolving definitions and elaboration of psychoanalysis. To dismiss any one of these concepts is not to dismiss psychoanalysis. In great part the purpose of this book is to demonstrate that psychoanalysis is a constantly changing, always diversified, body of thought. New ideas are developed and incorporated into old schemes or substituted for old schemes. Argument flourishes; unanimity never exists. It is the richness of the basic Freudian concepts that permits this diversity and forms a logical link even between wildly antagonistic theories.

Too often critics have talked of psychoanalysis as though it were some monolithic structure handed down, like the tablets of the law on Mount Sinai, in fixed and immutable form. In dismissing "the" explanation of psychoanalysis on any subject, the analytically unsophisticated psychiatrist may really be dismissing only "an" explanation or, even worse, an abandoned explanation. There is thus danger that he will reject in its entirety the psychoanalytic literature.

This is complicated by yet another difficulty. The psychoanalytic literature is primarily written for other pschoanalysts. As such, much of the literature is directed to the fine points and subtleties that intrigue the superspecialist. Those who are not psychoanalysts but are interested in dynamic psychiatry must not be put off by the often tendentious internal bickering that abounds within the field. Beyond this hyperspecialization, beyond some of the excessively technical language, will be found a viability of ideas in the psychoanalytic literature that can have great usefulness and adaptability to any laborer in the field of behavior. It is to demonstrate this viability, and variability, and to facilitate an understanding of one of the major clinical problems in psychiatry, that this book on depression is presented.

Contents

Epilogue

THE MEANING OF DESPAIR

The Meaning
of Despair

Depression holds an historic role in the development
of psychoanalytic thought. It was, in its way, responsible
for as much ambivalence, questioning of hypotheses and,
ultimately, revision of basic theory as were the traumatic
neuroses. And for much the same reason. Both of them
represented vast areas of unanswered and sometimes
seemingly unanswerable questions. They fall into that category of clinical phenomena (which would also include
nightmares and repetitive painful activity) that has baffled
psychiatrists because of the perversely nonadaptive, or at
least maladaptive, quality. Why should someone opt for
painful behavior? Why should someone cling to self-
recrimination, self-reproach, misery, and unhappiness? Almost every behavioral theory assumes the hedonic principle: It is "unnatural" for someone to embrace pain rather
than pleasure. But particularly because of the apparent
paradox, this type of behavior has forced theoreticians
over the years to reexamine and reevaluate extant theories,
and has prevented any static fixity of theory on the basis of
early authoritarian statements.

Depression is also of extreme interest because it was
the first clinical entity explained by Freud wherein an

emotion was seen as the central and focal etiological factor in the disease. This is not to say that Freud had not used emotion in talking about other diseases. However, it is in depression that an emotion, rather than a sexual wish, is first presented as the critical factor—that is, something gone wrong in the emotional system of the individual causes a neurosis. It is not just chance, therefore, that Sandor Rado, who eventually founded a theory of the neuroses based on emotion and emotional controls, first started his investigative work in depression.

The Basic Theory

ABRAHAM, FREUD, RADO. The first paper presented is by Karl Abraham, that modest and most undervalued first German psychoanalyst. This is the original psychoanalytic theory of depression. It is one of the few clinical entities (and this is in itself of interest) where the basic theory was not conceived by Freud. Freud acknowledged another man's contribution as the cornerstone on which he would elaborate his own theories.

Abraham made the comparison between grief and melancholy that became the crucial analogy that was to dominate thinkers in this field for some forty years. He started with the assumption that grief over loss of a loved object was an essentially normal phenomenon. Obviously, there is a relation between melancholy—that is, depression —and grief. The melancholic and the mourner look alike, they are sufferers, their reactions are in many ways similar. Yet mourning is assumed to be a normal phenomenon of human behavior. One does not think in terms of sending an

individual to a psychiatrist because he is crying or mourning the death of a loved one. But melancholy seems to be
grief gone haywire—extended, excessive, often unpreci-
pitated and seemingly unwarranted.

Abraham exploited the comparison between grief and
melancholy to explain the reason for melancholy. He said
that, while both represent the response to a loss, in melancholy there is an unconscious hostility at play, demonstrated
in the marked ambivalence of the melancholic. Abraham was
therefore stating (and this was a unique etiological explanation for his time) that the distinction between melancholy
and mourning is the presence of anger, here worded "unconscious hostility." The individual is likely to pass over
the bounds of normal mourning (grief) into abnormal
melancholia (depression) when his reaction to the lost
love is charged with anger (rage, unconscious hostility) as
well as love.

This brilliant and deceptively simple insight, based
on sharp clinical observation, is characteristic of the thinking
of Abraham. To this day a reading of Abraham in any subject
will reward the reader with sensitive and sensible perceptions. It is therefore a particular tragedy that so much of his
intelligence was dissipated by an unfortunate selection of
research interest—the problem of symptom choice. It is no
reflection on Abraham's ability that he was incapable of
solving this. To this day none of us can really say with any
great authority why an individual exhibits any symptom over
another. We can often "explain" a symptom, and explain it
with great accuracy in terms of the psychodynamic patterns
that went into it, but we know that we have seen similar psychodynamic patterns leading to different symptom solutions.
Abraham, like the early workers in cancer research, un-

fortunately chose to dedicate his life to what yet remains an unsolved problem.

Abraham started his theoretical work in the enthusiastic early days of the libido theory, when it was thought that all symptoms could be explained in terms of fixation points. Freud had related neurotic and normal behavior via the instrument of the developing sexual instinct. The child passes through various primitive early stages in his sexual development—oral, anal, phallic—before he achieves a unified adult sexual drive. For various constitutional or traumatic reasons any individual may retain a special interest or investment in an earlier phase. This is referred to as a fixation point. If in adult life a conflict obstructs normal libidinal outflow, there may occur a regression to this earlier point of sexual interest. Neurosis was explained in terms of the revival of this infantile sexuality and the defenses against it. Abraham therefore attempted to explain depression in terms of fixation.

Originally he saw depression as a function of anal fixation. Why? How *could* he have thought of it in terms of anality? If there is one fact that stands out to anyone who has seen a depressive patient it is the oral aspect. It is so obvious that there is hardly a theory of depression that does not in some way emphasize orality. However, the presence of hostility was the key dynamic in Abraham's explanation of depression. And at that time the libido theory offered only one explanation for hostility—anal sadism. Ergo, the explanation for depression had to be anal fixation. In addition, one could not explain two disparate phenomena with the same fixation, and orality was reserved for the more primitive diseases such as schizophrenia.

But Abraham was no fool and, like many men of his day, he was a great clinical observer. Thus, the oral aspect was obvious to him. This resulted in a reevaluation of the whole schema of fixation, which in turn led to the creation of a new developmental stage—the oral-sadistic phase. This is what Abraham explains in his paper. Hostility in depression is viewed in terms of the cannibalistic characteristic of the newly coined oral-sadistic phase of libido development. It is from this point that Freud built his theory in the paper *Mourning and Melancholia,* published in 1917.

Freud starts with Abraham's theory intact. He, too, stresses the relation between mourning and melancholia, and he sees both as a reaction to the loss of a loved object. He makes the distinction here that mourning is always in relation to a consciously perceived, realistically lost object; but melancholia, while it may be in relation to a similar object, is more frequently in relation to an unconsciously perceived, imagined loss of an object.

Mourning and melancholia share certain phenomena: (1) deflation of mood—in Freud's terms, painful dejection; (2) withdrawal of interest in the outside world; (3) inhibition of activity, and (4) loss of capacity to love. In addition, melancholia shows certain other features: (1) deflation of self-esteem; (2) self-accusation, and (3) delusional need for self-punishment. These extremely accurate clinical observations have withstood the test of time.

Freud then elaborates a theoretical system to explain all of the clinical features unique to the melancholic. First there is the loss of a loved object, real or imagined. This is followed by withdrawal of libido from the object; that is, all of the cathexis (sexual interest and energy) that was invested in this object is withdrawn from it as part of the separation phenomena. The rumination about the lost love is seen as the process of decathection, withdrawing the investment of sexual energy from the symbol of the loved one. Next, the ego is enraged with this object for leaving it. (Here again one sees Freud's debt to Abraham. Most theories from this point forward will cite rage as a critical determinant in the development of depression.) The presence or absence of rage is thus focal to this theory, too, in distinguishing between sick and healthy development (melancholia or mere mourning). With the anger there is a regression of part of the ego to an oral-sadistic level. At the same time, the ego is ambivalent and refuses to accept this loss of the loved object. The ego then splits and part regresses to an oral-receptive level. Then follows an introjection (swallowing up) of the object by the ego, and the ego then identifies with the now introjected object.

This process of introjecting an object for purposes of identification, termed narcissistic identification, has become an extremely important mechanism in psychoanalysis. Narcissistic identification is a peculiar form of relatedness. It is somewhere halfway between object love (love of another) and autoerotism. It has the trappings of self-love in that the cathexes seem to be in the self, and yet the cathexes are still invested in an object. However, now the object has been incorporated and is within the self. It is then identified with the self. This is not as primitive as paranoia, where the cathexis is indeed in the ego of the self. The libido that is withdrawn from the cathected objects in the paranoid or schizophrenic patient is reinvested in his own ego, creating a state called secondary narcissism, which simulates the primary narcissism of the newborn infant. Narcissistic identification is not that regressive, not that primitive. There is still an object if you will, but the object is within—fused and confused with one's self. This is that primitive halfway house between autoerotism (self-love), in which there is no external cathexis (either the self or part of the self being cathected), and object love.

After the introjection and identification of the object by the ego, the libido is reattached to the identified object (now equated with the ego). The sadistic part of the ego then attacks the object, now fused with the receptive part of the ego, for having left it. Consciously this is perceived as "a conflict between one part of the ego and its self-criticizing faculty" (a rudimentary anticipation of the yet-to-be developed concept of super-ego). This results in a deflation of the self-esteem, self-accusation, and need for self-punishment. The peculiar self-destructive and self-punishing behavior of the depressed patient is thus seen as an attempt to punish the abandoning love figure.

Freud's major modifications of Abraham's theory revolve around the concepts of introjection and incorporation. Introjection of a parent and parental standards as a means towards self-punishment, self-berating, and guilt eventually becomes elaborated by Freud into the concept of the super-ego. Freud's paper on depression has, therefore, an influence that extends well beyond the borders of the clinical entity discussed. Introjection becomes the vehicle by which conscience mechanisms are introduced into Freudian theories of normal development. And even in the restricted field of depression, it will be seen how introducing super-ego considerations (here still in the limited form of the ego ideal) will pave the way for a purely adaptational ego analysis of depression.

Abraham continued over the years to devote considerable thought to depression, being somewhat unhappy with his first theory. Because he was so involved with explaining neurosis purely in terms of vicissitudes of the sexual instinct, (feeling that, if only one could elaborate with scientific accuracy the true fixation points, one could define a specificity concerning symptom choice) his later explanations remained purely in id terms. As a result they were less progressive than Freud's early ideas. However, Abraham's four modifications to his original theory were extremely significant in their indirect influence. He said that: (1) There is an oral predisposition (this concept will be seen in the selection from Bibring). (2) There is an early injury due to narcissism (an infantile disappointment). (3) The disappointment occurs before the Oedipal complex is resolved. (4) There is a repetition of this disappointment later in life which reactivates the predisposing primary condition.

Here one sees that Abraham is in conformity with the general "two-step" theory of neurosis that Freud had popularized at this time; that is, the proposition that an infantile neurosis leaves the adult in a labile but essentially nonneurotic state. Such an adult is vulnerable to any traumatic occurrence that could reactivate his poorly resolved infantile neurosis.

Abraham, however, did more than perhaps he even imagined. The effect of introducing the prerequisites of an early injury due to narcissism and an oral predisposition is to reduce the role of the "loss of a loved object" (even though he does not so state it) to that of a precipitating stress. Many people will lose a loved object; only some will go into depression. Those who go into depression will be those who have an early narcissistic injury and an oral predisposition. In modern terms, he is saying that those who become depressed are essentially dependent people with certain basic defects in their self-esteem and self-pride system.

The classical psychoanalytic position on depression was brought to full form with the publication of Sandor Rado's 1928 paper. And what a paper that is! Fresh, concise, logical, ordered, and polished to brilliance, it epitomizes the author. This paper, forty years old, could have been written forty days ago.

Rado was, preeminently, a great teacher. The written word cannot convey the personal impact of this creative and provocative man. His paper suggests capacity for synthesizing the ideas of others and adding fresh emphasis, all with a clarity that obviates the need for much discussion. It is interesting that even in this early work when Rado was involved with the classical frame of reference (using purely the language of libido and id psychology) his definitions and his explanations were ego-oriented. It could be said that Rado was an ego analyst even before he was aware of it.

Three major foci are apparent in his theory. First is the emphasis on self-love and self-regard. Persons are predisposed to depression who have an intense craving for narcissistic gratification, an intense need to be loved and approved. (Here one clearly sees his debt to Abraham who, incidentally, was his analyst.) The second point of emphasis is on the emotions. Rage is placed in the forefront, and alongside it is a new respect for the significance of guilt.

It should be noted that this paper was written after Freud had defined the role of the super-ego. Every individual contains within him an incorporated parent—in the structure of the super-ego. The instrument for self-punishment is already available without the need for introjecting the lost love. Rado then explains the self-abusive behavior as the super-ego berating the ego. One can already see a reduction in the role of identification and cathexis, for this fundamental group of symptoms in depression is now explained as essentially a conscience mechanism.

Why does the ego endure it? Because of the sense of guilt arising from its original response to the loss, i.e. coercive rage. Self-punishment is seen as a way of winning love. It is an expiatory act. A plea for forgiveness for the attack of rage. This concept of expiation is the third significant feature of this paper. "That which could not be accomplished by rebellion, it now tries to achieve by remorseful self-punishment and expiation." "Guilt-atonement-forgiveness" is now seen as a key dynamic in depression.

With these significant alterations in classical theory, Rado had laid the groundwork for a much more radical departure from classical Freudian theory to follow.

The Theory Modified

RADO (1950), FENICHEL, BIBRING, KLEIN. Sandor Rado has been a student of depression all his life. As his basic psychological views altered, his concept of depression was naturally brought into line. And it is well known that his views altered considerably. This most articulate enunciator of classical Freudian theory was to become one of its most incisive and implacable critics.

When he broke with classical theory he abandoned most of its language, and all of its economics (energics). Introjection and narcissism, fundamental concepts in the early theory, had to be abandoned. In his "adaptational" dynamics Rado sees all neurotic behavior as products of misguided reparative maneuvers. The focal dynamic is no longer the vicissitudes of the libido but the emergency response mechanisms of the organism, specifically the emergency emotions of fear and rage. The neuroses are the result of emotional overreaction and the conflict of emotions becomes the central conflict. The essence of a purely adaptational analysis of depression was already extant in his first theory, so that most of the basic observations in the earlier work could be retained.

Rado says that depression is, in essence, an unconscious cry for love precipitated by an actual or imagined loss. Moreover, *the patient feels that the loss endangers his security.* Although Rado does not specifically state it, it is implied that only when the imagined loss is somehow or other linked to the security mechanism of the individual will one become depressed.

The overreaction that made depression a neurosis was an expiatory process of self-punishment. He punishes himself to reconcile himself with the mother. Nonetheless, he is still resentful of the deprivation by the mother. Resentment leads to coercive rage, which in cyclic fashion will generate more guilt and then more self-punishment for expiatory purposes. The guilt ultimately defeats the rage, which is then turned back on the self, further augmenting the self-abasement. This concept of retroflexed rage is, incidentally, one of the very earliest concepts of Freud which Rado borrows and elaborates. What we then see is an individual dominated by pure emotions—guilt, fear, and coercive rage. The self-punitive behavior so manifestly a part of clinical depression is now seen as indeed *self*-punitive. In Freudian theory the self-punishment is only an accidental and incidental result of the attack on the internalized mother.

The ambivalence found in depressed patients is now explained by the conflict between the coercive rage and the submissive fear. The usual pattern sees the coercive rage followed by a mood of gloomy repentance. This results in a regressive yearning for the alimentary security of the infant, which is why submissive fear eventually must defeat the coercive rage.

Since Rado no longer utilizes the concept of introjection and narcissistic identification, how can he explain the oral incorporative and cannibalistic elements so commonly features in the dreams of the depressed? He sees this cannibalism as a means of destroying the frustrating mother and, in so doing, using her for the food she denies. In addition this clears the way for the good, feeding mother to appear. The cannibalistic fantasy is now destroying for purposes of survival rather than retaining for purposes of love—an ingenious and fundamental alternative.

So far the one feature common to all the theories of depression presented has been the implicit equation of grief and melancholy. It was this analogy that dictated the central role of the "lost love object" in the etiology of depression. Unfortunately, theoretical brilliance is not always congruent with validity. There are numerous examples in medicine where a wrong theory has been perpetuated far beyond its reasonable alue because of the intellectual elegance of its conception and the esteem of its author.

Obviously, clinical experience indicated that depression was not always initiated by the loss of a loved object. Rather than carefully examining the other initiating factors to test for an alternative hypothesis, it was assumed that the seeming alternative precipitants must be merely symbolic representations of the lost love.

In my first dealings with depressed patients, I was

impressed that not one of the suicidal patients I examined
made attempts because of the breakup of a love affair. It
began to seem strange that people responded preponderantly
more to the representation of the fact than to the fact itself.
In retrospect the bias became obvious. In those early days
I was in a veteran's hospital and saw only male patients.
When I began to see women patients I observed that indeed
many of them became depressed when they were rejected
or abandoned in love. But what causes a man to become depressed? Almost invariably, it is a sense of personal failure,
usually in a career or financial matter. He has failed. He has
been fired from a job; he has been socially humiliated. A feeling of impotence and uselessness dominates his mood. I
began to think that at least in men the reverse of what Freud
had said might be true—that the love object, when it is a
precipitant, must really be a symbol of something more basic.
Later on I read the following, written not by a psychiatrist
but by a philosopher. In his essay *The Sickness Unto Death*,
Kierkegaard says:

Despair is never ultimately over the external object but always over ourselves. A girl loses her sweetheart and she despairs.
It is not over the lost sweetheart, but over herself-without-the-
sweetheart. And so it is with all cases of loss whether it be money,
power, or social rank. The unbearable loss is not really in itself
unbearable. What we cannot bear is in being stripped of the
external object. We stand denuded and see the intolerable abyss
of ourselves.

This was years before Freud. I think this is a quotation
of rare insight and truth. Fenichel comes surprisingly close
to saying the same thing.

Otto Fenichel was the author of the standard textbook
in psychoanalysis. To say this, however, is like describing

Tolstoy as a writer of popular Russian novels. The book is staggering in its erudition, obsessively complete in the variety of its considerations, with a tenacious capacity to seem up-to-date. For years I visualized its author as a venerable early pioneer in the field—under the assumption, I suppose, that the prodigious knowledge demonstrated could not have been assembled in less than seventy or eighty years. When I learned that he died in 1946 (while struggling through an internship in Los Angeles) at the age of 48, it seemed, and still seems, inconceivable.

Fenichel basically explains depression in terms of oral fixation, introjection, and so on, but he offers suggestions for a purely adaptational understanding. The amazing thing about Fenichel is the fertility of his imagination and the clarity of his vision. The number of original ideas and conceptions first suggested by him is astounding. He did not fully credit nor develop them himself because of his devotion to classical theory, with its emphasis on libido, id, and instinctual energy. Only when a rationale for pure ego psychology consistent with early Freudian theory was supplied to classic analysis by the writings of Kris, Lowenstein, and Hartmann, did one begin to see a revision of basic theories explaining neuroses in purely ego (adaptational) terms, such as Bibring did in his paper on depression.

Fenichel, however, clearly understood the critical importance of the relation between depression and self-esteem. He states that depression is a means of avoiding total dissipation of self-esteem. He also states that the precipitating experience in a depressed patient is either a loss of self-esteem or a loss of the supplies which would secure or even enhance the self-esteem. (One learns when reading Fenichel to adjust to certain patterns of expression. Whenever his

brilliant perceptions bring him into conflict with conserva-
tive theory, he minimizes the new observation by labeling
it "precipitating" as distinguished from fundamental or etiologic. Whenever he offers a new "precipitating stress" I
look for a possible new theory.) Here is the first basic theoretical shift in psychoanalytic literature (going further even
than Rado) from primary emphasis on the lost love object to
emphasis on the lost self-esteem.

The implications are clear, even if Fenichel does not
follow through. It is not essentially the loss of the love object
or its symbolic counterparts that causes depression. Indeed,
only when a loved object is invested with our self-esteem
does its loss produce a depression. What we are mourning is
our lost self-esteem, the love object merely being *symbolic
of it*. By extension, any loss of self-esteem or any symbol
of it should produce a depression. If a man is depressed over
the loss of a job, it is not because the job symbolizes a loved
object but, like a loved object, it can symbolize one's self-
esteem.

The loss of the loved object is then the instrument for
depression in those dependent people who perceive (even
if inaccurately) that particular loved object as the essential
instrument for survival. This is why women more frequently
than men go into depression over loss of a loved one. In
our culture security is invested in the male role. In her loss
a woman loses not only love but her survival mechanisms.
A woman asks how she is going to live, to educate her children, and so forth. In addition, a man is the major prestige
source for a woman—it is her husband's position that is often
her vicarious pride. On the other hand, a man's pride, masculinity, and self-confidence are based primarily on his professional career and personal attainments. More men jump

out of a window because of the loss of a business than because of the loss of a child. Why? Not because they love
their children less, but because in losing their businesses
they lose security, prestige, self-pride, and ultimately faith
and trust in themselves.

The early theorists, in comparing grief and depression,
observed that some mourners went on to depression and
related all melancholia to a lost love. If no loss occurred,
an imagined or symbolic one was assumed. If Abraham had
asked himself why most mourners do *not* go into depression,
he might have concluded that where depression does occur,
the loved one is a symbol and a vehicle for a more basic loss.

Fenichel has said:

Patients who react to disappointment in love with severe depressions are always persons to whom the love experience
meant not only sexual gratification but narcissistic gratification as
well. With their love they lose their very existence.

In stating this he shifts the emphasis from id to ego, from
sex to survival.

He does not, as did Rado, abandon the basic concept
of introjection as the pathognomonic feature in depression,
but postulates a specific utilization:

The oral sadistic introjection of the object whose love is wanted
as a narcissistic supply is the match that explodes the powder of
the dammed up narcissistic need.

With this statement the basis for depression is still the introjection of a loved object (in conformity with accepted
theory), but the difference lies in the purpose of introjection.
The purpose here is not retention of love, not libido cathexis
or discharge, but a source of "narcissistic supply." This match
explodes the powder of the dammed up *narcissistic*, not

sexual, need. Narcissistic need, as used here, means essentially ego drive, the drive for survival.

Although he comes to a new breakthrough in the understanding of depression with his elevation of the role of self-esteem, Fenichel ultimately falls back on an instinctual explanation. In general, when it came to summarizing his theories he was perhaps not venturesome enough, too respectful of the views of others, too modest in his self-appraisal. This is why Fenichel, for all his brilliance and imagination, is esteemed as a pedant rather than a pioneer—as a writer of textbooks rather than treatises. He abounded in intriguing new ideas, but lacked that special assurance (or vanity) of the creative person that would have permitted his presentation of a radically new theory without apology. It remained for others to borrow, expand, or rediscover many of Fenichel's concepts.

The groundwork had been well laid and it was Bibring who in classical analysis first chose to explain depression purely in terms of ego psychology. In the peculiar terminology of the ego psychologists who retain a libido frame of reference, he says it is the function of the ego fixated at oral-defense mechanisms. (The new ego psychologists, faced with attempting to explain neuroses in terms of adaptation without completely abandoning the earlier models, have evolved a whole new language based on tracing development in terms of the ego-instinct or ego-interest. This parallel with libido development is often clumsy and never completely successful.) After saying this, he goes on to say, in simpler, more meaningful terms:

Depression can be defined as the emotional expression (indication) of the state of helplessness and powerlessness of the ego, irrespective of what may have caused the break-down of the mechanism which established his self-esteem.

In a depressed patient, Bibring adds, certain narcissistic goals are maintained, and it is precisely the contrast of these goals with the ego's feeling or awareness of his helplessness to achieve them which produces depression. It is this exaggerated disparity which destroys one's confidence. The goals are: (1) a wish to be worthy and loved; (2) a wish to be strong and superior, and (3) a wish to be good and loving.

The first and third are often seen as identical phenomena. They are not, and I am glad that Bibring distinguishes them. It is the cynicism of our time that sees all loving and giving only in terms of wishing for reciprocity. The truth may be quite the contrary. It is indeed "better to give than to receive" because, whereas receiving *is* pleasurable and satisfies certain needs, it *does* place one in the position of being a recipient or dependent with the potential for ego diminution implicit in that position. By contrast, there is extra joy in giving because of the sense of one's self as a giver. This is ego-enhancing.

Under this system Bibring concludes that depression is not determined by a conflict between one's id and the ego. Nor is it determined by a conflict between the super-ego and the id or the environment. Rather, it stems primarily from within the ego itself, from an inner-system conflict.

Can there be a totally internalized conflict when speaking of the ego? Can there be a deflation of self-esteem without the interplay of an environment? I am not so sure. Is not success or failure essentially an environmentally determined phenomenon? After all, success and failure are not inborn, basic concepts. They are not even absolutes. The environment defines what success is, or failure. Thus I simply cannot conceive of an ego conflict that excludes both super-ego and environmental considerations. What may be deceptive is that the individual is reacting to his personal, distorted perception of the environment. In Erikson's terms he is responding to reality, not to actuality, by imposing on the current situation the circumstances of a previous time.

Again, the problem is in attempting to utilize the models of an id psychology for an ego-oriented psychology. Freud could be very logical and consistent. In evolving the libido theory he was always logical and consistent, even if he may not always have been right. But even though the individual is assuredly born with drives or instincts, the adult ego as we know it is not inborn but evolves. If you could raise a human being in an environment in which stimuli were reduced to the least possible, it is questionable whether it would survive, let alone develop an ego as we know it. It has been shown in child development studies that deprivation of major environmental factors leads to extreme deficits in ego development. Depression must involve an interplay between the environment and the ego; the environment, or an internalized representation, cannot be ignored.

At any rate, Bibring goes on to compare and contrast depression and anxiety. He sees anxiety as a reaction to danger, indicating the ego's anxiety to survive. The ego prepares for fight or flight. In depression the opposite takes place. The ego is paralyzed because it is *incapable* of meeting the danger.

Bibring says in summary that fixation is not all. There is also the ego's shocking awareness of its helplessness with regard to or in relation to its aspiration.

Depression is here now defined as a basic reaction of the ego, in the same way that anxiety is considered a basic reaction of the ego independent of the vicissitudes of the instinct. And I think correctly so. Just as anxiety is no longer a product of repressed libido, depression is no longer a product of the complicated vicissitudes of the libido. It is an independent phenomenon. It is an ego reaction, and it is indeed true that anything that lowers self-esteem without changing the narcissistic aims predisposes to depression. On that basis it is easy to see why one of the most common predispositions to depression is the starting of an analysis. A patient still unconsciously bound to his grandiose plans can see analysis as a humiliating experience.

A second common stimulus to depression in the course of analysis comes with the removal of favorite illusions, the weakening of neurotic defenses. For example, the obsessive patient sees himself as accomplishing his narcissistic aims via his obsessive work habits, and when you challenge these, deglamorize them, or make them less acceptable, depression can occur.

One of the interesting things about Bibring's paper is that he does not invalidate the other theories which are centered on aggression and narcissistic supplies. He offers a more cohesive and articulate system. Everything that Rado said about aggression and ambivalence is consistent with this theory. The same is the case with the observations of Fenichel. Bibring puts them in a more logical relationship.

The progression of these authors may seem to imply a logical and lineal direction in the devolpment of psychoanalytic theory. Melanie Klein will quickly lay that misapprehension to rest. If for no other reason than this, her paper should be included. However, there are ample other reasons. She is imaginative, original, always provocative, and never dull. Unfortunately, her direction has been countercurrent and her influence in this country almost nil. By contrast, her impact in England, where she resided, has been enormous. It is intriguing to speculate how much of this may be the force and magnetism of the person in distinction to the ideas, which frequently happens. I recall hearing Abram Kardiner reminisce about the effect that the young and attractive Melanie Klein had on the small group of Freud's early students. It was very much the person, not the postulates, that lingered in the memory.

Her theories at first glance seem atavistic. (At times she can sound like a Calvinist preacher.) She eschews the language and orientation of the ego psychologists and returns to the basic format of id psychology, in which all neurosis stems from a regression to a fixation point. A fixation point, however, must represent an earlier normal stage of development. Klein therefore postulates a new stage of development, which she refers to as "positions." The position occurring in the second half of the first year of life is called the normal depressive position; the depressed patient is one who has regressed to this depressive position. The regression results because the ego is threatened by the aggression of its own id. This aggression is a function of the death instinct, which plays a significant role in all her theories.

This may seem a far cry from Bibring, but consider for a moment what she must mean by a normal depressive stage of development. In most prevalent theories, the newborn infant is presumed to have no awareness of environment. This early phase, called primary narcissism or magical omnipotence, is assumed to be dominated by the ego's implicit sense of its power. During the first year of life the baby learns to distinguish self from environment—and how the mighty do fall! For far from being all-powerful, most powerful, or even of limited power, the developing child becomes cognizant of his smallness, vulnerability, and dependence. His very survival rests on the largesse of others. The first six to twelve months of life can therefore be seen as a rapid dissipation of self-esteem and self-confidence. Certainly by twelve months the child must have an awareness of his own helplessness. It is this which Klein calls the normal depressive position. To say, then, that the depressed patient regresses to this fixation point is to place the emphasis precisely where Bibring does—on helplessness and lowered self-esteem. The clinical awareness is the same. Only the frame of reference suggests antithesis.

The Theory in Contemporary Practice and Research

SPITZ, BOWLBY, LORAND, JACOBSON, LEVIN₀ The papers of Spitz and Bowlby do not contain any startling new hypotheses or radical alterations of theory. They are included because both represent the modern psychoanalyst at his best, and both demonstrate how far psychoanalysis has come since the early days of Sigmund Freud when the paucity of clinical material demanded extensive extrapolation from limited material.

René Spitz demonstrates the productive reciprocity that occurs from studying normal development. Freud gained great insight into normal psychology and development through its magnification and distortion in neuroses. Spitz shows how new insights into adult neuroses can emanate from direct observation of the developing child. The child analyst has generally pioneered in expanding the research method in psychoanalysis. That great innovator of child analysis, David Levy, showed how direct observation and the objective measurements of data associated with clinical medicine could be fused with the traditional theoretical approaches of psychoanalysis. In that tradition, Spitz utilized institutionalized children as an accidental experimental population to consolidate many ideas about anxiety, separation, and depression.

Bowlby had the opportunity (and good sense) to examine the displaced child of wartime England. Again, an accidental (the only kind feasible) experimental population was utilized to great advantage. While technically dealing with mourning, he succinctly illuminates that which is essential to an understanding of depression. More important, he demonstrates the sophisticated analyst, sufficiently confident in the methods of his own field to feel free to use the methods and findings of other behavioral sciences. He draws on the works of ethologists, animal psychologists, and anthropologists. It is an eclecticism that holds promise for the future. Too long has the analyst been secluded in his study. The years of isolation were years of introspection and fruitful deduction about the inner man, but the study of the ego now requires a man in action—reacting, and interacting— and has drawn the psychoanalyst back into the larger environment.

This book concludes with three papers on the treatment of depression. The papers were selected not because they are definitive, but because they are representative. They demonstrate how three highly respected psychoanalysts apply the special knowledge accumulated about a disease to modify in their various ways the therapeutic approach to it. Perhaps in demonstrating this they will reassure some of those who have assumed psychoanalysis is an unbending and inflexible uniform method, and will banish the confusion between the couch of Freud and the bed of Procrustes.

BASIC THEORY

Notes on the Psycho-Analytical Investigation and Treatment of Manic-Depressive Insanity and Allied Conditions[1]

KARL ABRAHAM

Whereas states of morbid anxiety have been dealt with in detail in the literature of psycho-analysis, depressive states have hitherto received less attention. Nevertheless the affect of depression is as widely spread among all forms of neuroses and psychoses as is that of anxiety. The two affects are often present together or successively in one individual; so that a patient suffering from an anxiety-neurosis will be subject to

[1] See references in chapter notes at back of book.

states of mental depression, and a melancholic will complain of having anxiety.

One of the earliest results of Freud's investigation of the neuroses was the discovery that neurotic anxiety originated from sexual repression; and this origin served to differentiate it from ordinary fear. In the same way we can distinguish between the affect of sadness or grief and neurotic depression, the latter being unconsciously motivated and a consequence of repression.

Anxiety and depression are related to each other in the same way as are fear and grief. We fear a coming evil; we grieve over one that has occurred. A neurotic will be attacked with anxiety when his instinct strives for a gratification which repression prevents him from attaining; depression sets in when he has to give up his sexual aim without having obtained gratification. He feels himself unloved and incapable of loving, and therefore he despairs of his life and his future. This affect lasts until the cause of it ceases to operate, either through an actual change in his situation or through a psychological modification of the displeasurable ideas with which he is faced. Every neurotic state of depression, just like every anxiety-state, to which it is closely related, contains a tendency to deny life.

These remarks contain very little that is new to those who regard the neuroses from the Freudian point of view, although surprisingly little has been written in the literature of psycho-analysis concerning the psychology of neurotic depression. But the affect of depression in the sphere of the psychoses awaits more precise investigation. This task is complicated by the fact that a good part of the diseases in question run a "cyclical" course in which there is an alteration between melancholic and manic states. The few preliminary studies[2] which have hitherto been published have only dealt with one of these two phases at a time.

During the last few years I have met with six undoubted cases of this kind in my practice. Two of these were light manic-depressive cases (so-called cyclothymia), one of whom I treated only for a short time. The third, a female patient, suffered from short but rapidly recurring states of depression accompanied by typical melancholic symptoms. Two more had succumbed to a depressive psychosis for the first time, but had previously shown a tendency to slight changes of mood in a manic or depressive direction. The last patient had been overtaken by a severe and obstinate psychosis at the age of forty-five.

Most psychiatrists, following Kraepelin, do not consider states of depression as belonging to manic-depressive insanity if they come on after the patient's fortieth year. Nevertheless, as the analysis proceeded this last case disclosed such a marked similarity in its psychic structure to those cases which did undoubtedly belong to the manic-depressive insanities that I should certainly class it in that group. I do not, however, intend this as a statement of opinion concerning the line of demarcation between the two psychoses. And I do not wish to discuss states of depression occurring in dementia præcox.

Even in my first analysis of a depressive psychosis I was immediately struck by its structural similarity with an obsessional neurosis. In obsessional neurotics*—I refer to severe cases—the libido cannot develop in a normal manner, because two different tendencies—hatred and love—are always interfering with each other. The tendency such a

---

* The following brief description adheres closely to Freud's characterization in his paper, "Notes upon a Case of Obsessional Neurosis" (1909).

person has to adopt a hostile attitude towards the external world is so great that his capacity for love is reduced to a minimum. At the same time he is weakened and deprived of his energy through the repression of his hatred or, to be more correct, through repression of the originally over-strong sadistic component of his libido. There is a similar uncertainty in his choice of object as regards its sex. His inability to establish his libido in a definite position causes him to have a general feeling of uncertainty and leads to doubting mania. He is neither able to form a resolution nor to make a clear judgement; in every situation he suffers from feelings of inadequacy and stands helpless before the problems of life.

I will now give as briefly as possible the history of a case of cyclothymia as it appeared after a successful analysis had been made.

The patient remembered that his sexual instinct had shown itself very precociously—before he was in his sixth year—and had set in with great violence. His first sexual object at that time had been a governess whose presence had excited him. She still figured very vividly in his phantasies. His emotional excitement had led him to practise onanism, which he had done by lying on his stomach and making rubbing movements. He had been discovered doing this by his nurse (formerly his wet-nurse), who expressly forbade him to do it, and whipped him whenever he disobeyed her. She also impressed upon him the fact that he would suffer for it all his life. Later, when he was at school he had been attracted in an erotic way by a school-fellow for a period of several years.

In his childhood and later he had never felt satisfied at home. He always had the impression that his parents favoured his elder brother, who was unusually clever, while he had only an average intelligence. He also believed that his younger brother, who was delicate, received greater attention from his mother than he did. The result of this was that he had a hostile attitude towards his parents, and one of jealousy and hatred towards his brothers. The intensity of this hate can be seen from a couple of impulsive acts which he carried out in his childhood. On two occasions when quarrelling over trifles he had become very violent towards his younger brother, and had knocked him down and seriously hurt him. Such violence is particularly remarkable when we learn that at school he was always the smallest and weakest among his contemporaries. He never made any real companions, but generally kept to himself. He was industrious, but had little to show for it. At puberty it became evident that his sexual instinct, which at first had shown itself so strongly, had become paralysed through repression. In contrast to his attitude in childhood he did not feel attracted to the female sex. His sexual activity was the same that he had carried out in childhood; but he did not perform it in the waking state but only in his sleep or half-asleep. He had no friends. He was quite aware of his lack of real energy when he compared himself with others. He found no encouragement at home; on the contrary, his father used to say contemptuous things about him in his presence. Added to all these depressing factors he suffered a definite psychic trauma: a teacher had the brutality to call him a physical and mental cripple in front of the whole class. His first attack of depression appeared soon after this.

Even later on he made no companions. He kept away from them intentionally, too, because he was afraid of being thought an inferior sort of person. Children were the only human beings he got on well with and liked, because with them he did not have his usual feeling of inadequacy. His life was a solitary one. He was positively afraid of women. He was capable of normal sexual intercourse, but had no inclination for it and failed to obtain gratification from it. His onanistic practices in his sleep were his chief sexual activity even in later years. He showed little energy in practical life; it was always difficult for him to form a resolution or to come to a decision in difficult situations.

Up to this point the patient's history coincided in all its details with what we find in obsessional neurotics. Nevertheless, we do not find obsessional symptoms in him but a circular parathymia that had recurred many times during the last twenty years.

In his depressive phase the patient's frame of mind was "depressed" or "apathetic" (I reproduce his own words) according to the severity of his condition. He was inhibited, had to force himself to do the simplest things, and spoke slowly and softly. He wished he was dead, and entertained thoughts of suicide. His thoughts had a depressive content. He would often say to himself, "I am an outcast," "I am accursed," "I am branded," "I do not belong to the world." He had an indefinite feeling that his state of depression was a punishment. He felt non-existent and would often imagine himself disappearing from the world without leaving a trace. During these states of mind he suffered from exhaustion, anxiety and feelings of pressure in the head. The depressive phase generally lasted some weeks, though it was of shorter duration at times. The intensity of the depression varied in different attacks; he would have perhaps two or three marked states of melancholy and probably six or more slighter ones in the course of a year. His depression gradually increased during the course of an attack until it reached a certain height, where it remained for a time, and then gradually diminished. This process was conscious to him and perceptible to other people.

When the patient was about twenty-eight years old a condition of hypomania appeared, and this now alternated with his depressive attacks. At the commencement of this manic phase he would be roused out of his apathy and would become mentally active and gradually even over-active. He used to do a great deal, knew no fatigue, woke early in the morning, and concerned himself with plans connected with his career. He became enterprising and be-lieved himself capable of performing great things, was talkative and inclined to laugh and joke and make puns. He noticed himself that his thoughts had something volatile in them; a slight degree of "flight of ideas" could be ob-served. He spoke more quickly, more forcibly and louder than usual. His frame of mind was cheerful and a little elevated. At the height of his manic phase his euphoria tended to pass over into irritability and impulsive violence. If, for example, someone disturbed him in his work, or stepped in his way, or drove a motor-car quickly past him, he responded with a violent affect of anger and felt inclined to knock the offender down on the spot. While in this state he used often to become involved in real quarrels in which he behaved very unfeelingly. In the periods of depression he slept well but during the manic phase he was very restless, especially during the second half of the night. Nearly every night a sexual excitement used to overtake him with sudden violence.

Although his libido had appeared very early and with great force in his childhood, the patient had for the most part lost the capacity for loving or hating. He had become incapable of loving, in the same manner as the obsessional neurotic. Although he was not impotent, he did not obtain actual sexual enjoyment, and he used to get greater satisfaction from a pollution than coitus. His sexual activities were in the main restricted to his sleep. In this, like the neurotic, he showed an auto-erotic tendency to isolate himself from the external world. People of this kind can only enjoy pleasure in complete seclusion; every living being, every inanimate object, is a disturbing element. It is only when they have achieved the complete exclusion of every external impression—as in the case when they are asleep— that they can enjoy a gratification of their sexual wishes, by dreaming them. Our patient expressed this in the following words: "I feel happiest in bed; then I feel as though I were in my own house."*

At puberty in especial the patient was made aware that he was behind his companions of the same age in many important respects. He had never felt their equal physically. He had also been afraid of being inferior mentally, especially in comparison with his elder brother. And now the feeling of sexual inadequacy was added. It was precisely at this time that his teacher's criticism ("a mental and physical cripple") struck him like a blow. Its great effect was explained by the fact that it recalled to his memory the prophecy of his wet-nurse, when she had threatened him with lifelong unhappiness because of his masturbation. Just when he was entering upon manhood therefore, and ought to have

---

* I might remark that the other male patients whose depressive psychoses I was able to analyse behaved in the same way. None of them were impotent, but they had all derived more pleasure from auto-erotic behaviour all along, and to have any relations with women was a difficult and troublesome business for them.

had masculine feelings like his companions, his old feelings of inadequacy received a powerful reinforcement. It was in this connection that he had had the first state of depression he could recollect.

As we so often see in the obsessional neuroses, the outbreak of the real illness occurred when the patient had to make a final decision about his attitude towards the external world and the future application of his libido. In my other analyses a similar conflict had brought on the first state of depression. For example, one of my patients had become engaged to be married; soon afterwards a feeling of incapacity to love overcame him, and he fell into a severe melancholic depression.

In every one of these cases it could be discovered that the disease proceeded from an attitude of hate which was paralysing the patient's capacity to love. As in the obsessional neuroses, other conflicts in the instinctual life of the patients as well can be shown to be factors in the psychogenesis of the illness. I should like to mention especially the patient's uncertainty as to his sexual rôle in this connection. In Maeder's case[3] a conflict of this kind between a male and female attitude was particularly pronounced; and in two of my patients I found a condition surprisingly similar to that described by him.

In their further development, however, the two diseases diverge from each other. The obsessional neurosis creates substitutive aims in place of the original unattainable sexual aims; and the symptoms of mental compulsion are connected with the carrying out of such substitutive aims. The development of the depressive psychoses is different. In this case repression is followed by a process of "projection" with which we are familiar from our knowledge of the psychogenesis of certain mental disturbances.

In his *Psycho-Analytic Notes upon an Autobiographical Account of a Case of Paranoia (Dementia Paranoides)*, Freud gives a definite formulation of the psychogenesis of paranoia. He sets out in short formulæ the stages which lead up to the final construction of the paranoic delusion. I will here attempt to give a similar formulation of the genesis of the depressive psychoses, on the basis of my analyses of depressive mental disturbances.

Freud considers that in a large portion at least of cases of paranoic delusions the nucleus of the conflict lies in homosexual wish-phantasies, i.e., in the patient's love of a person of the same sex. The formula for this is: "I (a man) love him (a man)." This attitude raises objections in the patient and is loudly contradicted, so that the statement runs: "I do not love him, I hate him." Since internal perceptions are replaced by external ones in paranoia, this hatred is represented as a result of the hatred endured by the patient from without, and the third formula is: "I do not love him—I hate him—because he persecutes me."

In the psychoses with which we are here concerned a different conflict lies concealed. It is derived from an attitude of the libido in which hatred predominates. This attitude is first directed against the person's nearest relatives and becomes generalized later on. It can be expressed in the following formula: "I cannot love people; I have to hate them."

The pronounced feelings of inadequacy from which such patients suffer arise from this discomforting internal perception. If the content of the perception is repressed and projected externally, the patient gets the idea that he is not loved by his environment but hated by it (again first of all by his parents, etc., and then by a wider circle of people). This idea is detached from its primary causal connection with his own attitude of hate, and is brought into association with other—psychical and physical—deficiencies.* It seems as though a great quantity of such feelings of inferiority favoured the formation of depressive states.

Thus we obtain the second formula: "People do not love me, they hate me . . . because of my inborn defects.† Therefore I am unhappy and depressed."

The repressed sadistic impulses do not remain quiescent, however. They show a tendency to return into consciousness and appear again in various forms—in dreams and symptomatic acts, but especially in an inclination to annoy other people, in violent desires for revenge or in criminal impulses. These symptomatic states are not usually apparent to direct observation, because for the most part they are not put into action; but a deeper insight into the patient's mind—as afforded in the catamnesis, for instance—will bring a great deal of this kind of thing to light. And if they are overlooked in the depressive phase there is more opportunity for observing them in the manic one. I shall have more to say about this subject later on.

It is more especially in regard to such desires to commit acts of violence or revenge that the patients have a tendency to ascribe their feelings to the torturing consciousness of their own physical or psychical defects, instead of to their imperfectly repressed sadism. Every patient who belongs to the manic-depressive group inclines to draw the same conclusion as Richard III, who enumerates all his own failings with pitiless self-cruelty and then sums up:

> And therefore, since I cannot prove a lover . . .
> I am determined to prove a villain.

* In many cases, and particularly in the slighter ones, the original connection is only partly lost; but even so the tendency to displacement is clearly recognizable.
† Cf. with this the etymology of the German word *hässlich* ("ugly") ="that which arouses hate."

Richard cannot love by reason of his defects which make him hateful to others; and he wants to be revenged for this. Each of our patients wishes to do the same, but cannot, because his instinctual activity is paralysed by repression.

New and morbid states, such as feelings of guilt, result from the suppression of these frequent impulses of hatred and revenge. Experience so far seems to show that the more violent were the person's unconscious impulses of revenge the more marked is his tendency to form delusional ideas of guilt. Such delusions, as is well known, may attain enormous proportions, so that the patient declares that he alone has been guilty of all sins since the world began, or that all wickedness originates from him alone. In these persons an insatiable sadism directed towards all persons and all things has been repressed in the unconscious. The idea of such an enormous guilt is of course extremely painful to their consciousness; for where there is a great degree of repressed sadism there will be a corresponding severity in the depressive affect. Nevertheless the idea of guilt contains the fulfillment of a wish—of the repressed wish to be a criminal of the deepest dye, to have incurred more guilt than everyone else put together. This, too, reminds us of certain psychic processes in obsessional neurotics, as, for instance, their belief in the "omnipotence" of their thoughts. They frequently suffer from anxiety lest they have been guilty of the death of a certain person by having thought about his death. The sadistic impulses are repressed in the obsessional neurotic also: because he cannot *act* in conformity with his original instincts he unconsciously gives himself up to phantasies of being able to kill by means of *thoughts*. This wish does not appear as such in consciousness but it takes the form of a tormenting anxiety.

As a result of the repression of sadism, depression,

anxiety, and self-reproach arise. But if such an important source of pleasure from which the active instincts flow is obstructed there is bound to be a reinforcement of the masochistic tendencies. The patient will adopt a passive attitude, and will obtain pleasure from his suffering and from continually thinking about himself. Thus even the deepest melancholic distress contains a hidden source of pleasure.

Before the actual state of depression sets in, many patients are more than usually energetic in their pursuits and manner of life. They often sublimate in a forced manner libido which they cannot direct to its true purpose. They do this so as to shut their eyes to the conflict within them, and to ward off the depressive frame of mind which is tending to break into consciousness. This attitude often succeeds for long periods, but never completely. The person who has to combat disturbing influences for a long time can never enjoy peace or security within himself. Any situation which requires a definite decision in the field of the libido will cause a sudden collapse of his psychic equilibrium which he has so laboriously kept up. When the state of depression breaks out his previous interests (sublimations) suddenly cease; and this leads to a narrowing of his mental outlook which may become so pronounced as to attain to monoideism.

When the depressive psychosis has become manifest its cardinal feature seems to be a mental inhibition which renders a rapport between the patient and the external world more difficult. Incapable of making a lasting and positive application of his libido, the patient unconsciously seeks seclusion from the world, and his auto-erotic trend manifests itself in his inhibition. There are other means, it is true, by which neuroses and psychoses can give symptomatic ex-

pression to an auto-erotic tendency. That it should be inhibition rather than some other symptom that appears in
this case is fully explained from the fact that the inhibition
is able to serve other unconscious tendencies at the same
time. I refer in particular to the tendency towards a "negation
of life." The higher degrees of inhibition in especial—i.e.,
depressive stupor—represent a symbolic dying. The patient
does not react even to the application of strong external
stimuli, just as though he were no longer alive. It is to be
expressly noted that in the foregoing remarks only two causes
of the inhibition have been considered. In every case analysis
revealed still further determinants, connected with the individual circumstances of the patient.

Certain features commonly present in states of depression become comprehensible if we accept the well-founded
conclusions of psycho-analytic experience. Take, for instance,
the frequent ideas of impoverishment. The patient complains,
let us say, that he and his family are exposed to starvation.
If a pecuniary loss has actually preceded the onset of his
illness, he will assert that he cannot possibly endure the blow
and that he is completely ruined. These strange ideas,
which often entirely dominate the patient's thoughts, are
explicable from the identification of libido and money—of
sexual and pecuniary "power"*—with which we are so
familiar. The patient's libido has disappeared from the world,
as it were. Whereas other people can invest their libido in
the objects of the external world he has no such capital to
expend. His feeling of poverty springs from a repressed perception of his own incapacity to love.

We very frequently meet with fears or pronounced

---

* The German word used, *Vermögen,* means both "wealth" and "capacity" in the sense of sexual potency.—*Trans.*

delusions centering round the same idea in states of depression connected with the period of involution. As far as my not very extensive psycho-analytical experience of these conditions goes, I have reason to believe that it is people whose erotic life has been without gratification who are liable to such delusions. In the preceding decade of their life they had repressed this fact and had taken refuge in all kinds of compensations. But their repressions are not able to cope with the upheaval of the climacteric. They now pass in review, as it were, their wasted life, and at the same time feel that it is too late to alter it. Their consciousness strongly resists all ideas connected with this fact; but not being strong enough to banish them completely, it has to allow them entrance in a disguised form. They are still painful in the form of delusion of impoverishment, but not as intolerable as before.

Viewed externally, the manic phase of the cyclical disturbances is the complete opposite of the depressive one. A manic psychotic appears very cheerful on the surface; and unless a deeper investigation is carried out by psychoanalytic methods it might appear that the two phases are the opposite of each other even as regards their content. Psycho-analysis shows, however, that both phases are dominated by the same complexes, and that it is only the patient's attitude towards those complexes which is different. In the depressive state he allows himself to be weighed down by his complex, and sees no other way out of his misery but death;* in the manic state he treats the complex with indifference.

* Some patients cling to the idea that they can be cured by the fulfilment of some external condition—usually one, however, which never can be fulfilled.

The onset of the mania occurs when repression is no longer able to resist the assaults of the repressed instincts. The patient, especially in cases of severe maniacal excitation, is as if swept off his feet by them. It is especially important to notice that positive and negative libido (love and hate, erotic desires and aggressive hostility) surge up into consciousness with equal force.

This manic state, in which libidinal impulses of both kinds have access to consciousness, once more establishes a condition which the patient has experienced before—in his early childhood, that is. Whereas in the depressive patient everything tends to the negation of life, to death, in the manic patient life begins anew. The manic patient returns to a stage in which his impulses had not succumbed to repression, in which he foresaw nothing of the approaching conflict. It is characteristic that such patients often say that they feel themselves "as though new-born." Mania contains the fulfillment of Faust's wish:

> Bring back my passion's unquenched fires,
>   The heavenly smart of bliss restore;
> Hate's strength—the steel of love's desires—
>   Bring back the youth I was once more.

The maniac's frame of mind differs both from normal and from depressive states, partly in its care-free and unrestrained cheerfulness, partly in its increased irritability and feeling of self-importance. The one or the other alteration can predominate according to the individuality of the patient or the different stages of the disease.

The affect of pleasure in mania is derived from the same source as is that of pleasure in wit. What I have to say about this is therefore in close agreement with Freud's theory of wit.[4]

Whereas the melancholiac exhibits a state of general inhibition, in the manic patient even normal inhibitions of the instincts are partly or wholly abolished. The saving of expenditure in inhibition thus effected becomes a source of pleasure, and moreover a lasting one, while wit only causes a transitory suspension of the inhibitions.

Economy of inhibition is, however, by no means the only source of manic pleasure. The removal of inhibitions renders accessible once more old sources of pleasure which had been suppressed; and this shows how deeply mania is rooted in the infantile.

The technique of the manic production of thoughts may be regarded as a third source of pleasure. Abolition of logical control and playing with words—two essential features of manic ideational processes—indicate an extensive "return to infantile freedom."

Melancholic inhibition of thought finds its reverse in the manic flight of ideas. In the melancholic phase there is a narrowing of the circle of ideas, in the manic phase a rapid change of the content of consciousness. The essential difference between flight of ideas and normal thinking is that whereas in thinking or speaking the healthy person consistently keeps in view the aim of his mental processes, the manic patient very easily loses sight of that aim.[5] This differentiation serves to characterize the external aspect of the flight of ideas, but not its significance for the manic subject. It is especially to be noted that the flight of ideas offers the patient considerable possibilities for obtaining pleasure. As has alreardy been said, psychic work is economized where the abolition of logical control is removed and where the sound instead of the sense has to be considered. But the flight of ideas has yet another function, and a double one: it makes it possible to glide by means of light allusions over those ideas that are painful to consciousness, for example, ideas of inadequacy; that is to say, it favours—like wit—transition to another circle of ideas. And it also permits of playful allusion to pleasurable things which are as a rule suppressed.

The similarity between the mind of the maniac and that of the child is characterized in a number of ways of which only one need be mentioned in this place. In the slighter states of manic exaltation the patient has a kind of careless gaiety which bears an obviously childish character. The psychiatrist who has had much to do with such patients can clearly see that his rapport with them is the same as with a child of about five years of age.

The severer forms of mania resemble a frenzy of freedom. The sadistic component-instinct is freed from its fetters. All reserve disappears, and a tendency to reckless and aggressive conduct takes its place. In this stage the maniac reacts to trifling occurrences with violent outbursts of anger and with excessive feelings of revenge. In the same way, when his exaltation had reached a certain height, the cyclothymic patient mentioned above used to feel an impulse to strike down anyone who did not at once make way for him in the street. The patients often have an excessive feeling of power, measuring it not by actual performance but by the violence of their instincts, which they are now able to perceive in an unusual degree. Fairly frequently there appear grandiose ideas which are very similar to children's boasts about their knowledge and power.

Arising from the case of cyclothymia already described at length, there is one important question which I cannot attempt to answer definitely. It remains to be explained why, when the patient was about twenty-eight, states of manic exalation should have appeared in addition to the depressive state which had already existed for a long time. It may be that it was a case where psychosexual puberty followed a long time after physical maturity. We often see the development of instinctual life delayed in a similar manner in neurotics. On this hypothesis the patient would not have experienced an increase of his instinctual life at puberty but have been overtaken, like a woman, by a wave of repression; and it would only have been towards the end of his third decade that a certain awakening of his instincts would have occurred in the form of the first manic state. And in fact it was at that age that his sexual interests turned more to the female sex and less towards auto-erotism than before.

I must now say a few words about the therapeutic effects of psycho-analysis.

The case I have most fully reported in these pages was so far analysed at the time when I read my paper at Weimar[6] that its structure was apparent in general. But there still remained a great deal of work to be done on it; and therapeutic results were only just beginning to be discernible. These have become more clearly visible during the last two and a half months. Naturally a definite opinion as regards a cure cannot yet be given, for after twenty years of illness, interrupted by free intervals of varying length, an improvement of two months' duration signifies very little. But I should like to record the result up to the present. In the period mentioned, no further state of depression has appeared, and the last one passed off very easily. In consequence of this the patient has been able to do continuous work. During the same period there did twice occur a changed frame of mind in a manic direction, which could not escape a careful observation; but it was of a far milder character than his previous states of exaltation. And, besides this, certain hitherto regularly observed phenomena were absent. Between these last two manic phases there has been no depressive one, as was usually the case, but a state which could be called normal, since no cyclothymic phenomena were present. For the rest we shall have to follow the further course of the case. There is only one more thing I should like to add: If the patient succeeds in permanently maintaining a state similar to that of the last two months, even this partial improvement will be of great value to him. In the other case of cyclothymia the period of observation has been too short to permit of an opinion regarding therapeutic results. But its pathological structure was found to be remarkably similar to that of the first case.

The third case described at the beginning of this paper showed the effectiveness of analysis in a striking manner, in spite of the fact that external circumstances obliged the treatment to cease after about forty sittings. Even in the early part of the treatment I was able to cut short a melancholic depression which had just developed in the patient, a thing which had never happened before; and as treatment proceeded its effect became more lasting and expressed itself in a distinct amelioration in the patient's frame of mind, and in a considerable increase of his capacity for work. In the months following the cessation of his analysis his state of mind did not sink back to its former level. It may be noted that in this case the preponderating attitude of hatred, the feeling of incapacity to love and the association of depression with feelings of inadequacy were clearly to be seen.

In the two above-mentioned cases of a melancholic depression occurring for the first time, a consistent analysis could not be carried out on account of external difficulties. Nevertheless, its effect was unmistakable. By the help of a psycho-analytical interpretation of certain facts and connections I succeeded in attaining a greater psychic rapport with the patients than I had ever previously achieved. It is usually extraordinarily difficult to establish a transference in these patients who have turned away from all the world in their depression. Psycho-analysis, which has hitherto enabled us to overcome this obstacle, seems to me for this reason to be the only rational therapy to apply to the manic-depressive psychoses.

The sixth case confirms this view with greater certainty, since I was able to carry the treatment through to the end. It had a remarkably good result. The patient came to me for treatment fifteen months after the onset of his trouble. Before this, treatment in various sanatoria had had only a palliative effect in relieving one or two symptoms. A few weeks after the commencement of psycho-analytic treatment the patient felt occasional relief. His severe depression began to subside after four weeks. He said that at moments he had a feeling of hope that he would once again be capable of work. He attained a certain degree of insight and said: "I am so egoistic now that I consider my fate the most tragic in the world." In the third month of treatment his frame of mind was freer on the whole; his various forms of mental expression were not all so greatly inhibited, and there were whole days on which he used to feel well and occupy himself with plans for the future. At this time he once said with reference to his frame of mind: "When it is all right I am happier and more care-free than I have ever been before." In the fourth month he said that he had no more actual feelings of depression. During the fifth month, in which the sittings no longer took place daily, distinct variations in his condition were noticeable, but the tendency to improvement was unmistakable. In the sixth month he was able to discontinue the treatment; and the change for the better in him was noticeable to his acquaintances. Since then six months have passed without his having had a relapse.

From a diagnostic point of view the case was quite clearly a depressive psychosis and not a neurosis of the climacteric period. I am unfortunately unable to publish details of the case; they are of such a peculiar kind that the incognito of the patient could not be preserved if I did. There are also other considerations which necessitate a quite special discretion—a fact which is greatly to be regretted from a scientific point of view.

There is one objection that might be raised regarding the therapeutic results obtained in this case, and that is that I had begun treating it precisely at that period when the melancholia was passing off, and that it would have been cured without my doing anything; and from this it would follow that psycho-analysis did not possess that therapeutic value which I attribute to it. In answer to this I may say that I have all along been careful to avoid falling into an error of this kind. When I undertook the treatment I had before me a patient who was to all appearances unsusceptible to external influence and who had quite broken down under his illness; and I was very sceptical as to the result of the treatment. I was the more astonished when, after overcoming considerable resistances, I succeeded in explaining certain ideas that completely dominated the patient, and observed the effect of this interpretative work. This initial improvement and every subsequent one followed directly upon the removal of definite products of repression. During the whole course of the analysis I could most distinctly observe that the patient's improvement went hand in hand with the progress of his analysis.

In thus communicating the scientific and practical results of my psycho-analyses of psychoses showing exaltation and depression I am quite aware of their incompleteness, and I hasten to point out these defects myself. I am not in a position to give as much weight to my observations as I could have wished, since I cannot submit a detailed report of the cases analysed. I have already mentioned the reasons for this in one of the cases. In three other very instructive cases motives of discretion likewise prevented me from communicating any details. Nor will intelligent criticism reproach me for adopting this course. Those who take a serious interest in psycho-analysis will make good the deficiencies in my work by their own independent investigations. That further investigations are very greatly needed I am fully aware. Certain questions have not been considered at all or only barely touched upon in this paper. For instance, although we have been able to recognize up to what point the psychogenesis of obsessional neuroses and cyclical psychoses resemble each other, we have not the least idea why at this point one group of individuals should take one path and the other group another.

One thing more may be said concerning the therapeutic aspect of the question. In those patients who have prolonged free intervals between their manic or depressive attacks, psycho-analysis should be begun during that free period. The advantage is obvious, for analysis cannot be carried out on severely inhibited melancholic patients or on inattentive maniacal ones.

Although our results at present are incomplete, it is only psycho-analysis that will reveal the hidden structure of this large group of mental diseases. And moreover, its first therapeutic results in this sphere justify us in the expectation that it may be reserved for psycho-analysis to lead psychiatry out of the impasse of therapeutic nihilism.

Mourning and Melancholia

SIGMUND FREUD

Dreams having served us as the prototype in normal life of narcissistic mental disorders, we will now try to throw some light on the nature of melancholia by comparing it with the normal affect of mourning.[1] This time, however, we must begin by making an admission, as a warning against any over-estimation of the value of our conclusions. Melancholia, whose definition fluctuates even in descriptive psychiatry, takes on various clinical forms the grouping together of which into a single unity does not seem to be established with certainty; and some of these forms suggest somatic rather than psychogenic affections. Our material, apart from such impressions as are open to every observer, is limited to a small number of cases whose psychogenic nature was indisputable. We shall, therefore, from the outset drop all claim to general validity for our conclusions, and we shall console ourselves by reflecting that, with the means of investigation at our disposal to-day, we could hardly discover anything that was not typical, if not of a whole class of disorders, at least of a small group of them.

The correlation of melancholia and mourning seems

[1] See references in chapter notes at back of book.

justified by the general picture of the two conditions.[2] Moreover, the exciting causes due to environmental influences are,
so far as we can discern them at all, the same for both
conditions. Mourning is regularly the reaction to the loss
of a loved person, or to the loss of some abstraction which
has taken the place of one, such as one's country, liberty,
an ideal, and so on. In some people the same influences
produce melancholia instead of mourning and we consequently suspect them of a pathological disposition. It is also
well worth notice that, although mourning involves grave
departures from the normal attitude to life, it never occurs
to us to regard it as a pathological condition and to refer
it to medical treatment. We rely on its being overcome after
a certain lapse of time, and we look upon any interference
with it as useless or even harmful.

The distinguishing mental features of melancholia are
a profoundly painful dejection, cessation of interest in the
outside world, loss of the capacity to love, inhibition of all
activity, and a lowering of the self-regarding feelings to a
degree that finds utterances in self-reproaches and self-re-
vilings, and culminates in a delusional expectation of punishment. This picture becomes a little more intelligible when we
consider that, with one exception, the same traits are met
with in mourning. The disturbance of self-regard is absent
in mourning; but otherwise the features are the same. Profound mourning, the reaction to the loss of someone who is
loved, contains the same painful frame of mind, the same
loss of interest in the outside world—in so far as it does
not recall him—the same loss of capacity to adopt any new
object of love (which would mean replacing him) and the
same turning away from any activity that is not connected
with thoughts of him. It is easy to see that this inhibition

and circumscription of the ego is the expression of an exclusive devotion to mourning which leaves nothing over for other purposes or other interests. It is really only because we know so well how to explain it that this attitude does not seem to us pathological.

We should regard it as an appropriate comparison, too, to call the mood of mourning a "painful" one. We shall probably see the justification for this when we are in a position to give a characterization of the economics of pain.[3]

In what, now, does the work which mourning performs consist? I do not think there is anything far-fetched in presenting it in the following way. Reality-testing has shown that the loved object no longer exists, and it proceeds to demand that all libido shall be withdrawn from its attachments to that object. This demand arouses understandable opposition—it is a matter of general observation that people never willingly abandon a libidinal position, not even, indeed, when a substitute is already beckoning to them. This opposition can be so intense that a turning away from reality takes place and a clinging to the object through the medium of a hallucinatory wishful psychosis.[4] Normally, respect for reality gains the day. Nevertheless its orders cannot be obeyed at once. They are carried out bit by bit, at great expense of time and cathectic energy, and in the meantime the existence of the lost object is psychically prolonged. Each single one of the memories and expectations in which the libido is bound to the object is brought up and hypercathected, and detachment of the libido is accomplished in respect of it.[5] Why this compromise by which the command of reality is carried out piecemeal should be so extraordinarily painful is not at all easy to explain in terms of economics. It is remarkable that this painful unpleasure is taken as a matter of course by us. The fact is, however, that when the work of mourning is completed the ego becomes free and uninhibited again.[6]

Let us now apply to melancholia what we have learnt about mourning. In one set of cases it is evident that melancholia too may be the reaction to the loss of a loved object. Where the exciting causes are different one can recognize that there is a loss of a more ideal kind. The object has not perhaps actually died, but has been lost as an object of love (e.g. in the case of a betrothed girl who has been jilted). In yet other cases one feels justified in maintaining the belief that a loss of this kind has occurred, but one cannot see clearly what it is that has been lost, and it is all the more reasonable to suppose that the patient cannot consciously perceive what he has lost either. This, indeed, might be so even if the patient is aware of the loss which has given rise to his melancholia, but only in the sense that he knows *whom* he has lost but not *what* he has lost in him. This would suggest that melancholia is in some way related to an object-loss which is withdrawn from consciousness, in contradistinction to mourning, in which there is nothing about the loss that is unconscious.

In mourning we found that the inhibition and loss of interest are fully accounted for by the work of mourning in which the ego is absorbed. In melancholia, the unknown loss will result in a similar internal work and will therefore be responsible for the melancholic inhibition. The difference is that the inhibition of the melancholic seems puzzling to us because we cannot see what it is that is absorbing him so entirely. The melancholic displays something else besides what is lacking in mourning—an extraordinary diminution in his self-regard, an impoverishment of his ego on a grand

scale. In mourning it is the world which has become poor
and empty; in melancholia it is the ego itself. The patient
represents his ego to us as worthless, incapable of any
achievement and morally despicable; he reproaches himself,
vilifies himself and expects to be cast out and punished. He
abases himself before everyone and commiserates with his
own relatives for being connected with anyone so unworthy.
He is not of the opinion that a change has taken place in
him, but extends his self-criticism back over the past; he
declares that he was never any better. This picture of a
delusion of (mainly moral) inferiority is completed by sleeplessness and refusal to take nourishment, and—what is psychologically very remarkable—by an overcoming of the
instinct which compels every living thing to cling to life.

It would be equally fruitless from a scientific and a
therapeutic point of view to contradict a patient who brings
these accusations against his ego. He must surely be right
in some way and be describing something that is as it seems
to him to be. Indeed, we must at once confirm some of his
statements without reservation. He really is as lacking in
interest and as incapable of love and achievement as he
says. But that, as we know, is secondary; it is the effect of the
internal work which is consuming his ego—work which is
unknown to us but which is comparable to the work of
mourning. He also seems to us justified in certain other
self-accusations; it is merely that he has a keener eye for the
truth than other people who are not melancholic. When in
his heightened self-criticism he describes himself as petty,
egoistic, dishonest, lacking in independence, one whose sole
aim has been to hide the weaknesses of his own nature, it
may be, so far as we know, that he has come pretty near
to understanding himself; we only wonder why a man has

to be ill before he can be accessible to a truth of this kind. For there can be no doubt that if anyone holds and expresses to others an opinion of himself such as this (an opinion which Hamlet held both of himself and of everyone else[7]), he is ill, whether he is speaking the truth or whether he is being more or less unfair to himself. Nor is it difficult to see that there is no correspondence, so far as we can judge, between the degree of self-abasement and its real justification. A good, capable, conscientious woman will speak no better of herself after she develops melancholia than one who is in fact worthless; indeed, the former is perhaps more likely to fall ill of the disease than the latter, of whom we too should have nothing good to say. Finally, it must strike us that after all the melancholic does not behave in quite the same way as a person who is crushed by remorse and self-reproach in a normal fashion. Feelings of shame in front of other people, which would more than anything characterize this latter condition, are lacking in the melancholic, or at least they are not prominent in him. One might emphasize the presence in him of an almost opposite trait of insistent communicativeness which finds satisfaction in self-exposure.

The essential thing, therefore, is not whether the melancholic's distressing self-denigration is correct, in the sense that his self-criticism agrees with the opinion of other people. The point must rather be that he is giving a correct description of his psychological situation. He has lost his self-respect and he must have good reason for this. It is true that we are then faced with a contradiction that presents a problem which is hard to solve. The analogy with mourning led us to conclude that he had suffered a loss in regard to an object; what he tells us points to a loss in regard to his ego.

Before going into this contradiction, let us dwell for a

moment on the view which the melancholic's disorder affords of the constitution of the human ego. We see how in him one part of the ego sets itself over against the other, judges it critically, and, as it were, takes it as its object. Our suspicion that the critical agency which is here split off from the ego might also show its independence in other circumstances will be confirmed by every further observation. We shall really find grounds for distinguishing this agency from the rest of the ego. What we are here becoming acquainted with is the agency commonly called "conscience"; we shall count it, along with the censorship of consciousness and reality-testing, among the major institutions of the ego,[8] and we shall come upon evidence to show that it can become diseased on its own account. In the clinical picture of melancholia, dissatisfaction with the ego on moral grounds is the most outstanding feature. The patient's self-evaluation concerns itself much less frequently with bodily infirmity, ugliness or weakness, or with social inferiority; of this category, it is only his fears and asseverations of becoming poor that occupy a prominent position.

There is one observation, not at all difficult to make, which leads to the explanation of the contradiction mentioned above [at the end of the last paragraph but one]. If one listens patiently to a melancholic's many and various self-accusations, one cannot in the end avoid the impression that often the most violent of them are hardly at all applicable to the patient himself, but that with insignificant modifications they do fit someone else, someone whom the patient loves or has loved or should love. Every time one examines the facts this conjecture is confirmed. So we find the key to the clinical picture: we perceive that the self-reproaches are reproaches against a loved object which have been shifted away from it on to the patient's own ego.

The woman who loudly pities her husband for being tied to such an incapable wife as herself is really accusing her *husband* of being incapable, in whatever sense she may mean this. There is no need to be greatly surprised that a few genuine self-reproaches are scattered among those that have been transposed back. These are allowed to obtrude themselves, since they help to mask the others and make recognition of the true state of affairs impossible. Moreover, they derive from the pros and cons of the conflict of love that has led to the loss of love. The behaviour of the patients, too, now becomes much more intelligible. Their complaints are really "plaints" in the old sense of the word. They are not ashamed and do not hide themselves, since everything derogatory that they say about themselves is at bottom said about someone else. Moreover, they are far from evincing towards those around them the attitude of humility and submissiveness that would alone befit such worthless people. On the contrary, they make the greatest nuisance of themselves, and always seem as though they felt slighted and had been treated with great injustice. All this is possible only because the reactions expressed in their behavior still proceed from a mental constellation of revolt, which has then, by a certain process, passed over into the crushed state of melancholia.

There is no difficulty in reconstructing this process. An object-choice, an attachment of the libido to a particular person, had at one time existed; then, owing to a real slight or disappointment coming from this loved person, the object-relationship was shattered. The result was not the normal one of a withdrawal of the libido from this object and a displacement of it on to a new one, but something different, for whose coming-about various conditions seem to be necessary. The object-cathexis proved to have little power of resistance and was brought to an end. But the free libido was not displaced on to another object; it was withdrawn into the ego. There, however, it was not employed in any unspecified way, but served to establish an *identification* of the ego with the abandoned object. Thus the shadow of the object fell upon the ego, and the latter could henceforth be judged by a special[9] agency, as though it were an object, the forsaken object. In this way an object-loss was transformed into an ego-loss and the conflict between the ego and the loved person into a cleavage between the critical activity of the ego and the ego as altered by identification.

One or two things may be directly inferred with regard to the preconditions and effects of a process such as this. On the one hand, a strong fixation to the loved object must have been present; on the other hand, in contradiction to this, the object-cathexis must have had little power of resistance. As Otto Rank has aptly remarked, this contradiction seems to imply that the object-choice has been effected on a narcissistic basis, so that the object-cathexis, when obstacles come in its way, can regress to narcissism. The narcissistic identification with the object then becomes a substitute for the erotic cathexis, the result of which is that in spite of the conflict with the loved person the love-relation need not be given up. This substitution of identification for object-love is an important mechanism in the narcissistic affections; Karl Landauer[10] has lately been able to point to it in the process of recovery in a case of schizophrenia. It represents, of course, a *regression* from one type of object-choice to original narcissism. We have elsewhere shown that identification is a preliminary stage of object-choice, that it is the first way —and one that is expressed in an ambivalent fashion—in which the ego picks out an object. The ego wants to incorporate this object into itself, and, in accordance with the oral or cannibalistic phase of libidinal development in which it is, it wants to do so by devouring it.[11] Abraham is undoubtedly right in attributing to this connection the refusal of nourishment met with in severe forms of melancholia.[12]

The conclusion which our theory would require—namely, that the disposition to fall ill of melancholia (or some part of that disposition) lies in the predominance of the narcissistic type of object-choice—has unfortunately not yet been confirmed by observation. In the opening remarks of this paper, I admitted that the empirical material upon which this study is founded is insufficient for our needs. If we could assume an agreement between the results of observation and what we have inferred, we should not hesitate to include this regression from object-cathexis to the still narcissistic oral phase of the libido in our characterization of melancholia. Identifications with the object are by no means rare in the transference neuroses either; indeed, they are a well-known mechanism of symptom-formation, especially in hysteria. The difference, however, between narcissistic and hysterical identification may be seen in this: that, whereas in the former the object-cathexis is abandoned, in the latter it persists and manifests its influence, though this is usually confined to certain isolated actions and innervations. In any case, in the transference neuroses, too, identification is the expression of there being something in common, which may signify love. Narcissistic identification is the older of the two and it paves the way to an understanding of hysterical identification, which has been less thoroughly studied.[13]

Melancholia, therefore, borrows some of its features from mourning, and the others from the process of regression from narcissistic object-choice to narcissism. It is on the one hand, like mourning, a reaction to the real loss of a loved object; but over and above this, it is marked by a determinant which is absent in normal mourning or which, if it is present, transforms the latter into pathological mourning. The loss of a love-object is an excellent opportunity for the ambivalence in love-relationships to make itself effective and come into the open.[14] Where there is a disposition to obsessional neurosis the conflict due to ambivalence gives a pathological cast to mourning and forces it to express itself in the form of self-reproaches to the effect that the mourner himself is to blame for the loss of the loved object, i.e. that he has willed it. These obsessional states of depression following upon the death of a loved person show us what the conflict due to ambivalence can achieve by itself when there is no regressive drawing-in of libido as well. In melancholia, the occasions which give rise to the illness extend for the most part beyond the clear case of a loss by death, and include all those situations of being slighted, neglected or disappointed, which can import opposed feelings of love and hate into the relationship or reinforce an already existing ambivalence. This conflict due to ambivalence, which sometimes arises more from real experiences, sometimes more from constitutional factors, must not be overlooked among the preconditions of melancholia. If the love for the object—a love which cannot be given up though the object itself is given up— takes refuge in narcissistic identification, then the hate comes into operation on this substitutive object, abusing it, debasing it, making it suffer and deriving sadistic satisfaction from its suffering. The self-tormenting in melancholia, which is without doubt enjoyable, signifies, just like the corresponding phenomenon in obsessional neurosis, a satisfaction of trends of sadism and hate[15] which relate to an object, and which have been turned round upon the subject's own self in the ways we have been discussing. In both disorders the patients usually still succeed, by the circuitous path of self-punishment, in taking revenge on the original object and in tormenting their loved one through their illness, having resorted to it in order to avoid the need to express their hostility to him openly. After all, the person who has occasioned the patient's emotional disorder, and on whom his illness is centered, is usually to be found in his immediate environment. The melancholic's erotic cathexis in regard to his object has thus undergone a double vicissitude: part of it has regressed to identification, but the other part, under the influence of the conflict due to ambivalence, has been carried back to the stage of sadism, which is nearer to that conflict.

It is this sadism alone that solves the riddle of the tendency to suicide which makes melancholia so interesting— and so dangerous. So immense is the ego's self-love, which we have come to recognize as the primal state from which instinctual life proceeds, and so vast is the amount of narcissistic libido which we see liberated in the fear that emerges as a threat to life, that we cannot conceive how that ego can consent to its own destruction. We have long known, it is true, that no neurotic harbours thoughts of suicide which he has not turned back upon himself from murderous impulses against others, but we have never been able to explain what interplay of forces can carry such a purpose through to execution. The analysis of melancholia now shows that the ego can kill itself only if, owing to the return of the object-cathexis, it can treat itself as an object—if it is able to direct against itself the hostility which relates to an object and which represents the ego's original reaction to objects in the external world.[16] Thus in regression from narcissistic object-choice the object has, it is true, been got rid of, but it has nevertheless proved more powerful than the ego itself. In the two opposed situations of being most intensely in love and of suicide the ego is overwhelmed by the object, though in totally different ways.[17]

As regards one particular striking feature of melancholia that we have mentioned, the prominence of the fear of becoming poor, it seems plausible to suppose that it is derived from anal erotism which has been torn out of its context and altered in a regressive sense.

Melancholia confronts us with yet other problems, the answer to which in part eludes us. The fact that it passes off after a certain time has elapsed without leaving traces of any gross changes is a feature it shares with mourning. We found by way of explanation that in mourning time is needed for the command of reality-testing to be carried out in detail, and that when this work has been accomplished the ego will have succeeded in freeing its libido from the lost object. We may imagine that the ego is occupied with analogous work during the course of a melancholia; in neither case have we any insight into the economics of the course of events. The sleeplessness in melancholia testifies to the rigidity of the condition, the impossibility of effecting the general drawing-in of cathexes necessary for sleep. The complex of melancholia behaves like an open wound, drawing to itself cathectic energies—which in the transference neuroses we have called "anticathexes"—from all directions, and emptying the ego until it is totally impoverished.[18] It can easily prove resistant to the ego's wish to sleep.

What is probably a somatic factor, and one which cannot be explained psychogenically, makes itself visible in the regular amelioration in the condition that takes place towards evening. These considerations bring up the question whether a loss in the ego irrespectively of the object—a purely narcissistic blow to the ego—may not suffice to produce the picture of melancholia and whether an impoverishment of ego-libido directly due to toxins may not be able to produce certain forms of the disease.

The most remarkable characteristic of melancholia, and the one in most need of explanation, is its tendency to change round into mania—a state which is the opposite of it in its symptoms. As we know, this does not happen to every melancholia. Some cases run their course in periodic relapses, during the intervals between which signs of mania may be entirely absent or only very slight. Others show the regular alternation of melancholic and manic phases which has led to the hypothesis of a circular insanity. One would be tempted to regard these cases as non-psychogenic, if it were not for the fact that the psycho-analytic method has succeeded in arriving at a solution and effecting a therapeutic improvement in several cases precisely of this kind. It is not merely permissible, therefore, but incumbent upon us to extend an analytic explanation of melancholia to mania as well.

I cannot promise that this attempt will prove entirely satisfactory. It hardly carries us much beyond the possibility of taking one's initial bearings. We have two things to go upon: the first is a psycho-analytic impression, and the second what we may perhaps call a matter of general economic experience. The impression which several psycho-analytic investigators have already put into words is that the content of mania is no different from that of melancholia, that both disorders are wrestling with the same "complex," but that probably in melancholia the ego has succumbed to the complex whereas in mania it has mastered it or pushed it aside. Our second pointer is afforded by the observation that all states such as joy, exultation or triumph, which give us the normal model for mania, depend on the same economic conditions. What has happened here is that, as a result of some influence, a large expenditure of psychical energy, long maintained or habitually occurring, has at last become unnecessary, so that it is available for numerous applications and possibilities of discharge—when, for instance, some poor wretch, by winning a large sum of money, is suddenly relieved from chronic worry about his daily bread, or when a long and arduous struggle is finally crowned with success, or when a man finds himself in a position to throw off at a single blow some oppressive compulsion, some false position which he has long had to keep up, and so on. All such situations are characterized by high spirits, by the signs of discharge of joyful emotion and by increased readiness for all kinds of action—in just the same way as in mania, and in complete contrast to the depression and inhibition of melancholia. We may venture to assert that mania is nothing other than a triumph of this sort, only that here again what the ego has surmounted and what it is triumphing over remain hidden from it. Alcoholic intoxication, which belongs to the same class of states, may (in so far as it is an elated one) be explained in the same way; here there is probably a suspension, produced by toxins, of expenditures of energy in repression. The popular view likes to assume that a person in a manic state of this kind finds such delight in movement and action because he is so "cheerful." This false connection must of course be put right. The fact is that the economic condition in the subject's mind referred to above has been fulfilled, and this is the reason why he is in such high spirits on the one hand and so uninhibited in action on the other.

If we put these two indications together,[19] what we find is this. In mania, the ego must have got over the loss of the object (or its mourning over the loss, or perhaps the object itself), and thereupon the whole quota of anticathexis which the painful suffering of melancholia had drawn to itself from the ego and "bound" will have become available. Moreover, the manic subject plainly demonstrates his liberation from the object which was the cause of his suffering, by seeking like a ravenously hungry man for new object-cathexes.

This explanation certainly sounds plausible, but in the first place it is too indefinite, and, secondly, it gives rise to more new problems and doubts than we can answer. We will not evade a discussion of them, even though we cannot expect it to lead us to a clear understanding.

In the first place, normal mourning, too, overcomes the loss of the object, and it, too, while it lasts, absorbs all the energies of the ego. Why, then, after it has run its course, is there no hint in its case of the economic condition for a phase of triumph? I find it impossible to answer this objection straight away. It also draws our attention to the fact that we do not even know the economic means by which mourning carries out its task. Possibly, however, a conjecture will help us here. Each single one of the memories and situations of expectancy which demonstrate the libido's attachment to the lost object is met by the verdict of reality that the object no longer exists; and the ego, confronted as it were with the question whether it shall share this fate, is persuaded by the sum of the narcissistic satisfactions it derives from being alive to sever its attachment to the object that has been abolished. We may perhaps suppose that this work of severance is so slow and gradual that by the time it has been finished the expenditure of energy necessary for it is also dissipated.[20]

It is tempting to go on from this conjecture about the work of mourning and try to give an account of the work of melancholia. Here we are met at the outset by an uncertainty. So far we have hardly considered melancholia from the topographical point of view, nor asked ourselves in and between what psychical systems the work of melancholia goes on. What part of the mental processes of the disease still takes place in connection with the unconscious object-cathexes that have been given up, and what part in connection with their substitute, by identification, in the ego?

The quick and easy answer is that "the unconscious (thing-) presentation[21] of the object has been abandoned by the libido." In reality, however, this presentation is made up of innumerable single impressions (or unconscious traces of them), and this withdrawal of libido is not a process that can be accomplished in a moment, but must certainly, as in mourning, be one in which progress is long-drawn-out and gradual. Whether it begins simultaneously at several points or follows some sort of fixed sequence is not easy to decide; in analyses it often becomes evident that first one and then another memory is activated, and that the laments which always sound the same and are wearisome in their monotony nevertheless take their rise each time in some different unconscious source. If the object does not possess this great significance for the ego—a significance reinforced by a thousand links—then, too, its loss will not be of a kind to cause either mourning or melancholia. This characteristic of detaching the libido bit by bit is therefore to be ascribed alike to mourning and to melancholia; it is probably supported by the same economic situation and serves the same purposes in both.

As we have seen, however, melancholia contains something more than normal mourning. In melancholia the relation to the object is no simple one; it is complicated by the conflict due to ambivalence. The ambivalence is either constitutional, i.e. is an element of every love-relation formed by this particular ego, or else it proceeds precisely from those experiences that involved the threat of losing the object. For this reason the exciting causes of melancholia have a much wider range than those of mourning, which is for the most part occasioned only by a real loss of the object, by its death. In melancholia, accordingly, countless separate struggles are carried on over the object, in which hate and love contend with each other; the one seeks to detach the libido from the object, the other to maintain this position of the libido against the assault. The location of these separate struggles cannot be assigned to any system but the *Ucs.*, the region of the memory-traces of *things* (as contrasted with *word*-cathexes). In mourning, too, the efforts to detach the libido are made in this same system; but in it nothing hinders these processes from proceeding along the normal path through the *Pcs.* to consciousness. This path is blocked for the work of melancholia, owing perhaps to a number of causes or a combination of them. Constitutional ambivalence belongs by its nature to the repressed; traumatic experiences in connection with the object may have activated other repressed material. Thus everything to do with these struggles due to ambivalence remains withdrawn from consciousness, until the outcome characteristic of melancholia has set in. This, as we know, consists in the threatened libidinal cathexis at length abandoning the object, only, however, to draw back to the place in the ego from which it had proceeded. So by taking flight into the ego love escapes extinction. After this regression of the libido the process can become conscious, and it is represented to consciousness as a conflict between one part of the ego and the critical agency.

What consciousness is aware of in the work of melancholia is thus not the essential part of it, nor is it even the part which we may credit with an influence in bringing the ailment to an end. We see that the ego debases itself and rages against itself, and we understand as little as the patient what this can lead to and how it can change. We can more readily attribute such a function to the *unconscious* part of the work, because it is not difficult to perceive an essential analogy between the work of melancholia and of mourning. Just as mourning impels the ego to give up the object by declaring the object to be dead and offering the ego the inducement of continuing to live, so does each single struggle of ambivalence loosen the fixation of the libido to the object by disparaging it, denigrating it and even as it were killing it. It is possible for the process in the *Ucs.* to come to an end, either after the fury has spent itself or after the object has been abandoned as valueless. We cannot tell which of these two possibilities is the regular or more usual one in bringing melancholia to an end, nor what influence this termination has on the future course of the case. The ego may enjoy in this the satisfaction of knowing itself as the better of the two, as superior to the object.

Even if we accept this view of the work of melancholia, it still does not supply an explanation of the one point on which we were seeking light. It was our expectation that the economic condition for the emergence of mania after the melancholia has run its course is to be found in the ambivalence which dominates the latter affection; and in this we found support from analogies in various other fields. But there is one fact before which that expectation must bow. Of the three preconditions of melancholia—loss of the object, ambivalence, and regression of libido into the ego—the first two are also found in the obsessional self-reproaches arising after a death has occurred. In those cases it is unquestionably the ambivalence which is the motive force of the conflict, and observation shows that after the conflict has come to an end there is nothing left over in the nature of the triumph of a manic state of mind. We are thus led to the third factor as the only one responsible for the result. The accumulation of cathexis which is at first bound and then, after the work of melancholia is finished, becomes free and makes mania possible must be linked with regression of the libido to narcissism. The conflict within the ego, which melancholia substitutes for the struggle over the object, must act like a painful wound which calls for an extraordinarily high anticathexis.—But here once again, it will be well to call a halt and to postpone any further explanation of mania until we have gained some insight into the economic nature, first, of physical pain, and then of the mental pain which is analogous to it.[22] As we already know, the interdependence of the complicated problems of the mind forces us to break off every enquiry before it is completed—till the outcome of some other enquiry can come to its assistance.[23]

The Problem of Melancholia

SANDOR RADO

The insight which psycho-analysis has gained into the clinical picture of melancholia is the result of the investigations of Freud and Abraham. Abraham was the first to turn his attention to this subject. As early as 1911 he asserted[1] that melancholia represents a reaction (comparable to that of grief) to the loss of love (the object). Some years later Freud, having in the interval begun his researches into the nature of narcissism, took the decisive step which led to the analytical elucidation of the subject of melancholia.[2] He recognized that in melancholia the object which has been renounced is set up again within the ego and that thus in his self-reproaches the patient is continuing his aggressive tendencies against that object. The first conditioning factor in this process he showed to be the regression from an object-relation to a narcissistic substitute for it and, next, the predominance of ambivalence, which replaces love by hate and oral incorporation. In a later work Freud supplemented this hypothesis by the observation that the cruelty of the super-ego in melancholia results from the defusion of instincts which accompanies the act of identification.[3] In 1923 Abra-

[1] See references in chapter notes at back of book.

ham published a second and comprehensive work on melancholia.[4] By a number of excellent individual observations he was able to confirm Freud's conclusions in all points and he added several important clinical discoveries. He emphasized the melancholiac's incapacity for love—an incapacity springing from his ambivalence—indicated the large part played in the mental productions of such patients by cannibalistic and oral instinctual impulses and revealed in the history of their childhood a "primal depression" from which they had suffered at the height of their Œdipus development as a reaction to the double disappointment of their love for mother and father.

We now understand the mechanism of melancholia in so far as Freud has dissected it into its separate parts and Abraham has traced the forces at work in it to elementary impulses of the component instincts. But the plan according to which these separate mental acts are combined to form the whole structure of melancholia, its origin and its specific meaning are still wholly obscure.

I shall endeavour to indicate to you to-day how far the analysis of the ego and its narcissism enable us to penetrate deeper into the nature of melancholia.

The most striking feature in the picture displayed by the symptoms of depressive conditions is the fall in self-esteem and self-satisfaction.* The depressive neurotic for the most part attempts to conceal this disturbance; in melancholia it finds clamorous expression in the patients' delusional self-accusations and self-aspersions, which we call "the delusion of moral inferiority." On the other hand, there are in the

* *Selbstgefühl,* usually translated by the neutral word "self-regard," is used by this author in a more positive sense and is variously translated here, by self-respect, self-esteem and self-satisfaction, as well as by self-regard.

behaviour of melancholiacs many phenomena which are in complete contradiction to the patient's general self-abasement. Freud gives the following description of this remarkable inconsistency in such patients[5]; "They are far from evincing towards those around them the attitude of humility and submission that alone would befit such worthless persons; on the contrary, they give a great deal of trouble, perpetually taking offence and behaving as if they had been treated with great injustice."

He adds the explanation that these latter reactions are still being roused by the mental attitude of rebellion, which has only later been converted into the contrition of the melancholiac. As observation shews, the acute phase of melancholia (or depressive conditions) is regularly preceded by such a period of arrogant and embittered rebellion. But this phase generally passes quickly and its symptoms are then merged into the subsequent melancholic phase. In the transitory symptoms which occur during analytic treatment we have an impressive picture of this process. Let us now endeavour to throw some light on this rebellious phase from the patient's previous history and a consideration of the type of persons who are subject to it.

We will begin by describing the characteristics which may be recognized in the ego of persons predisposed to depressive states. We find in them, above all, an intensely strong craving for narcissistic gratification and a very considerable narcissistic intolerance. We observe that even to trivial offences and disappointments they immediately react with a fall in their self-esteem. Their ego then experiences an urgent craving to relieve in some way or other the resulting narcissistic tension. The ego may be completely absorbed by this and be paralysed for all further activities. A stronger individual, on the other hand, will scarcely react at all to such frustrations, will endure without harm trivial variations in the degree of his self-esteem and will accommodate himself to the inevitable delay in its restoration. Those predisposed to depression are, moreover, wholly reliant and dependent on other people for maintaining their self-esteem; they have not attained to the level of independence where self-esteem has its foundation in the subject's own achievements and critical judgment. They have a sense of security and comfort only when they feel themselves loved, esteemed, supported and encouraged. Even when they display an approximately normal activity in the gratification of their instincts and succeed in realizing their aims and ideals, their self-esteem largely depends on whether they do or do not meet with approbation and recognition. They are like those children who, when their early narcissism is shattered, recover their self-respect only in complete dependence on their love-objects.

Thus the favourite method employed by persons of this type for increasing their self-respect is that of attracting to themselves narcissistic gratification from *without*. Their libidinal disposition is easy to comprehend; the instinctual energies which they direct towards objects retain strong narcissistic elements, and therefore passive narcissistic aims prevail in their object-relations. Freud postulated that the melancholiac's "object-choice conforms to the narcissistic type"; this characteristic may be regarded as a special instance of my general statement.[6]

Besides dependence on the love-object we find in persons prone to depressive states a number of secondary characteristics which must be present in order to make up this typical disposition. Such persons are never weary of court-

ing the favour of the objects of their libido and seeking for
evidences of love from them; they sometimes expend an
astonishing skill and subtlety in this pursuit. This applies
not only to the objects of ther purely sexual feelings: they
behave in exactly the same way in relations in which their
sexual instinct is inhibited in its aim and sublimated. They
are wont to have a considerable number of such relations,
for they are most happy when living in an atmosphere permeated with libido. But as soon as they are sure of the affection or devotion of another person and have entered into a
fairly secure relation with him or her their behaviour undergoes a complete change. They accept the devoted love of
the beloved person with a sublime nonchalance, as a matter
of course, and become more and more domineering and
autocratic, displaying an increasingly unbridled egoism,
until their attitude becomes one of full-blown tyranny. They
cling to their objects like leeches (to use a phrase of Abraham's) and feed upon them, as though it were their intention
to devour them altogether. But all this takes place without
their self-critical faculty being aware of it; as a rule they are
just as unaware of the wooing character of their attitude as
of its subsequent reversal or of the tenacity with which
their sadism fastens on their love-objects. Taking this attitude into consideration we can hardly wonder that they react
with embittered vehemence to aggression on the part of
others or to the threat of withdrawal of love and that they
feel the final loss of the object of their tormenting love to be
the greatest injustice in the world.

Such, approximately, is the process leading to the in-
dignant rebellion which precedes the turning of the subject's
aggressive tendencies against himself in melancholia. Let us
for the moment leave out of consideration the introjection

of the object, to which process Freud has traced the reversal of mood in this disease, and let us try to see how melancholia can be accounted for on the same psychological premises as have explained the patient's passing into the phase of rebellion. It will then be obvious that his contrition can only be a reaction to the failure of his rebellion—a fresh weapon (the last one) to which his ego has recourse in order to carry out its purpose. That which it could not accomplish by rebellion it now tries to achieve by remorseful self-punishment and expiation. The ego does penance, begs for forgiveness and endeavours in this way to win back the lost object. I once described melancholia as a great despairing cry for love, and I believe that our present context justifies us in so conceiving of it.[7]

But, you will object, this cannot be so, for the melancholiac has surely withdrawn his interest from the object: it exists for him no longer. How can he be striving to be reconciled to this object and to recapture its affection? You are right; but the melancholiac has transferred the scene of his struggle for the love of his object to a different stage. He has withdrawn in narcissistic fashion to the inner world of his own mind and now, instead of procuring the pardon and love of his object, he tries to secure those of his super-ego. We know that his relation to the object was marked by the predominance of the narcissistic desire to be loved, and it is quite easy for this aspiration to be carried over to his relation with his own super-ego. It is as if the ego of the melancholiac were to say to his super-ego: "I will take all the guilt upon myself and submit myself to any punishment; I will even, by ceasing to care for my bodily welfare, offer myself as an expiatory sacrifice, if you will only interest yourself in me and be kind to me." Thus it seems that in melancholia there is an attempt to decide the conflict with the object on a field other than the real one: there is a narcissistic flight from the object-relation to that with the super-ego and, by this regressive step, the ego is removed from reality.

From this behaviour of the melancholiac we may venture to divine the processes which once took place within him at the time when the formation of his super-ego was in progress. He was a child of a narcissistic disposition, whose self-esteem depended entirely on his parents' love. What an improvement in his mental situation when he began actively to reproduce their requirements in his own mind! He was then able to say to them: "There is no need for you to correct me any more, for I tell myself what you expect of me and, what is more, I will do it." But there were also times when he was naughty and his parents were very angry. Then he understood that he had only to pay the penalty and to ask for forgiveness, in order to be reconciled to them. The next time he offended, it occurred to him that he might do penance of his own accord and punish himself, in order quickly to win his parents' forgiveness. Incidents of this sort are related to us in our patients' analyses and children are known actually to carry out this idea. We can easily imagine that, later, this process takes place in the child without his knowing it. He begins *unconsciously* to reproduce within his mind the punishments anticipated from his parents and, in doing so, he unconsciously *hopes to win love*. Some unmerited narcissistic injury, e.g. an estrangement from his parents through no fault of his own, is probably the original motive for such an unconscious attempt at reparation. In some such way we may reconstruct the process by which the person who subsequently succumbs to melancholia (and certainly he is not alone in this respect) produces the mechanism of self-punishment.

But, as soon as the active reproduction of parental punishment ceases to have reference in the conscious mind to
the parents themselves and is carried out unconsciously, the
intention is no longer that the subject should be reconciled
to them but to the super-ego, which is their internal mental
representative. Instead of the early process of putting matters right in actual fact with the parents, we have the purely
psychical process by which he puts them right with his
super-ego, as happens later in melancholia. But in relation to
external reality this inner process remains entirely inef-
fective. With the unconscious reproduction of parental punishments the oral-narcissistic process of introjection (the
formation of the super-ego) has overstepped the limits of its
social usefulness: self-punishment is a part of the infantile
relation to the object, a survival which controverts reality
and takes an inward direction. In its dread of losing love
the infantile ego has clearly gone too far; its narcissistic
craving remains unsatisfied, even when it submits itself to the
destructive effects of self-punishment. In so far, then, as the
ego in melancholia gives itself up to this mechanism, it has
broken off its relations with reality and jeopardized its existence in vain.

We have seen how self-punishment takes place in the
hope of absolution and has its origin in the longing for love.
Now I am sure you will share my critical suspicion that the
close connection between *guilt, atonement* and *forgiveness,*
so deeply rooted in our mental life, cannot possibly owe its
enormous importance simply to the experiences of the growing child in the course of his training. It is certainly a momentous step when the child begins to grasp the idea of
guilt and to experience the peculiar quality of the sense of
guilt. But it seems as though he were already prepared for
this experience, so as to understand straight away the next

conception: that of punishment and expiation and, above all, that of final forgiveness. Our study of melancholia enables us actually to see into the history of this mental structure—a history reaching back to the primal dawn of the mind—and to lay bare the ultimate foundations of experience upon which it is built. Here I may refer to a conclusion which I have already suggested elsewhere.[8] Briefly it is this: that, when the child passes from the period of suckling, he carries with him, indelibly stamped on his mind, a sequence of experiences which *later* he works over so as to form the connection: guilt—atonement—forgiveness. You can observe in the nursery how the infant, if its craving for nourishment awakens in the absence of the mother, flies into an impotent rage, kicks and screams, and then, exhausted by this reaction to its helplessness, falls wholly a prey to the torments of hunger. But you know also that this cruel experience is finally followed with *unfailing certainty* by the reappearance of the mother and that in drinking at her breast the child experiences that oral-narcissistic bliss which Freud is certainly right in describing as the prototype, never again attained to, of all subsequent gratifications.[9] The whole process constitutes a *single* sequence of experiences, countless times repeated, of whose responsibility in determining future development we surely need no further proofs. From the paroxysm of rage in the hungry infant proceed all the later forms of *aggressive reaction* to frustration (e.g. devouring, biting, striking, destroying, etc.) and it is on these that the ego, in the period of latency, concentrates its whole sense of guilt. The hypercathexis of the impulses of aggression with manifest feelings of guilt is the consequence of a normal advance in development, which the material produced in our analyses enables us to follow without effort, while the knowledge arrived at by Freud makes it easily intelligible. At the height of the phallic phase the infantile ego (intimidated by the dread of castration—loss of love) has to renounce its dangerous Œdipus wishes and to secure itself against their recurrence. To do this it forms out of the primary function of self-observation a powerful institution (the super-ego) and develops the capacity for becoming aware of the criticisms of this institution in the form of a dread of conscience (the sense of guilt). The newly-acquired reaction of conscience deals a death-blow to the Œdipus complex, but the impulses embodied in that complex undergo different fates. The genital impulse succumbs to repression; its motor elements are inhibited and the group of ideas (incest-phantasies, onanism) which were cathected by it vanish from consciousness and leave no trace behind them. The aggressive impulse, on the other hand, cannot be warded off in so effectual a manner. Its driving force is, it is true, paralysed by the setting up of a powerful anti-cathexis, but the ideas cathected by it are retained in consciousness. Evidently the ego is incapable of erecting a barrier against the manifestations of aggression as it does against those of gross sensuality. The former are constantly presented to it by the unavoidable impressions of daily life and not least by the aggressive measures adopted by those who train the child. Education must therefore content itself with *condemning* his acts of aggression in the most severe terms and causing him to attach to them the ideas of guilt and sin. The close relation between genitality and repression on the one hand and aggression and defence through reaction on the other—a relation to which Freud has recently drawn attention[10]—thus has its roots in the child's practical situation. Subsequently, the repressed guilt connected with genitality (i.e. the guilt which is incapable of entering consciousness) hides itself behind the guilt of aggression, which persists undisguised in the conscious mind; and thus the sadistic impulse (which, genetically, goes back to the infant's outbreak of rage) also becomes the manifest carrier of the whole feeling of incest-guilt, this being displaced from its genital source. The torments of hunger are the mental precursors of later "punishments" and, by way of the discipline of punishment, they come to be the primal mechanism of self-punishment, which in melancholia assumes such a fatal significance. At the bottom of the melancholiacs' profound dread of impoverishment there is really simply the dread of starvation (that is, of impoverishment in physical possessions), with which the vitality of such part of his ego as remains normal reacts to the expiatory acts which threaten the life of the patient in this disease. But drinking at the mother's breast remains the radiant image of unremitting, forgiving love. It is certainly no mere chance that the Madonna nursing the Child has become the emblem of a mighty religion and thereby the emblem of a whole epoch of our Western civilization. I think that if we trace the chain of ideas, *guilt—atonement—forgiveness,* back to the sequence of experiences of early infancy: *rage, hunger, drinking at the mother's breast,* we have the explanation of the problem why the hope of absolution and love is perhaps the most powerful conception which we meet with in the higher strata of the mental life of mankind.

According to this argument, the deepest fixation-point in the melancholic (depressive) disposition is to be found in the "situation of threatened loss of love" (Freud[11]), more precisely, in the hunger-situation of the infant. We shall learn more about it if we examine more closely that experience of "oral-narcissistic bliss" which is vouchsafed to him in his extremity. I have elsewhere tried to demonstrate that pleasurable stimulation of the mouth-zone does not constitute the whole of the oral-libidinal gratification but should rather be regarded as its more conspicuous antecedent.[12] I thought there was reason to refer the climax of this enjoyment to the subsequent, invisible part of the process, which I termed "the alimentary orgasm" and which I have assumed to be the precursor, along the road of evolution, of the later genital orgasm. We now see that the alimentary orgasm of the infant at the mother's breast is a phenomenon with important consequences, whose influence radiates out into the whole of his later life. It satisfies the egoistic cravings of the little human being for nourishment, security and warmth, fulfils the longings of his budding object-instincts and, by the blending of all these factors its induces in him a kind of narcissistic transport which is inseparably connected with them. It is perhaps more correct to say that this tremendous experience of gratification contains, as yet inextricably combined, all the components which subsequent development will differentiate and carry forward to different fates. But it comes to the same thing: we cannot fail to recognize that the infant's dawning ego acquires in this narcissistic gratification that mental quality which it will later experience as "self-satisfaction." This feeling is, in its origin, the reaction of the dawning ego to the experience which is biologically the most important to it, namely, that of alimentary orgasm. Later on the principal incentives for stimulating self-esteem will be the ego's developments in the direction of power and all the forms of activity by which it obtains gratification—we can actually distinguish within self-esteem a progress from the oral to a sadistic-anal and thence to a genital level (corresponding to the varying technique of acquisition)—but the peculiar quality of the experience persists as a specifically differentiated memory-symbol of that early ego-reaction which was conditioned by the alimentary orgasm.

If we take into consideration the fact that the quality of feeling which is experienced as self-esteem (as this has already been described by Bernfeld[13]), can, by the addition of fresh factors, advance in successive stages to the pitch of exaltation, triumph, ecstasy and intoxication, we may feel that the chain of connected ideas is brought to a satisfactory end. I discovered already some time ago through another channel that states of intoxication in adults are derived from the experience of blissful repletion in the process of nutrition. Now it is precisely for melancholia that the genetic sequence here worked out: *alimentary orgasm—self-satisfaction—intoxication*—is of importance. As we have heard, the melancholiac tries to restore his seriously diminished self-esteem by means of love. His behaviour strikes us as morbid, because it is related not to the object but to his own super-ego. But it leads to a result which is entirely logical though none the less pathological. I refer to mania, in which disease, as Freud has recognized,[14] the ego is once more merged with the super-ego in unity. We may add that this process is the faithful, intra-psychic repetition of the experience of that fusing with the mother that takes place during drinking at her breast. The earliest (oral) technique for the renewal of self-satisfaction is revived on the psychic plane and results —as is psychologically perfectly correct—in the transports of mania. The manic condition succeeds the phase of self-punishment with the same regularity with which formerly, in the biological process, the bliss of satiety succeeded to hunger. We know, further, that the ego has yet another pathological method to which it can resort in order to bolster up its tottering self-esteem. This method also takes the alimentary orgasm as its prototype: it consists of a flight into the pharmacotoxic states to which the victims of drug-addiction have recourse.

Let us go back to our earlier statement that the ego, finding that its rebellion against the loss of its object is futile, changes its psychological technique, confesses that it is guilty and passes into a state of remorseful contrition. Here the question arises exactly why and of what does the ego feel itself guilty? In depressive neurotics we need to get through a great deal of work in order to answer this question with any certainty. With the melancholiac, however, who in this respect is so frank with us, we have only to listen attentively and then we easily arrive at the inner meaning of his self-reproaches. He feels guilty because by his aggressive attitude he has himself to blame for the loss of the object, and in this we certainly cannot contradict him. We observe, too, that this confession of guilt by the ego is modelled on infantile prototypes and its expression is strongly reinforced from infantile sources. Nevertheless, precisely the most striking characteristics of the melancholiac's atonement would still be incomprehensible were it not that we know that this behaviour is contributed to very largely from another quarter.

There is indeed another psychic process at work, parallel with the melancholic atonement. It has its origin in the sadistic trend of hostility to the object, which has already shown its force in the ambivalent character of the love-relation, which later supplied the fuel for rebellious reactions, and which brought the ego over to the other view, namely, that the object alone was to blame for the quarrel, having provoked the rigour of the ego by its caprice, unreliability and spite. Freud's discovery, which I mentioned at the beginning of this paper, revealed to us the surprising fact that in melancholia this overmastering aggressive tendency of the id proves stronger than the ego. When the latter has failed ignominiously to carry through the claims of its hostile impulses towards the object (i.e. when the phase of rebellion collapses) and thereupon adopts an attitude of masochistic remorse towards the super-ego, the aggressive tendency of the id goes over to the side of the super-ego and forces the ego itself, weakened by its expiatory attitude, into the position of the object. Thereafter the super-ego visits upon the ego all the fury which the ego would otherwise have been capable of visiting upon the object. In the past the ego sallied forth into the world in order to find gratification for its narcissistic craving for love, but the demands of its sadism brought it to grief; now, turning away from reality, it seeks for narcissistic gratification within the mind itself, but, here again, it cannot escape the overpowering force of the aggressive instinct. The self-punishments assume forms very different from that of the expiation which may have hovered before the imagination of the ego, and are carried to a degree far in excess of it. In its remorse the ego turned, full of confidence, to a benevolent being, whose punishments would be but light; now it has to bear the consequences of its infantile trustfulness and weakness. Since, in its perplexity, it cannot rid itself of the hope of the forgiveness which shall save it, it submits to the rôle of object, takes upon itself the whole guilt of the object and suffers without resistance the cruelties of the super-ego. Its own self is now almost annihilated—only its various dreads (expressed in distorted forms) betray that the core of the ego still exists. Such total capitulation on the part of the ego to the sadism of the id would be incomprehensible, if it were not that we realize that it falls a victim to the indestructible infantile illusion that only by yielding and making atonement can it be delivered from its *narcissistic* distress.

This, then, is the change of grouping which the "synthetic function" brings about in the ego of the melancholiac. From instinctual processes whose origin and trend are diametrically opposed it succeeds in organizing the mental activities into one great and unified whole, these heterogeneous elements appearing as operative factors which are mutually dependent and complementary. The repentant ego desires to win the forgiveness of the offended object and, as an atonement, submits to being punished by the super-ego instead of by the object. In the undreamed-of harshness of the super-ego the old tendency of hostility to the object is expending its fury on the ego, which is thrust into the place of the hated object. Thus, the result of this synthetic process is a very extensive loss of the relation to reality and complete subjection of the ego to the unrestrained tyranny of the sadistic super-ego, which, as Freud remarks, has arrogated to itself the consciousness (and, we may now add, also the "synthetic function") of the melancholic personality.

Here we must pause, for we cannot suppress our astonishment at this conclusion. This, so to speak, symmetrical solution which we have discovered for the conflicts of the ambivalent instinctual impulses is certainly tempting in form, and in content it is based in all its elements on assured data acquired by observation, but it appears to contain a hopeless contradiction. According to our construction the object would have to undergo two different processes of incorporation, being absorbed not only by the super-ego but by the ego—an idea which at first sight we cannot grasp and which we mistrust. Either our explanation is erroneous or we still lack insight into certain fundamental relations. I hope to be able to shew that the latter is true and that the difficulty can be solved. But, in order to do this, we must go back a little further.

Freud has assumed, for good reasons, that sensory perception is at the outset entirely controlled by the pleasure-principle. Only what is pleasurable is perceived; that which is painful is, as far as possible, ignored. It is a long time before this latter also gains psychic representation in the child. When it does so, the period begins in which the world clearly consists, in the child's view, of two kinds of ideas: those of things which are pleasurable and those of things which are painful. But there are certain tricky things which are sometimes a source of pleasure and sometimes of pain: the mother, for instance, according to whether she caresses her child with a happy smile or is angry and disregards or even hurts it. It is easy for us to say that it is one and the same mother in two different moods. It signifies an enormous advance when the child reaches the point of being able to make this synthesis; at first he is incapable of such an achievement of thought. He is still wholly dominated by the pleasure-principle, and he distinguishes between these two impressions as objects which are "good" or "bad," or, as we may say, as his "good mother" or his "bad mother." The experiences and recollections connected with the mother do not form in the child's mind *one* continuous series, as we should expect in the case of adults. His perceptions and memory-images of the *one* real object produce *two* series, sharply differentiated according to their hedonic value.

This primitive mode of functioning of the dawning intellectual activity acquires a lasting importance in our mental life from the fact that it is connected with the ambivalence of instinctual life. The "good" (pleasure-conferring) and the "bad" (frustration-inflicting) mothers become for the child *isolated objects* (instinct-representations) of his love and his hate. This duality of the objects persists in such thinking as is instinctually controlled, even when the child from the purely intellectual standpoint grasps the complete idea of "mother" (including both her "good" and her "bad" moods). As soon as he comes under the influence of a strong love-impulse his whole real knowledge about the bad side of his mother is simply blotted out; and, conversely, when his hate-impulses break through, there is nothing in the mother who is now "bad" to remind him that this mother is also wont to be good. It is easy to understand this behaviour: it means that the still weak ego is avoiding the conflict of ambivalence by turning with its love to a mother who is *only* loveable and with its hate to another mother who deserves *only* hate. While in this condition the child, from his subjective standpoint, cannot yet be described as "ambivalent" at all; ambivalence is established only when education succeeds in causing him to relate the two contrary discharges of instinct to the one real mother-object, that is, when he has "learnt to know" what he is doing. By this means education compels him to repress at any rate the worst part of his aggressive tendencies. His aggression, warded off by the ego, then remains in the unconscious fastened upon the isolated representation "bad mother," a fact which ensures the continuance of this partial idea. When the child has recognized the sad truth that his mother is sometimes "good" and sometimes "bad," there arises in him in his craving for love the constantly increasing longing for a mother who is "always only good." The isolated image of the "good" mother now persists in his mind as a strongly-cathected *wish-idea*.

I would note here that persons who have the care of little children reveal in their behaviour an instinctive knowledge of the duality of the child's conception. When a nurse, after scolding her little charge, desires to soothe him, she makes use of a certain comforting expedient. "The naughty boy has gone away," she says, "there is only our good boy here now." Or if, perhaps, she perceives that she has been unjust to the little boy, she will give herself one or two slaps in front of him and then say of herself "Naughty Marie has gone away: there is only good Marie here now." You observe how this innocent game confirms the child's instinctive view that bad people are there to be slain, for to be "away" means to be dead. We may say, further, that in this double idea we have the origin of the good and evil spirits which primitive man conceives of as "possessing" people or things, and also of the idea of a "double" which in dreams, myths and other creations of the unconscious is so often met with as an expression of ambivalence.

The child's longing for a father and mother who shall be always "only good" is constantly being reinforced by the threats with which he is menaced (castration) and by painful punishments, and it finally provides the motive force for the formation of the super-ego. In saying this we are only expressing in a somewhat modified form a discovery of Freud's which has become familiar to us. Our formulation of it is designed to bring into prominence the part played in psychology by these pairs of ideas. We gain a clear picture of the situation in the phase in which the super-ego is being formed, if we attribute to the infantile ego the following train of thought:—

"My parents must never punish me any more, they must *only* love me. Their image within my mind—my super-ego—will now see to it that they need never again be angry with me. Of course my super-ego also must love me. But if the function of my super-ego is to secure for me my parents' love, then it must be able to compel me to desist from certain actions. If necessary, it must be very severe with me and, nevertheless, I shall love it."

According to this description the formation of the super-ego is an attempt of the ego to realize its desire to transform the alternately "good" and "bad" parents into parents who are "only good." In pursuit of this intention the ego must above all renounce its genital and sadistic impulses, in so far as they are directed against the parents (Œdipus libido of the id). Moreover, it must make up its mind to accord to the internalized parents (the super-ego) the right to be angry and severe on occasion; nevertheless, the ego will not cease to love them and to desire their love. In taking this decision the ego makes over to the super-ego the control of those instinctual energies of the id whose activity it has itself renounced.

Thus the parental institution set up within the mind (introjected) is in all points a creation of the ego. The ego in the first instance constructs this institution from its "good parents" and also from the behaviour of the "bad parents." That is to say, the ego *loves* the internalized parents just as it loves its "good parents" in reality, but it must not allow itself to *hate* them like its "bad parents," even if they behave like "bad parents." We see then that the super-ego when it comes into being takes over from the ego the group of ideas relating to "good parents" together with the cathexis pertaining to it, whilst it borrows from the group of ideas relating to the "bad parents" only its *content*. The erotic and aggressive forces with which the super-ego has to work are placed at its disposal by the ego when the latter abandons its own right to employ them; they are drawn from the instinct-reservoir of the id. The sadistic tendency (of hostility to the parents), so far as it resists this fate, is banished by the ego unaltered into the realm of the repressed, where it already finds a representation in the isolated partial idea of the "bad parents." A similar fate overtakes that remainder of the crudely sensual sexual trend which refuses to be turned inwards (in the form of desexualization and surrender to the super-ego). Thus the ego strives earnestly to give to its old dream of parents who are "only good" living realization in the real parents.

At this point I must again emphasize the one-sided orientation and the schematic character of the account which I have just given. My purpose was simply to define the type of individuals, feminine in their narcissism, to which persons of depressive disposition conform. With this type the mere "danger of loss of love" is sufficient to compel formation of the super-ego. The purely masculine type, whose narcissism is of a different character and which surrenders only to the pressure of threatened castration, does not concern us here.

We can now return from this excursion back to the question of melancholic introjection. The individual who is later to succumb to melancholia retains all his life, in consequence of the exaggerated ambivalence of his instinctual disposition, very considerable residues of his infantile duplicating mode of thinking. When he gives play alternately to his ambivalent impulses and thus succeeds in completely withdrawing his consciousness from the light or dark side of the object, as the occasion requires, he is behaving in a manner hardly different from that of the child. It is only clinical observation of this phenomenon, so entirely characteristic of neurotic ambivalence, which enables us by reasoning *a posteriori* to throw light upon the corresponding processes in the development of the child. When, with the outbreak of melancholia, the strong current of regressive processes begins to flow, the subject's idea of his latest love-object, which has hitherto corresponded to reality, must also give way in the end to the archaic demands made on the function of thought by his ambivalence, which has now broken free of all restraint. The "good object," whose love the ego desires, is introjected and incorporated in the super-ego. There, in accordance with the principle which, as we have just remarked, governs the formation of this institution, it is endowed with the prescriptive right (formerly so vehemently disputed in relation to the real object), to be angry with the ego—indeed, very angry. The "bad object" has been split off from the object as a whole, to act, as it were, as "whipping-boy." It is incorporated in the ego and becomes the victim of the sadistic tendency now emanating from the super-ego. As you see, the logical inconsistency is really entirely cleared up.

This conclusion now enables us to discover in its fullest implications the hidden meaning of the mechanism of melancholia. For consider: The worst fault by which the "bad object" has incurred guilt, according to the reproach of the ego, is its ambivalence, by which it has "provoked" the ego's hostility. Now if the "bad object" which resides within the ego is chastised and finally destroyed, all that remains is the object purged of its "bad" element, i.e. the "good object"; moreover, the hostility of the ego (of the id) is satisfied and has spent itself. Nothing now stands in the way of the purified ego's uniting itself with the object, which is also purged of offence, in reciprocal love! When the subject

swings over to mania this, the goal of the melancholic process
(in the region of the pathological) is fully attained. The
"bad object" (as Abraham recognized[15]) is expelled from the
ego by an anal act and this is synonymous with its being
killed. The ego, freed of its own aggressive tendencies and
its hated enemy, heaves a sigh of relief and with every sign
of blissful transport unites itself with the "good object,"
which has been raised to the position of the super-ego.

Thus we come to realize that the process of melancholia
represents an attempt at reparation (cure) on a grand scale,
carried out with an iron psychological consistence. It is designed to revive the ego's self-regard, which has been annihilated by the loss of love, to restore the interrupted love-
relation, to be as it were a prophylactic measure against the
ego's ever suffering such severe injury again and, with this
end in view, to do away with the causes of the mischief,
namely, the ambivalence of the ego and that of the object.
As to attaining any *real* effect by this line of action, the crucial point is that it does not take place on the right plane, in
relation to the object-world, but is carried out, subject to a
narcissistic regression, entirely between the separate institutions in the patient's mind. It cannot restore to the ego the
lost object; the final reconciliation with the object (after
this has been replaced by the super-ego) is accomplished
not as a real process in the outside world but as a change of
the situation (cathexis) in the psychic organization. From
this purely psychic act, however, there ensues an important
real result: the restoration of the subject's self-esteem—indeed, its leap into the exaltation of mania. The difference is
clear to us: the melancholic process, set going by a grievous
shattering of the subject's narcissim, can by means of a
purely psychic shifting of cathexis attain to its *narcissistic*

goal (the restoration of self-esteem), even though reality be thereby ignored. Once passed into the state of mania, the ego immediately finds its way back into the object-world. With all its energy released by the sudden change in cathexis it rushes upon reality and there expends its violence. What determines the behaviour of the manic patient is the oral derivation of the psychogenic transport; it is a striking fact that in mania the adult with his manifold potentialities of action and reaction reproduces the uninhibited instinctual manifestations which we observe in the euphoria of the satiated suckling. That the quality of the reactions of a period of life in which the super-ego did not as yet exist should be the pattern upon which is modelled the manic state (the basis of which is a temporary withdrawal of the super-ego) is exactly what we should expect.

The productive energy of the melancholic process is not exhausted when the manic phase has been brought about. When the last echoes of that phase have died away—or sometimes immediately on its passing—this energy finds outlet in the obsessive tinge which it imparts to the subject's character in the "interval of remission." One of Abraham's most memorable contributions to our knowledge is his discovery and description of this peculiarity of character.[16] This issue is due to the preponderance of sadistic-anal instinctual energies and is based on a renunciation of the oral restoration of self-esteem in mania. The ego has grown stronger and endeavours to avert in the sphere of reality the dangers with which it is threatened by its ambivalence. Thanks to the subject's full recognition of reality, this endeavour is crowded with considerable success in the direction of cure. The ego, its wits sharpened by its painful experiences, erects widely-flung psychic bulwarks to restrain its ambivalence; through this excess of reaction-formations its character now becomes like that of the obsessional neurotic. But this change in character does more than merely guard the ego against the perils of its ambivalence. By means of the extensive ideal-formation the dangerous aggressive impulses are directed into social channels and thus, by way of fulfilment of the ideal, they minister to narcissistic gratification in accordance with reality. As we know, the power of this mental structure to resist fresh strains varies extraordinarily with different individuals. But it would be premature to try to make any more exact pronouncement at the present time either on this point or on the other economic problems of the manifold courses taken by melancholia.

In conclusion I should like to devote a few remarks to the problem of *neurotic* depression. Observation shows that the depressive process, in so far as it has caught in its grip the ego of the person suffering from a transference-neurosis, is carried out in exact accordance with the mechanism of true melancholia. That is to say that neurotic depression also has as its basis a narcissistic turning-away from reality, the external object being replaced by psychic institutions and an endeavour being made to solve the conflicts on the intra-psychic plane instead of in the outside world, and by means of a regressively activated oral technique. But there is this difference: these processes almost wholly consume the ego of the melancholic and destroy those functions in him which relate to reality, while in a transference-neurosis they are as it were merely superimposed upon an ego which is, indeed, neurotic but is more or less intact. In the depressive neurotic the object and, with it, the relation to reality, are preserved: it is only that the patient's hold on them is loosened and the weakly ego has begun to give up the struggle with the world

—a struggle which it feels to be unbearable—to turn in-wards in a narcissistic fashion and to take refuge in the oral-narcissistic reparation-mechanism. Thus, neurotic depression is a kind of partial melancholia of the (neurotic) ego; the further the depressive process extends within that ego at the cost of its relations to the object and to reality, the more does the condition of narcissistic neurosis approximate to melan-cholia. Accordingly, in an acute access of depression we should expect the issue to turn upon whether in the narcissistic ma-chinery of the ego the oral mechanisms gain the upper hand or whether the sadistic-anal (and genital) mechanisms, whose hold upon the object-world is firmer, are strong enough to safeguard the ego from the plunge into melancholia.

THE THEORY
MODIFIED

Psychodynamics of Depression from the Etiologic Point of View

SANDOR RADO

In the study of disordered behavior we will find our chief help is the etiologic point of view. In order to keep etiology the center of investigative interest, we have evolved the working concept of "pathogenic phenotypes." The problem thus posed is to disclose the causative chain of events which produces each of these disease-prone phenotypes as its effect. Genetically, this etiologic chain is a chain of interactions of genotype and environment. We must learn to correlate more effectively clinical observation and material drawn from genetics, pathologic anatomy, physiology, biophysics, biochemistry, and psychodynamics. There can be no true progress unless we leave our cozy pigeon-holes and join forces for the common task.

Within this framework we tentatively speak of the "class of moodcyclic phenotypes," which is characterized, among other manifestations, by the high incidence of depressive spells. These depressive spells are the topic of our present symposium. My assignment is to outline their specific psychodynamics which presumably represent the terminal links in the etiologic chain.

In the circumstances we must resort to schematic presentation and limit ourselves to the essentials. First we shall sketch the clinical picture of a spell of depression:

The patient is sad and in painful tension. He is intolerant of his condition, thereby increasing his distress. His self-esteem is abased, his self-confidence shattered. Retardation of his initiative, thinking, and motor actions makes him incapable of sustained effort. His behavior indicates open or underlying fears and guilty fears. He is demonstratively preoccupied with his alleged failings, shortcomings, and unworthiness; yet he also harbors a deep resentment that life does not give him a fair deal.

He usually has suicidal ideas and often suicidal impulses. His sleep is poor; his appetite and sexual desire are on the wane or gone. He takes little or no interest in his work and ordinary affairs and shies away from affectionate as well as competitive relationships. All in all, he has lost his capacity to enjoy life. He is drawn into a world of his own imagination, a world dedicated to the pursuit of suffering rather than to the pursuit of happiness.

Such attacks may be occasioned by a serious loss, failure, or defeat; or may seem to come from the clear blue sky. Their onset may be sudden or gradual; their duration, from a few days or weeks to many months. Their severity ranges from mildly neurotic to fully psychotic.

Often in the neurotic and almost always in the psychotic cases there are conspicuous physical symptoms, such as loss of weight and constipation.

In some patients spells of depression alternate with spells of elation while in others no spells of elation occur.

The depressive spell has a hidden pattern of meaning. Since the patient's subjective experience contains only disjointed fragments of this pattern, the observer must penetrate psychoanalytically into the unconscious (or, as we prefer to say, "nonreporting") foundations of the patient's subjective experience.[1] In this light, the depressive spell is a desperate cry for love, precipitated by an actual or imagined loss which the patient feels endangers his emotional (and material) security. In the simplest case the patient has lost his beloved one. The emotional overreaction to this emergency unfolds, unbeknown to the patient himself, as an expiatory process of self-punishment. By blaming and punishing himself for the loss he has suffered, he now wishes to reconcile the *mother* and to reinstate himself into *her* loving care. The aim-image of the patient's repentance is the emotional and alimentary security which he, as an infant, enjoyed while clinging to his mother's feeding breast. The patient's mute cry for love is patterned on the hungry infant's loud cry for help. His most conspicuous morbid fears (such as his fear of impoverishment, his hypochondriac concern for his digestive organs) are revivals of the infant's early fear of starvation.[2] The expiatory process is governed by the emergency principle of repair: in the organism the pain of lost pleasure tends to elicit activity aimed at recapturing the lost pleasure.

However, the patient's dominant motivation of repentance is complicated by the simultaneous presence of a strong resentment. As far as his guilty fear goes, he is humble and

[1] See references in chapter notes at back of book.

yearns to repent; as far as his coercive rage goes, he is resentful.

In the forephase of the depressive spell the patient tends
to vent his resentment on the beloved person, the one by
whom he feels "let down" or deserted. He wants to force
this person to love him.* When the patient feels that his
coercive rage is defeated, his need for repentance gains the
upper hand; his rage then recoils and turns inward against
him, increasing by its vehemence the severity of his self-
reproaches and self-punishments. As a superlative bid for
forgiveness, the patient may thus be driven to suicide. When
he attempts to finish his life, he appears to be acting under
the strong illusion that this supreme sacrifice will reconcile
the mother and secure her nourishing graces—forever.[3]

A significant feature must be added to the characterization of the love-hungry patient's coercive rage. This rage
proposes to use the patient's teeth as coercive weapons. The
infant's teeth enhanced his alimentary delight; but rage remembers the destructive power of biting and chewing. In the
non-reporting reaches of his mind, the enraged patient is
set to devour the frustrating mother herself as a substitute
for food. Moreover, her disappearance from the scene will
enable the smiling mother to reappear with her dependable
offerings of food. In dire need, prehistoric tribesmen may
have devoured their chieftain (later, their totem animal)
with similar ideas in mind. Sometimes this "cannibalistic"
feature is clearly revealed in the depressed patient's dreams.
Fasting, the temporary cessation of biting and chewing, is in
turn one of the earliest and most enduring forms of punish-

---

* According to an anecdote, the father of Frederick the Great was
overheard shouting as he beat one of the lackies, "You must love me,
you rascal."

ment and self-punishment in our civilization ("tooth for tooth"). It appears in the cultural patterns of expiation and reappears in the depressive version of expiation for the same psychodynamic reasons.*

The patient takes pride not in his repentance, but in his coercive rage, even after defeat has retroflexed and forced this rage to subserve his repentance. Thus he punishes himself not only for his defiance, but also, in continued defiance, for his inexcusable failure to terrorize the beloved one (the mother) in the first place. Furthermore, the retroflexion of rage is never complete; the expiatory process is continuously complicated by a residue of straight rage which remains directed against the environment. The merciless, though unconscious, irony with which the patient blames even the failings of the beloved one on himself demonstrates spectacularly this residue of straight rage. By reducing his self-reproaches to absurdity, he succeeds in venting his resentment on the beloved one at the height of his forced contrition and self-disparagement.

The extreme painfulness of depression may in part be explained by the fact that in his dependent craving the patient is torn between coercive rage and submissive fear, and thus strives to achieve his imaginary purpose, that of regaining the mother's love, by employing two conflicting methods at the same time.

The struggle between fear and rage underlies the clinical distinction between retarded depression and agitated depression. If rage is sufficiently retroflexed by the prevailing guilty fear, the patient is retarded; if the prevailing guilty fear is shot through with straight environment-directed rage,

* Another version of morbid fasting is known to the medical profession as "anorexia nervosa."

he is agitated. Whenever antagonistic tensions of equal or nearly equal strength compete for *immediate* discharge, they tend to produce an interference pattern of discharge. We call this psychodynamic mechanism discharge-interference. His retarded behavior, on the other hand, is explained as an inhibitory effect on the combined action of guilty fear and pain.

Based on these findings, we view depression as a process of miscarried repair. To a healthy person a serious loss is a challenge. He meets the emergency by calming his emotions, marshalling his remaining resources, and increasing his adaptive efficiency. Depressive repair miscarries because it results in the exact opposite. Anachronistically, this repair presses the obsolete adaptive pattern of alimentary maternal dependence into service and by this regressive move it incapacitates the patient still more.[4]

Historically, this theory developed as follows. Retroflexed rage is one of Freud's early clinical discoveries; he described it as "sadism (aggression) turned against the self." In 1917, Freud suggested that the depressed patient's ego metamorphoses into a replica of the lost love-object.[5] This replacement by identification, Freud continued, serves the patient's ambivalence, his hate as well as his love, for at the same time he turns his sadism against himself and thus hits the love-object in himself.

In 1924, a significant paper by Abraham initiated a tacit reconsideration of this hypothesis of "identification with the lost love-object."[6] Abraham showed that the identification amounts to a forceful fantasy of devouring and thus destroying the hated love-object.

In 1927, the present writer introduced three points.[7] First, that the depressed patient reverts to the infant's first love-object (source of security), the mother. Second, that the patient has the same idea as had the infant: to destroy the *frustrating* aspect of the beloved one (formed in the split-off image of the "frustrating mother"), while retaining the *gratifying* aspect of the beloved one (formed in the split-off image of the "gratifying mother"). Third, that the depressive process is a process of expiation, overchaged by retroflexed rage. In 1932, he added that when the depressed patient voices his reproaches as self-reproaches, he does so ironically.[8] In recent years, closer study of the failures of emergency adjustment has shown that the entire depressive process must be evaluated from the adaptational point of view, and interpreted as a process of miscarried repair.[9]

The motivational organization which we hold to be specific of the depressive spell is composed of three primary constituents: the alteration of mood to one of sustained gloomy repentance; the regressive yearning for the alimentary security of the infant; and the struggle between the excessive emergency emotions, in which submissive fear defeats coercive rage. The first two of these three constituents are altogether peculiar to the depressive spell, but the third is not. A similarly grave conflict between the excessive emergency emotions is a primary constituent also in the obsessional and the paranoid patterns. However, in these contexts the relative strength of the contending forces is different, and so is their disordering effect.

In the nonreporting foundations of the obsessional pattern the coercive use of the teeth is eclipsed in actual effectiveness by the coercive use of the hands and of the trampling feet. In certain circumstances, the infant may also resort to the coercive use of defecation. In the infant's experience, the hands could be used both ways, to fondle or to beat; and the control of reputedly poisonous feces too could be used either to obey and accomodate or to have fun and defy. The coercive use of the extremities (which includes the infant's "murderous" impulses as well) was the enraged infant's response to maternal discipline in general; enraged bowel defiance his reaction to the mother's particular effort to impose bowel "regularity" upon him. With the progressing biologic maturation of the infant, the struggle for power between him and the mother is thus extended and intensified. In the pattern under consideration the combined forces of straight rage and prohibited desire are about as strong as the combined forces of guilty fear and retroflexed rage. This makes the struggle between obedient submission and defiant coercion interminable. Must he let mother have her way, or can he force her to let him have his way and still love him? Although the emotions concerned are repressed to an astonishing extent, their conflicting tensions penetrate into the range of awareness and raise havoc with the patient's intellect. The see-saw of the patient's doubts, doings and undoings, side-tracked precautions and side-tracked temptations, token transgressions and token self-punishments, is a product of discharge-interference. The function of these symptoms is to insure discharge. The formation of interference patterns explains the puzzling fact that the discharge, though forced, is nonetheless slow and torturous. Wherever the desire or demand is irrepressible or inescapable, such as in the areas of evacuation, sex and work, the patient may obtain satisfaction through "pain-dependent pleasure behavior".[10] The patterns of pain-dependence are interference patterns of discharge, composed of two antagonistic sets of tensions: guilty fear and retroflexed rage on the one hand and, on the other, defiant rage and inhibited desire. Each of these patterns derives its special characteristics from the particular pleasure organization involved; the inhibition of desire is automatized, varies in severity, and results from parental prohibition in early life. To sum up: the obsessive patient experiences less emotional turmoil; but he tends to become pain-dependent and is forced to squander his finest resources on a hopeless and unending task. *

In the paraniod pattern on the other hand, straight environment-directed rage rises to dominance; hence the patient's proneness to violence.[13] This differential dynamics may help to explain the clinical observation stressed already by Abraham, that during the intervals between depressive spells the behavior of moodcyclic patients often shows an obsessive pattern; and we may add, occasionally a paranoid pattern.[14] These patterns tend to disappear during the depressive spell; but the patient's pain-dependence persists.

Knowledge of the specific dynamics of depression has proved helpful in treatment. Here I shall mention but one point of technique which this dynamics has put into sharp relief.

The therapist's intuitive reaction to the depressed patient is to treat him with overwhelming kindness. This may indeed reassure the patient and lessen his predicament, but it also may defeat completely the therapist's purpose and drive the patient into utter despair. If, at the moment, the patient's craving for affection is stronger, kindness will win. If his guilty fear and retroflexed rage are stronger, kindness will lose; because in the latter case the patient will feel: "This man is so kind to me and I am such an unworthy

* By using the concept of emergency behavior,[11] adaptational pyschodynamics supplies the answers to the questions Freud raised in 1926.[12]

person." The fresh bout of self-reproaches thus provoked may increase the danger of suicide. When the therapist finds that retroflexed rage has reached an alarming degree, he may therefore treat the patient harshly in order to provoke a relieving outburst of rage. Here the danger is that the patient may break the treatment. These are, of course, hardly more than palliative measures designed to keep the patient alive and the treatment going.[15]

Concerning the psychodynamic aspect of shock treatment, observers have suggested that in the patient's unconscious mind such treatment registers as a punishment. Even if it does, the question of the physiologic mode of action of shock treatment still remains.

In order to balance the picture, I shall now enumerate some of the unsolved problems:

Our tentative generalizations derive from the psychoanalytic study of a limited number of cases. In order to establish their range of validity it will be necessary to repeat such studies on a much larger scale.

The strength of fear and rage in relation to one another, and the strength of both in relation to the patient's capacity for love, joy and happiness in life, are problems almost untouched. A closely related task is to explore the *physiologic* basis of such psychodynamic mechanisms as *discharge-summation* through the joint of confluent tensions, and *discharge-interference* through the alternate action of competing tensions.

In the case of unoccasioned depression a "precipitating loss" exists only in the patient's unconscious imagination; thus this "loss" is an effect of the patient's emotional disturbance, rather than its cause. Even in occasioned depression, it is not infrequently the patient's emotional overreaction that makes this "loss" appear to him so severe. Hence, the patient's emotional overreaction need not be due to a precipitating loss, failure, or defeat. His sudden guilty fear and hidden craving for alimentary security may be due to other as yet unknown causes. He then may invent a "precipitating event" in order to make the expiatory pattern complete, as if rationalizing his depression. The problem is to disclose the mechanism responsible for the sharp rise in the patient's guilty fear and for his regressive dependence for emotional security on the feeding mother.

There is a good deal of work to be done at the *physiologic* level of inquiry. Even the expiatory process itself may be the human elaboration of a biologic pattern formed at lower stages of the evolutionary scale.

Treated or untreated, after a period of time the depressive spell spends its fury and subsides; we do not know why or how.

Psychodynamics, so far, has offered no clue to explain why some depressed patients are subject also to spells of elation and others are not.

The incidence of depressive spells is not limited to the class of moodcyclic phenotypes. Such spells also occur in almost every other pathogenic type. We encounter depressions in drug-dependent patients, neurotics, schizophrenics, general paretics, patients afflicted with severe physical illness, etc. The question arises whether or not significant psychodynamic differences exist between depressive spells that occur in different pathogenic contexts. Further psychoanalytic investigation may provide an answer to this question.

In the failues of emergency adjustment the ultimate factor discernible by psychodynamic analysis is the patient's emotional overreaction to danger in terms of pain, fear, and rage. This trait is traceable to early life; the most constant among its early manifestations is the infant's emotional over-reaction to parental discipline with its threats of punishment. At the present stage of inquiry an investigative program must include the *physiologic* and *genetic* aspects of this emotional overreaction. In our view, this problem is of surpassing importance to the psychodynamics of all disordered behavior.[16] Concerning depression, the program must also include the problem of the moodcyclic *genotype*.

The value of the cooperation of the geneticist depends on the degree of precision with which the psychiatrist can classify the clinical material and formulate the problem for him. The same applies to the cooperation expected from our colleagues in the fields of pathologic anatomy, physiology, biophysics, and biochemistry. Hence, the first item on our agenda must be to improve the scientific standards of clinical observation and description, and put the interpretation of the patient's behavior firmly on the basis of adaptational psychodynamics. We must abandon obsolete methods and concepts without costly delay. Semantics and cybernetics warn us with increasing urgency that by using undefined (and often enough, undefinable) language we can communicate nothing but confusion. Our responsibility is to keep pace with the general advance of science, evolve a sound, consistent, and verifiable conceptual scheme, and keep it continuously up to date.

Depression and Mania

OTTO FENICHEL

Depression and Self-Esteem

The understanding of the impulse neuroses and addictions provides the background prerequisite for the study of that most frequent and also most problematic mechanism of symptom formation, depression. To a slight degree, depression occurs in nearly every neurosis (at least in the form of neurotic inferiority feelings); of high degree it is the most terrible symptom in the tormenting psychotic state of melancholia.

Depression is based on the same predisposition as addiction and pathological impulses. A person who is fixated on the state where his self-esteem is regulated by external supplies or a person whose guilt feelings motivate him to regress to this state vitally needs these supplies. He goes through this world in a condition of perpetual greediness. If his narcissistic needs are not satisfied, his self-esteem diminishes to a danger point. He is ready to do anything to avoid this. He will try every means to induce others to let him participate in their supposed power. On the one hand the pregenital fixation of such persons manifests itself in a tendency to react to frustrations with violence; on the other hand their oral dependence impels them to try to get what they need by ingratiation and submissiveness. The conflict between these contradictory devices is characteristic for persons with this predisposition.

Methods of ingratiation often reveal in analysis that simultaneously they are methods of rebellion. Sacrifice and prayer, the classic methods of ingratiation, are often thought of as a kind of magical violence used to force God to give what is needed. Many depressive attitudes are precisely such condensations of ingratiation and aggressiveness.

These persons, in their continuous need of supplies that give sexual satisfaction and heighten self-esteem simultaneously, are "love addicts," unable to love actively; they passively need to feel loved. Besides, they are characterized by their dependence and their narcissistic type of object choice. Their object relationships are mixed up with features of identification and they tend to change objects frequently because no object is able to provide the necessary satisfaction. They require a behavior on the part of their objects that permits or encourages their participation by enabling them to feel at one with the partner. Without giving any consideration to the feelings of their fellow men they demand of them an understanding of their own feelings. They are always bent upon establishing a "good understanding" with people, though they are unable to fulfill their own part of such an understanding; this need compels them to attempt to deny their ever-present readiness to react hostilely.

In consonance with the early fixation of persons of this kind, the personality of the object is of no great importance. They need the supplies, and it does not matter who provides them. It does not necessarily have to be a person; it may be a drug or an obsessive hobby. Some persons of this type fare worse than others; they not only need supplies, but simultaneously fear getting them, because they unconsciously consider them dangerous.

As in the case of drug addicts, "love addicts," too, may become incapable of getting the desired satisfaction, which in turn increases their addiction. The cause for this decisive incapacity is the extreme ambivalence connected with their oral orientation.[1]

The understanding of this archaic type of regulation of self-esteem will be facilitated by a recapitulation of the developmental stages of guilt feelings. In the life of the infant, the stages of hunger and satiety alternate. The hungry infant remembers having been satisfied previously and tries to force the return of this state by asserting his "omnipotence" in screaming and gesticulation. Later on, the infant loses belief in his omnipotence; he projects this omnipotence onto his parents and tries to regain it through participation in their omnipotence. He needs this participation, the feeling of being loved, in the same way that previously he needed milk. Now the succession of hunger and satiety is replaced by the succession of states in which the child feels alone and therefore experiences a kind of self-depreciation—we called it annihilation—and states in which he feels loved and his self-esteem is re-established. Still later, the ego acquires the ability to judge by anticipating the future. Then the ego creates (or rather uses) states of "minor annihilations" or small "diminutions" in self-esteem as a precaution against the possibility of a real and definite loss of narcissistic supplies. Still later, the superego develops and takes over the inner regulation of self-esteem. No longer is the feeling of being loved the sole prerequisite for well-being, but the

[1] See references in chapter notes at back of book.

feeling of having done the right thing is now necessary. Conscience develops its warning function; "bad conscience" again creates states of minor annihilations or small diminutions in self-esteem to warn against the danger of a definite loss of narcissistic supplies, this time from the superego. Under certain circumstances the warning signal of the conscience may fail and turn into the tormenting feeling of complete annihilation of melancholia, in the same way that in anxiety hysteria the warning signal of anxiety may suddenly turn into a complete panic. The explanation of such failure of conscience was postponed. The study of depression is the place to come back to it.

A severe depression represents the state into which the orally dependent individual gets when the vital supplies are lacking; a slight depression is an anticipation of this state for warning purposes.

The motives of defense against instinctual drives are anxiety or guilt feeling. In the same way that an anxiety motivating defense is still manifest in anxiety hysteria, a guilt feeling motivating defense is manifest in some simple depressions.

After times of long deprivation and frustration, everybody tends to become apathetic, slow, retarded, uninterested. Apparently even normal persons need a certain amount of external narcissistic supplies, and if these supplies cease entirely, they get into the situation of infants not sufficiently taken care of. These states are models of "simple depressions." There are transitory states between "depressions" of this kind and regressions to a passive state of hallucinatory wish fulfillment in which no demands are directed toward the real world any more and life is supplanted by an objectless passive vegetative existence, as in some catatonic states.

Neurotic depressions are desperate attempts to force an object to give the vitally necessary supplies, whereas in the psychotic depressions the actual complete loss has really taken place and regulatory attempts are aimed exclusively at the superego.[2]

This, however, is not an absolute difference. In neurotic depressions, too, guilt feelings and the fear of being abandoned by the superego play an important part; the affection of external objects, then, is needed for the purpose of contradicting the accusing superego. And in psychotic depressions, where the struggle takes place on a narcissistic level, the ambivalence toward external objects still remains recognizable.

Orality in Depression

The pregenitality of these patients exhibits itself first of all in their anal orientation. Abraham showed that the personality of manic-depressive persons in the free intervals resembles, to a great extent, that of compulsive neurotics.[3] Combinations of depressions with compulsion neurosis are frequent. Very often money plays a significant role in the clinical picture (fear of loss of money and of poverty in depressions). Behind this anal orientation, definite trends of an oral fixation always are apparent. The refusal to eat is not only the most widespread clinical symptom of melancholia; it is a concomitant of every depression. Occasionally, this symptom alternates with bulimia.

In the chapter on organ neurosis a type of neurotic depression was mentioned in which the depressive phases were combined with bulimia, whereas the phases in which the patients restricted their eating were the ones in which they felt well.

Cannibalistic fantasies are demonstrable in the delusions of melancholia, and also in less severe types of depression, where they may be observed in dreams or as the unconscious significance of one or another symptom. Depressed patients frequently return to oral-erotic activities of their childhood—for instance, to thumbsucking. In addition, depressed persons show various oral traits of character.[4]

The unconscious ideas of depressed persons, and frequently their conscious thoughts also, are filled with fantasies of persons or parts of persons they may have eaten. To those who have no experience in analysis, it cannot be too strongly emphasized how literally this oral incorporation is conceived of as devouring.[5]

In a previous chapter, a patient was mentioned who could not eat fish because fish have "souls" and therefore represented the patient's father who had died when she was in her first year of life. She had neurotic gastrointestinal symptoms and believed that her "diaphragm" ached. In these symptoms she was warding off her Oedipus wish which had assumed the form of a desire to eat her dead father. It turned out that in the dialect of German which she spoke, the word for diaphragm, *Zwerchfell,* was pronounced as if spelled *Zwergfell* (*Zwerg* meaning dwarf); she imagined that a little dwarf, jumping about, made a hubbub in her belly. Her *Zwerchfell* was her devoured father, or, rather, his devoured penis.

Children show often enough that they believe emotionally in the possibility of eating a person and of being eaten up, even long after this idea has been rejected intellectually.

The characteristic receptive orality goes hand in hand with a receptive skin eroticism, that is, with a longing for a reassuring warmth.

A patient with a severe anxiety was unable to go to bed at night because she could not achieve the necessary relaxation and because she unconsciously regarded her not going to bed as a way of compelling fate to supply her needs. She managed to achieve a relative rest and relaxation by two acts that were love substitutes: (*a*) she would drink, and (*b*) she would sit on the radiator and enjoy its warmth.

Aims of incorporation also mark a difference between the anality met with in depressions and the anality of compulsion neurotics. The anality of the depressed person does not attempt to retain its object; it aims rather at incorporating, even if the object has to be destroyed for this purpose. Abraham has demonstrated that this type of anality corresponds to the older subtype of the anal-sadistic stage. A regression to this earlier anal level is obviously a decisive step. With the partial loss of objects attendant upon this stage, the patient is free from all restraint and his libido regresses further back to orality and narcissism.[6]

Outline of the Problems in the Mechanisms of Depression

Experiences that precipitate depressions represent either a loss of self-esteem or a loss of supplies which the patient had hoped would secure or even enhance his self-esteem. They are either experiences which for a normal person would also imply loss of self-esteem, such as failures, loss of prestige, loss of money, a state of remorse, or they imply the loss of some external supplies, such as a disappointment in love or the death of a love partner; or further they may be tasks which the patient has to fulfill and which, objectively or subjectively, make him more aware of his "inferiority" and narcissistic needs; paradoxically, even experiences that for a normal person would mean an increase in self-esteem may precipitate a depression if the success frightens the patient as a threat of punishment or retaliation, or as an imposition for further tasks, thus augmenting his need for supplies.

Patients who react to disappointments in love with severe depressions are always persons to whom the love experience meant not only sexual gratification but narcissistic gratification as well. With their love, they lose their very existence. They are afraid of such a loss, and usually very jealous. The intensity of the jealousy does not at all correspond to the intensity of the love. The most jealous persons are those who are not able to love but need the feeling of being loved. After any loss, they try at once to find a substitute for the lost partner, by drinking, for example, or by looking for another partner immediately, an act which may increase their jealousy, namely, on a projective basis; their longing for another partner is projected and the patient thinks that his partners are looking for a new object.

In the phenomenology of depression, a greater or lesser loss of self-esteem is in the foreground. The subjective formula is "I have lost everything; now the world is empty," if the loss of self-esteem is mainly due to a loss of external supplies, or "I have lost everything because I do not deserve anything," if it is mainly due to a loss of internal supplies from the superego.

The patients try to influence the persons around them to return their lost self-esteem. Frequently they try to captivate their objects in a way characteristic for masochistic characters, by demonstrating their misery and by accusing the objects of having brought about this misery, and by enforcing and even blackmailing their objects for affection. This can be more readily observed in neurotic depressions than in psychotic ones because the ingratiating attitude of the neurotic is directed more toward external objects.

It can even be observed in simple neurotic inferiority feeings and in "bad moods,"[7] which very often take the form "I am no good"; latent guilt feelings are common in neurotics because they feel that their warded-off "bad" impulses are still operative within them.

Neurotic inferiority feelings are generally rooted in the failure of the Oedipus complex; they mean: "Because my infantile sexuality ended with a failure, I am inclined to believe that I shall always be a failure."[8] They are also intimately connected with the castration complex, so that the patient, for instance, in comparisons he draws between himself and others, unconsciously is comparing genitals. But these circumstances alone do not determine the neurotic inferiority feelings. Their actual source is an awareness of the impoverishment of the ego due to the unconscious neurotic conflicts.[9] Many a simple "neurotic depression" is due to the circumstance that since the greater percentage of the available mental energy is used up in unconscious conflicts, not enough is left to provide the normal enjoyment of life and vitality. Still another determinant of neurotic feelings of inferiority arises from the latent guilt feeling because of the continued effectiveness of the warded-off impulses. Persons who tend to develop depressions try to get rid of the guilt feeling by influencing objects to give them affection; if the form of this influence becomes more sadistic, further guilt feelings are aroused and a vicious circle is created.

Even psychotically depressed persons are prone to accuse objects of not loving them and to behave sadistically toward external objects. This can be seen in certain modes of behavior of these patients which strictly contradict their conscious feeling that they themselves are the worst creatures of all. The depressed patient, who seemingly is so extremely submissive, is actually often successful in dominating his entire environment. Analysis shows that this is a manifestation of an intense oral sadism.

In one of his plays, Nestroy has a melancholic say: "If I could not annoy other people with my melancholia, I wouldn't enjoy it at all."

Again it must be stressed that the borderline between neurotic depressions, with ambivalent struggles about narcissistic supples between the patient and his objects, and psychotic depressions, where the conflict has become internalized, is not a sharp one. Conflicts between the superego and the ego are effective in everyone who has narcissistic needs. And remnants of hope for external help may still be effective in severe depressive psychoses.[10]

Since depression always starts with an increase in narcissistic needs, that is, with the feeling "Nobody loves me," it might be expected that the patient will feel that everybody hates him. Actually, delusions of this kind do occur. However, the feeling of being universally hated occurs more frequently in cases representing transition states to delusions of persecution. The classic depressions tend rather to feel that they are not hated as much as they should be, that their depravity is not sufficiently apparent to others. The characteristic position is not so much "Everybody hates me" as "I hate myself." The depressed patient obviously can love himself no more than he can the external object. The depressed patient is as ambivalent toward himself as he is toward objects. But the two components of the ambivalence are stratified differently. In relation to the object, the love impulses (or at least the impulses toward being loved) are more manifest, while the hate is hidden. In relation to his own ego, it is the hate that becomes vociferous, while the primary narcissistic overestimation of the ego remains concealed. Only analysis reveals that the depressed patient often behaves very arrogantly and inflicts himself upon his objects.

Hostility toward the frustrating objects has been turned into hostility toward one's own ego. This self-hatred appears in the form of a sense of guilt, that is, of a discord between the ego and the superego. The existence of the psychic agency known as the superego was first recognized through the study of depression.[11] The effectiveness of the superego becomes definitely evident only when it is at odds with the ego; this, to be sure, is true in all states of bad conscience, but to an extreme degree in depressions.

A redirection of hostility, originally aimed at objects, against the ego and the resulting pathological conflicts within the personality are met with also in phenomena outside of the realm of depression. In hypochondriasis and in some pregenital conversion symptoms, conflicts between the individual and external objects are transposed into the personality, where they continue in the form of conflicts between the ego and the superego or between the ego and certain organs; and certain compulsive symptoms are designated as manifestations of the ego's attacks on the superego. The internalization of the originally external conflict is accomplished in depression in the same way as in these phenomena: by an introjection, that is, by the fantasy that the ambivalently loved object has been devoured and now exists within the body. This introjection is simultaneously a sexual fantasy of the patient whose sexuality is orally directed.

It is characteristic for depression, especially for psychotic depression, that the attempts to re-establish the last narcissistic equilibrium by means of the introjection of objects fail. The introjection, because of its sadistic nature, is perceived as a danger or guilt, and the struggles originally carried on with the external object are continued within the patient's "stomach" with the introjected object. The fact that in the superego another introjected object is already present and becomes involved in this struggle complicates the picture. The depressed person, after the introjection of the object, experiences no rage of the kind "I want to kill him (me)," but rather the feeling "I deserve to be killed." It is, as a rule, the superego which turns against the ego with the same rage that this ego previously used in its struggle with the object. The ego, in turn, acts toward this superego as it formerly acted toward the object. The outcome is that the struggle *subject vs. introject* becomes complicated in two ways: in the foreground is the struggle *superego vs. ego+introject;* but the ego, in its ambivalence toward the superego, changes it also into a struggle of *ego vs. superego +introject.*[12]

Mourning and Depression

To clarify this introjection and its consequences, Freud compared the depression with the related normal phenomenon of mourning.[13] If a child loses an object, the libidinal strivings, no longer bound to the object, flood the child and may create panic. In "grief" the adult person has learned to control this flood by retarding the necessary process of loosening. The tie to the lost object is represented by hundreds of separate memories; for each of these memories the dissolution of the tie is carried through separately and this takes time. Freud designated this process the "work of mourning." Carrying out this work is a difficult and unpleasant task which many persons try further to retard by holding onto the illusion that the lost person still lives, and thus postponing the necessary work. An apparent lack of emotion in mourners may also be due to an identification with the dead person.

The illusion that the lost person still lives and the identification with him are closely related. Every mourner tends to simplify his task by building up a kind of substitute object within himself after the real object has departed. For this he uses the same mechanism all disappointed persons, including the depressed ones, employ—namely, regression from love to incorporation, from object relationship to identification. It can often be observed that a mourning person in one or other respects begins to resemble the lost object, that, for example, as Abraham reported, his hair becomes gray like the hair of the person he mourns[14]; he develops cardiac symptoms if the object died of heart disease; he assumes one of the peculiarities of speech or gestures of the lost person. Freud pointed out that this process is not limited to the case of loss through death but holds good in the case of a purely mental loss as well. He referred to women who, after separation, take on traits of their lovers.[15] Bulimia (institutionalized in the form of funeral repasts, reminiscent of the totem festivals of savages),[16] which unconsciously means the idea of eating the dead person, and the refusal of food, which means the rejection of this idea, come within the limits of normal grief. All this gives evidence of an identification with the dead person, subjectively perceived as an oral incorporation occurring on the same level as in psychotic depression but of lesser intensity.

The study of the folklore of death and burial customs offers convincing evidence for the universality of introjection as a reaction to the loss of an object.[17] Black mourning apparel is a remnant of primitive mourning in sackcloth and ashes, which represents an identification with the dead person.[18]

All this supports Freud's formulation: "It may well be that identification is the general condition under which the id will relinquish its objects."[19] Many persons who have lost one of their parents early in childhood show signs of an oral fixation and tend to establish, along with their object relationships proper, extensive identifications, that is, to incorporate their objects.

Apparently, for a normal person it is easier to loosen the ties with an introject than with an external object. The establishment of an introjection is a means of facilitating the final loosening. Mourning consist of two acts, the first being the establishment of an introjection, the second the loosening of the binding to the introjected object.

Mourning becomes more complicated or even pathological if the relationship of the mourner to the lost object was an extremely ambivalent one. In this case the introjection acquires a sadistic significance; the incorporation then not only represents an attempt to preserve the loved object but also an attempt to destroy the hated object. If a hostile significance of this kind is in the foreground, the introjection will create new guilt feelings.

A case of death is always likely to mobilize ambivalence. The death of a person for whom one had previously wished death may be perceived as a fulfillment of this wish. The death of other persons may cause feelings of joy because death came to somebody else, not to oneself. Narcissistically oriented persons, in the painful state of mourning, tend unconsciously to reproach their dead friends for having brought them into this painful state. These reactions create guilt feelings and remorse. Actually, even in normal death rituals, symptoms of remorse are never lacking.

Beggars and dishonest firms are well aware of the remorseful mood of mourners and know how to take advantage of it.

The identification with the dead also has a punitive significance: "Because you have wished the other person to die, you have to die yourself." In this case, the mourner fears that because he has brought about death through the "omnipotence" of his death wish, the dead person may seek revenge and return to kill him, the living. This fear of the dead in turn increases the ambivalence. The mourner tries to pacify the dead one (*de mortuis nil nisi bonum*) as well as to kill him again and more effectively. The pious rituals of holding vigils at the side of the bier and of throwing sand into the grave or of erecting monuments of stone are traceable to archaic measures which are intended to prevent the dead from coming back.[20] Grief in general is a "taming" of the primitive violent discharge affect, characterized by fear and self-destruction, to be seen in mourning savages. Such outbursts are all the stronger the more ambivalent the attitude toward the lost object was. Our "mourning," extended over a period of time, is a defense against being overwhelmed by this primitive affect.[21]

In summary it may be stated that mourning is characterized by an ambivalent introjection of the lost object, a continuation of feelings toward the introject that once had been directed toward the object, and the participation of guilt feelings throughout the process.

Similar mechanisms may be operative in other types of sadness. The affective state of being sad is characterized by a decrease in self-esteem. A slightly sad person needs consolation, pity, "supplies." A very sad person withdraws from objects and becomes narcissistic by incorporating the unsatisfactory object; and after its introjection the struggle for the re-establishment of self-esteem is continued on the intrapsychic level.

Under certain conditions the narcissistic need and the conflicts around introjection in a mourning or sad person will be more intense than usual. This is the case if (*a*) the lost object has not been loved on a mature level but rather used as a provider of narcissistic supplies, (*b*) the previous relationship to the object has been ambivalent, (*c*) the person has been orally fixated and has had unconscious longings for a sexualized "eating."

The types described above as predisposed for the development of depressions have all these three characteristics: an increased narcissistic need, an increased ambivalence, and an increased orality. If such a person loses an object, he hates the object for having left him, tries to compel the object by violent magical means to make up for this loss, continues these attempts after an ambivalent introjection of the object, and, in attempting to decrease his guilt feelings, actually intensifies them. The highly cathected continuation of the struggle against the introject constitutes depression. Depression is a desperate attempt to compel an orally incorporated object to grant forgiveness, protection, love, and security. The destructive elements liberated by this coercion create further guilt feelings and fears of retaliation. The depressed person is in an untenable position since he is afraid that the granting of the supplies, of which he is in such desperate need, may simultaneously signify the object's or introject's revenge.

Ambivalence may also enter the picture of mourning in conditions other than depression, as, for example, in obsessive self-reproaches following a death. Pathognomonic for depression is the depth and the definite and full character of the regression, which extends beyond the later anal phase into orality and narcissism.[22]

The Pathognomonic Introjection

It has been stated that depression is a loss of self-esteem, either a complete breakdown of all self-esteem or a partial one intended as a warning against the possibility of a complete one. This formulation must now be supplemented by the statement that the depressed person tries to undo this loss and actually aggravates it by a pathognomonic introjection of the ambivalently loved object. This supplies the key to the failure of the warning signal of the conscience and to the resultant feelings of utter annihilation. The oral-sadistic introjection of the object, whose love is wanted as a narcissistic supply, is the match that explodes the powder of the dammed-up narcissistic need.

The introjetcion, then, is not only an attempt to undo the loss of an object. Simultaneously it is an attempt to achieve the *unio mystica* with an omnipotent external person, to become the lost person's "companion," that is, food comrade, through becoming his substance and making him become one's own substance. Ambivalence, however, gives this introjection a hostile significance. The wish to force the object to give his consent to the union ends in the attainment of punishment for the violence of this wish. After the introjection, the struggle for forgiveness is continued on a narcissistic basis, the superego now struggling with the ego.

The depressed patient complains that he is worthless and acts as if he has lost his ego. Objectively he has lost an object. Thus ego and object are somehow equated. The sadism that once referred to the object has now been turned against the ego.

This turning against the ego was discovered by Freud in analyzing the self-reproaches of depressed patients.[23] Apparently meaningless self-reproachful statements proved to have a meaning if the name of the hated object was substituted for "I." The self-reproaches were originally reproaches against the object. Thus the introjection at the basis of depression really is the opposite of the defense mechanism of projection: the bad characteristics of an object which one dare not become aware of because one fears the hatred they would arouse are perceived in one's own ego instead. The depressed patient says "I am bad because I am a liar" when he wants to say "I am angry with X because he has lied to me"; or "I am bad because I am a murderer" when he wants to say "I am angry with X; he has treated me badly as if he wanted to murder me."

Some self-reproaches in depressed persons, however, impress one as being more or less objectively correct, rather than as delusions. Like paranoiacs, depressed persons are very sensitive to those portions of reality that are suitable to their mental needs, and react to them exaggeratedly.

By virtue of the introjection, a part of the patient's ego has become the object; as Freud puts it: "The shadow of the object has fallen on the ego."[24] This identification, in contradistinction to hysterical identification, must be called a narcissistic identification, for here the object is entirely replaced by an alteration of the ego.[25] "Regression from object relationship to identification," "regression to narcissism," and "regression to orality" are terms that mean one and the same thing looked upon from different viewpoints.

It will be recalled that Helene Deutsch reported a similar identification with a hatred object in the psychogenesis of agoraphobia.[26] The question arises, then, as to the way in which the identification in depression differs from that found in agoraphobia. The answer is not difficult. There is relatively less regression to the oral level in agoraphobia. "This difference is that the identification in agoraphobia is affected at a higher level of libidinal development and is consequently transient and corrigible."[27]

The Conflict Between the Superego and the Ego

After the introjection, the sadism enlists on the side of the superego and attacks the ego that has been altered by the introjection. Not rage, but guilt feeling is felt. The sadism of the superego in depression exceeds the sadism found in the superego of compulsion neurotics as much as the depressed patients ambivalence exceeds that of the compulsion neurotic. The superego treats the ego in the same way that the patient unconsciously had wished to treat the object that was lost.

But there are still further complications. It has been mentioned that the struggle in melancholia does not always have the form *superego vs. ego+introject,* but sometimes the form *ego vs. superego+introject;* that is, the recently introjected object may also join with the superego.

Freud explained the depressive self-reproaches as accusations directed against the introjected object.[28] Abraham added that often complaints appear to come counterwise from the introjected object in the form of accusations that the real object actually had made against the patient.[29] This enlistment of the introjected object on the side of the superego is in consonance with Freud's basic idea that the superego, too, originated in an introjection of objects.

Abraham reported a case in which two objects were introduced, the one into the superego, the other into the ego. The self-reproaches of this patient corresponded to complaints made by an introjected mother about an introjected father.[30]

In melancholic depressions the delusion of being poisoned is not rare, originating in the feeling of becoming destroyed by some orally introjected force. Weiss demonstrated that this delusion reflects an introjection of the object into the superego.[31]

Such an interpretation does not necessarily conflict with the interpretation of this idea, on a more superficial level, as a fantasy of being impregnated. The dangerous introject, felt as a poison, may have different meanings on different levels; it may represent child and penis as well as breast and milk. The feeling of being poisoned contains a piece of psychological truth. The patient has introjected an object that now disturbs him from within. Thus the far-reaching hypochondriacal delusions in severe melancholia represent a distorted recognition of the process of introjection. The fear of being eaten up by something inside the body is a retaliation fear for the sadistic introjection. This "something" may be rationalized as a pathogenic virus, which forms a bridge to the more common phobia of being infected. And it is the idea of being eaten up by an introjected object that makes so many neurotics fear the mysterious disease of cancer.[32]

In melancholia it seems as if the main emphasis of the personality has been shifted from the ego to the superego. The patient's conscience represents his total personality; the ego altered by the introjection is the mere object of this conscience and is entirely subdued by it.

Freud has described a similar situation in a mood that is the very opposite of depression—humor.[33] The mood of humor, too, is achieved by a displacement of the emphasis of the personality from the ego to the superego. The difference is that in humor the overcathected superego is the friendly and protective positive ego-ideal; in depression, it is the negative, hostile, punishing conscience.

The superego has a double aspect. It represents a protective and a punitive power. Under normal circumstances the first aspect prevails and occasional punishments are accepted for purposes of conciliation. In depression, regression has abolished the first aspect of the superego. The ego, nevertheless, continues its attempts to achieve reconciliation. The whole depressive process appears as an attempt at reparation, intended to restore the self-esteem that has been damaged. The cutting off of narcissistic supplies has disturbed the entire psychic equilibrium. In the depressive process, the object that is believed to have brought this disturbance about is punished and destroyed for this very reason; but the object has become, by introjection, a part of the patient himself. In its attempt to destroy the bad object, the depressive ego meets the fate of Dorian Gray, who had to die in order to destroy his portrait.

The ego, persecuted by its superego to such a degree, has no other means at its disposal than has the ego of the compulsion neurotic when it is at odds with its superego: it reacts with submissiveness as well as with attempts at rebellion. The latter, however, cannot be successful because of the power the sadistic superego has acquired. Manifestly, in depressions the ego is more helpless and yielding to the attacks of the superego; the rebellious attitudes operate in a more hidden way only.

In the discussion of the submissiveness of the compulsion neurotic, it was stated that in yielding to its fate, the ego tries to ingratiate itself with the superego in the hope of achieving forgiveness. It chooses submission and even punishment as a "lesser evil," and besides it can, under certain circumstances, even obtain masochistic pleasure through these inflictions. The same is attended by the ego of depressed patients. The sadism of the superego, however, dooms the hope for forgiveness to failure and increases the suffering beyond any possibility of enjoyment.

Self-reproach in depression is not only (from the re-proaching superego's point of view) an attempt to attack the introjected object; in addition it represents (from the re-proached ego's point of view) a courting of the superego and a plea for forgiveness intended to convince the superego how much its accusations have been taken to heart.

With such an attitude the ego only repeats what it did at the time when the superego was created. The little boy, during the construction of his superego, said to his father: "You need not be angry with me; I will take care of that myself." By building a superego, he introjected the angry behavior of the father, thereby eliminating the necessity of the father's external anger, and preserving his "good" father as a real person. In the same spirit the melancholic person says to his superego (and the neurotically depressed patient to his object): "Look, I am a good boy, accepting all punish-ments; now you must love me again." But the melancholic patient fails in this attempt. The inordinate sadism, inherent in the oral-instinctual orientation and remobilized by the regression, has been given over to the superego, and the full fury with which the ego unconsciously had wished to attack the object is now loosed against the ego.[34]

Suicide

The depressed patient's strong tendency toward suicide reflects the intensity of this struggle. In trying to appease the superego by submissiveness, the ego has reckoned incorrectly. The intended forgiveness cannot be achieved because the courted part of the personality, through the regression, has become inordinately cruel and has lost the ability to forgive.

The suicide of the depressed patient is, if examined from the standpoint of the superego, a turning of sadism against the person himself, and the thesis that nobody kills himself who had not intended to kill somebody else is proved by the depressive suicide. From the standpoint of the ego, suicide is, first of all, an expression of the fact that the terrible tension the pressure of the superego induces has become unbearable. Frequently the passive thought of giving up any active fighting seems to express itself; the loss of self-esteem is so complete that any hope of regaining it is abandoned. The ego sees itself deserted by its superego and lets itself die."[35] To have a desire to live evidently means to feel a certain self-esteem, to feel supported by the protective forces of a superego. When this feeling vanishes, the original annihilation of the deserted hungry baby reappears.

Other suicidal acts have a much more active character. They assert themselves as desperate attempts to enforce, at any cost, the cessation of the pressure of the superego. They are the most extreme acts of ingratiatory submission to punishment and to the superego's cruelty; simultaneously they are also the most extreme acts of rebellion, that is, murder—murder of the original objects whose incorporation created the superego, murder, it is true, of the kind of Dorian Gray's murder of his image. This mixture of submission and rebellion is the climax of the accusatory demonstration of misery for the purpose of coercing forgiveness: "Look what you have done to me; now you have to be good again."

"Neurotically" depressed children frequently have suicidal fantasies, the love-blackmailing tendency of which is obvious: "When I am dead the parents will regret what they have done to me and will love me again."[36] When melancholic patients try to blackmail their cruel superego in a similar manner, they are worse

off than children who court real parents capable of forgiveness
and love.

This means that suicide is carried out because hopes
and illusions of a relaxing gratification are connected with
the idea of suicide. Actually analyses of attempts at suicide
frequently show that the idea of being dead or of dying has
become connected with hopeful and pleasurable fantasies.

Hopes of this kind are more in the foreground in suicides
that are not of the melancholic type and in which introjection
and struggles between the superego and the ego do no play any
part.[37] What is often striven for in suicidal attempts is not "destruction of the ego" but some libidinous aims which, through displacement, have become connected with ideas that objectively bring
self-destruction, although they have not been intended as such.[38]
Such ideas may be the hope of joining a dead person, a libidinous
identification with a dead person,[39] the oceanic longing for a
union with the mother,[40] or even simply orgasm itself,[41] the attainment of which, through certain historical events, may have become represented by the idea of dying. The specific fantasies
that are connected with the idea of dying[42] can often be surmised
from the method by which the suicide is attempted or planned.[43]

The hopeful illusions that are connected with the idea
of suicide in melancholia are the attainment of forgiveness
and reconciliation, which are to be enforced by the simultaneous maximal submission and rebellion, a killing of the punishing superego, and the regaining of union with the protecting
superego—a reunion that puts an end to all losses of self-
esteem by bringing back the original paradise of oceanic
omnipotence.[44]

Self-destructive actions during melancholic states, carried
out as self-punishment, as an expression of certain delusions or
without any rationalization, have been designated "partial sui-

cides."[45] This term is absolutely correct in so far as the underlying unconscious mechanisms are identical with those of suicide.

Sometimes, for reasons unknown, the ego's hopes seem not to have been entirely in vain. A mere change of cathexis frees the ego from the terrible forces within itself. The hopes which are illusionary in the case of suicide are to a certain degree actually achieved in mania. The bad superego is destroyed, and the ego seems united to a purified protective superego in narcissistic love. In still other cases, a depression may end without any mania, as a normal mourning ends after a certain time. The factors, doubtlessly quantitative in nature, that determine whether or when the result is to be a suicide, a manic attack, or a recovery are still unknown.

The Decisive Regression and its Causes

The difference between a neurotic and a psychotic depression, it has been stated, is determined by the depth of the narcissistic regression. "Narcissistic regression" means that the object relationships are replaced by relations within the personality; the patient loses his object relationships by regressing into a phase where no objects yet existed. Depressed patients become aware of this withdrawal of object cathexes by the painful sensation of feeling the world and themselves as "empty." This withdrawal of object cathexes, however, is not necessarily a total one. Except in cases of severe melancholia, there are always remainders of objects as well as more or less successful attempts to regain the lost objective world.[46]

The ego came into being with the awareness of objects. The establishment of objects simultaneously established the ego. In a psychosis, the conception of objects and therewith

the structure of the ego are disturbed by a regression to the
time before the establishment of the ego. The psychosis re-
awakens the factors that were characteristic of the archaic
ego while in the process of coming into being. However,
this "repetition" is not identical with the original; all psychoses contain elements that do not represent the repetition of
infantile factors but remainders of the prepsychotic adult
personality.

What determines whether or not a fatal narcissistic regression occurs?

The first possibility is that an unknown organic factor
may be decisive. Actually, many psychiatrists believe that
manic-depressive psychoses cannot be fully understood in
mental terms. This view has been defended even more
tenaciously in regard to manic-depressive psychoses than in
regard to schizophrenia. Yet somatic research has revealed
little in the way of positive findings for the one group or
the other.

There are three considerations that suggest the operation
of somatic factors.

1. The strict periodicity that frequently characterizes the
alternations of mood. This periodicity appears to be independent
of any external event and to indicate the operation of a biological
factor.

2. Even in cases where the cycle is not markedly periodic,
the spontaneity of the mood alternations which frequently occur
without any apparent external precipitation argues against their
being purely psychogenic.

3. In no other neurosis is there such definite evidence of
heredity, the same type of disorder recurring in successive genera-
tions.

None of these arguments, however, is too decisive. The
periodicity, it is true, seems to be endogenous in origin, but

what appears periodically may well be understandable in psychological terms. The apparent absence of precipitating causes for the swings of mood will not be too impressive for analysts because this argument does not take into account the existence of the unconscious. So-called endogenous depressions have been distinguished from reactive depressions, according to the presence or absence of a demonstrable precipitating cause. But how would this type of differentiation stand the test if, for example, applied to hysterical seizures? Some of these appear to be brought on by immediate precipitating events, but some of them arise spontaneously and without apparent external reason. Yet nobody distinguishes between "endogenous" and "reactive" hysterical seizures; instead it is assumed that apparently spontaneous attacks have an unconscious precipitating cause that escaped the notice of the observer. The same applies to depressions. In other neurotic disorders, likewise, a discrepancy between a slight provocation and an intense reaction is not attributed to an organic factor, which would be inaccessible to psychological study, but the discrepancy is understood as the effect of a displacement. It should be noted, moreover, that it is by no means true that the reactive cases (the cases with obvious precipitating factors) are the slight ones and the endogenous ones the severe. Often a severe and clearly psychotic depression may follow the death of a husband or wife; and often definitely nonpsychotic depressions or even mere bad moods occur spontaneously without the patient or an observer being able to assign any precipitating causes and unconscious dispositional causes.[47] This holds good for the manic-depressive group as well. A person predisposed to illness by oral and early ego fixation may fall ill as a result of mild precipitating circumstances that are not readily observable; however, even one with relatively little predisposition may fall ill if severe and obvious circumstances appear.

Nor does heredity, though more conspicuous than in other neuroses or psychoses, separate the manic-depressive disorders from other mental disturbances, where its effectiveness was not considered a hindrance to study them from a psychological point of view. Constitution and experience, as etiological factors, again form a complementary series. The manic-depressive disorders surely give no reason to change this point of view. The organic constitutional influence, which is undoubtedly present, need not be the sole determinant. Psychoanalytic study makes it probable that this constitution consists in a relative predominance of oral eroticism, just as in compulsion neurosis it consists in an enhanced anal eroticism.

What kind of accidental experiences favor the subsequent development of depressions?

In the discussion of the differential etiology of compulsion neurosis it was stated that those patients tend to react to conflicts with an anal regression, and thus with a compulsion neurosis, who, as children, under the influence of anal fixations, have used the same type of defense. This holds true for oral regression and depression as well. There is no depression that would not represent a repetition of a first decisive reaction to childhood difficulties, which formed the pattern for the later breakdown. The struggle to maintain their self-esteem is carried on by depressed patients in a way similar to that which they used as children under the influence of oral fixations. Abraham showed that persons who tend to become depressed uniformly have suffered frustrations in childhood to which they responded by means of a similar mechanism. These frustrations connoted severe injuries to their narcissistic needs and, in conformity with the pregenital fixation, occurred very early in life. Thus Abraham was able to formulate as an etiological prerequisite for the development of later psychotic depressions: "a severe injury to infantile narcissism through a combination of disappointments in love; the occurrence of the first great disappointment in love before the Oedipus wishes were successfully mastered; the repetition of the original disappointment in later life is the event precipitating the illness."[48] The subsequent depressions follow the path opened up by the infantile "primal depression," which fixed the fateful tendency to react in an analogous way to future disappointments.

A woman patient with a sexual perversion of the type of extreme submissiveness, whose life was a constant struggle for narcissistic supplies and whose behavior frequently was impulsive in character like that of an addict, apparently produced this neurotic behavior to escape from depressions. She was successful in her attempts and did not suffer from depressions of a severe nature in adult life. One day, the patient had a nightmare, the content of which she had forgotten; she was only able to describe the feelings in the dream. These feelings had been horrible; she described them with the exact same words that melancholics use to describe the most severe sensations of their depressions. The world, in her dream, had lost all value for her. She felt entirely drained, without connection to anybody else, and completely annihilated; simultaneously she felt as if she had committed the most dreadful sins. She cried in her dream and even after she awoke.

The phenomenon of a "psychosis in a dream" in a person who does not suffer from it when awake seemed strange. In the analysis of this dream, however, it was discovered that it was not so strange after all. What occurred in this dream was something that frequently occurs in dreams: forgotten memories became manifest. The depression in the dream was the repetition of a "primal depression" which the patient had experienced in her fourth year of life when a little brother was born. This primal depression had been forgotten, and her neurosis served the purpose of avoiding a repetition of this dreadful experience of her childhood.

The content of the "injuries to infantile narcissism," which precipitate the primary depression, may vary. These injuries may be extraordinary experiences of abandonment and loneliness, or they may, in especially predisposed individuals, consist in the usual and unavoidable disappointments such as the birth of siblings, experiences of minor humiliations, penis envy, or the frustrations of the Oedipus longings.

Abraham called the injuries causing primary depressions "pre-oedipal" to indicate that frustrations have this effect only when experienced as a "loss of essential narcissistic supplies." Usually a child who feels deprived in this way turns toward another person who may give what the first object had denied, that is, from mother to father or vice versa. He is worse off if "a combination of disappointments in love"[49] occur. The Oedipus complex of subsequent manic-depressive patients, therefore, is frequently a "complete," that is, bisexual, one, both components of which have terminated in a narcissistic injuries.[50]

Now at last we are in a position to understand which conditions actually make for the predisposition for subsequent depressions. The decisive narcissistic injuries must have taken the form of severe disappointments in the parents, at a time when the child's self-esteem was regulated by "participation in the parents' omnipotence." At this time, a dethroning of the parents necessarily means a dethroning of the child's own ego. Probably it is not only so that after disappointments of this type the child asks for subsequent compensating external narcissistic supplies throughout his life, thus disturbing the development of his superego; he also tries to compensate for his parents' insufficiencies by the development of a specially "omnipotent," that is, strict and rigid, superego, and subsequently needs external narcissistic supplies in order to outweigh the unbearable demands of this qualitatively different superego.

That it is, in the last analysis, the "oceanic feeling"[51] of union with an "omnipotent" mother for which depressed persons are longing is manifest in those forms of depression called nostalgia.[52]

A child of four or five experiencing a "primal depression," an adult person suffering from nostalgia, and any person exposed for a long time to severe deprivations and frustrations—they all are psychologically again in the situation of a narcissistically hungry infant lacking the necessary external care.

Impulsive behavior and drug addiction can be utilized as a means of fighting off depressions, because these disorders represent other means of attaining the same end: the provision of the needed narcissistic supplies. Since depressions are states that develop if these supplies are missing, addictions and impulse neuroses, in so far as they still are able to achieve their end, are suitable for evading depressions.

The formulation can now be made that the disposition for the development of depressions consists in oral fixations which determine the reaction to narcissistic shocks. The experiences that cause the oral fixations may occur long before the decisive narcissistic shocks; or the narcissistic injury may create a depressive disposition because it occurs early enough to still be met by an orally oriented ego. It may also occur that certain narcissistic shocks, because they are connected with death (and the reaction to death is always oral introjection of the dead person), create the decisive oral fixation.

Regarding the factors that create oral fixations in the first place, the same holds true as for other fixations: the determinants are extraordinary satisfactions, extraordinary frustrations, or combinations of both, especially combinations of oral satisfaction with some reassuring guarantee of security; actually traumatic experiences in the nursing period can be found more often in subsequent manic-depressive patients than in schizophrenics.

In addition to the pregenital fixation, Freud emphasized the importance of a narcissistic orientation as an etiological prerequisite for depressions;[53] without such orientation a regression from object love to identification would not occur with such intensity. Before the onset of the illness the narcissism may show itself in the type of object choice[54] and in the receptive and ambivalent nature of the patient's love.

In clinical psychiatry, the involutional melancholias are differentiated from the true manic-depressive disorders. Psychoanalytically, not much is known about the structure and mechanisms of involutional melancholias; they seem to occur in personalities with an outspoken compulsive character of an especially rigid nature.[55] In the climacterium the compulsive defensive systems fail; in these cases the decisive oral regression seems to be due to physical alterations of the economy of the libido.

Cyclothymia and variations in mood represent transitional states between the manic-depressive disease and normality. The existence of these intermediate states shows that the manic-depressive state is but a morbid exaggeration of something universally present—namely, of struggles around the maintenance of self-esteem. There are multifarious problems in normal psychology—for example, the heightening and reduction of self-esteem (referred to sometimes as the instinct for self-assertion), moods and humors, sadness and joy, the nature of grief—all of which find their counterparts among the manifestations within the manic-depressive field. All these normal phenomena differ from manic-depressive phenomena first by the relatively small amounts of energy invested and second by the absence of the narcissistic regression.

Under difficult social circumstances and in unstable times the number of depressions and depressive suicides increases. This fact has been used as an objection to the psychoanalytic theory of depression, in contrast to the often raised objection based on heredity. Perhaps depression is nothing but a "human way of reacting to frustrations and misery"? But the connection is a more complicated one. It may suffice to state that a society that cannot provide necessary satisfactions for its members necessarily creates a vast number of persons with an orally dependent character. Unstable times and economic depressions, by depriving people of their satisfactions as well as of their power and prestige and habitual ways of regulating self-esteem, increase their narcissistic needs and their oral dependence. On the other hand persons who, as a result of childhood experiences, have developed an orally dependent character are worse off under such social conditions, since they are unable to take frustrations without reacting in a depressive way.

Mania

Until now only the depressive side of the manic-depressive phenomena has been discussed. Actually, this side is understood analytically much better than is mania.

Descriptively, an immense increase in self-esteem forms the center of all manic phenomena. The statement that conscience seems to be either abandoned or very limited in its effectiveness has the same meaning, because "feelings of conscience" and "decrease in self-esteem" are essentially identical. All problems of mania can be attacked from the point of view of this increase in self-esteem or decrease in conscience. All activities, after the abandonment of inhibitions, are intensified. The patients are hungry for objects, not so much because they need to be sustained or taken care of by them but to express their own potentialities and to get rid of the now uninhibited impulses that seek discharge. The patient is not only hungry for new objects; he also feels freed because hitherto effective blockings have fallen away, and he is more or less overwhelmed by this breaking down of dams; the freed impulses as well as the energies, which hitherto had been bound in the efforts to restrain these impulses, now flow out, using any available discharge.

In other words: what the depression was striving for seems to be achieved in the mania; not only narcissistic supplies, which again make life desirable, but a total narcissistic victory is at hand; it is as if all the supply material imaginable is suddenly at the patient's disposal, so that the primary narcissistic omnipotence is more or less regained and life is felt to be incredibly intensified.[56]

Freud stated that in the manic state the difference between the ego and the superego apparently disappears.[57] Whereas in melancholia the ego is entirely powerless and the superego omnipotent, in mania the ego has regained omnipotence, either by triumphing in some way over the superego and taking back the omnipotence or by being united with the superego and participating in its power.[58] The mirthful mood of the manic has to be interpreted economically as a sign of a saving in psychic expenditure.[59] It demonstrates that the tension between the superego and the ego, which previously had been extremely great, must have been released abruptly. In mania the ego has somehow succeeded in freeing itself from the pressure of the superego; it has terminated its conflict with the "shadow" of the lost object, and then, as it were, "celebrates" this event.

As has been stated, the manic-depressive patient is ambivalent toward his own ego. In depressions he demonstrates the hostile element of this ambivalence. Mania brings to the surface the other aspect of this ambivalence: his extreme self-love.

What has made this change possible? In the same way that a bad conscience is the normal model for the morbid state of depression, mania has a normal model in the feeling of "triumph."[60] Analysis of this feeling shows that triumph is felt whenever an expenditure becomes superfluous—an expenditure that had previously been necessary in the ambivalent reactions of a powerless subject to a powerful object. Triumph means "Now I am powerful again" and is felt the more intensely the more suddenly the change from lack of power to power is achieved. Triumph is a derivative of the pleasure the child feels whenever his growing ego achieves the feeling "I no longer need to be afraid, because I can master something which until now I looked upon as dangerous; now I am as powerful as omnipotent grownups are." The methods by which participation in the reassuring power is achieved vary from the (original) killing of the omnipotent tyrant for the purpose of taking his place to an ingratiatory submission for the purpose of having the tyrant permit the participation. A man feels "elated" whenever he feels that he is rid of an obligation, liability, or general dependence hitherto effective (rebellious type of triumph), or whenever he achieves external or internal forgiveness, or whenever he passes any kind of "examination," when he is loved again or has the feeling of having done the right thing (ingratiatory type of triumph).

Is a similar real liberation from the superego's pressure achieved in mania? The clinical picture seems to indicate that this is the case.

There is no doubt that the depressive pressure is ended, that the triumphant character of mania arises from the release of energy hitherto bound in the depressive struggle and now seeking discharge. An abundance of impulses, most of them oral in nature, make their appearance and, together with the heightened self-esteem, produce the feeling "life is rich," as contrasted to the oppressive "emptiness" experienced in depression.

The apparent hypergenitality of the typical maniac has an oral character and aims at the incorporation of everybody. Abraham described this condition when he stated that the "mental metabolism" is increased in mania. The patient is hungry for new objects, but he also gets rid of objects very quickly and dismisses them without any remorse.[61]

"Incorporation of everybody" has been confirmed by the findings of Lewin,[62] according to which multiple indentifications are characteristic for manic states. He described a patient whose manic attacks corresponded to an acting out of a primal scene in identification with both parents.[63] The typical "nongenuine" behavior patterns of maniacs may be due to temporary and relatively superficial identifications with external objects.

In all societies the institution of "festivals" is found, that is, of occasions when superego prohibitions are periodically undone. Institutions of this kind are certainly based on a social necessity. Any society that creates chronic dissatisfaction in its members needs institutions through which the dammed-up tendencies toward rebellion may be "channelized"; through them a form of discharge of strivings hostile to existing institutions is provided, which entails the least possible injury to these institutions. Once a year, under ceremonial guarantees, under specified conditions, and in an institutionalized way, rebellious impulses are permitted to express themselves. From time to time the "superego is abolished"; the powerless are permitted to play "participation," and this creates a good mood in them and enables them to obey for another year.[64]

The good mood felt at festivals is certainly a correlate of mania. Freud stated that the periodicity of cyclothymia as well as of festivals may, in the final analysis, be based on a biological necessity. All differentiations in the psychic apparatus may need a temporary abolition from time to time. In sleep, the ego is submerged nightly into the id from which it arose. Similarly, in festivals and in mania the superego may be drawn back in the ego.[65]

The tragedy is succeeded by the satyr play; after the serious worship of God comes the merry fair in front of the church; tragedy and satyr play, worship and the fair have the same psychological content; but this content is met with by different attitudes of the ego. That which is threatening and serious in tragedy and worship is play and fun in satyr plays and the fair.[66] No doubt, this sequence goes back to a cycle of being hard pressed by a strict authority and of casting it off. An original sequence of pressure by authority and rebellion against it probably was later supplanted by a sequence of pressure by authority and institutionalized festivals. On an intrapsychic basis the same sequence is represented by the cycle of guilt feelings and unscrupulousness; later by the sequence of guilt feelings and forgiveness. What once took place between chiefs and subjects has become internalized and takes place between superegos and egos.

Freud, in *Totem and Taboo*, gave a phylogenetic hypothesis as to how this cycle might have come into being.[67]

The manic-depressive cycle is a cycle between periods of increased and decreased guilt feelings, between feelings of "annihilation" and of "omnipotence," of punishment and of new deed; this cycle, in the last analysis, goes back to the biological cycle of hunger and satiety in the infant.

However, one decisive difference seems to remain between the normal model of triumph—based either on a real victory over external or internal tyranny or on a successful achievement of participation—and the pathological phenomenon of a manic attack.

The exaggerated manner of all manic expressions does not give the impression of genuine freedom. Actually, the analysis of a mania shows that the patient's fears of his superego as a rule are not entirely overcome. Unconsciously they are still effective, and the patient suffers in mania under the same complexes as he did in the depressive state. But he succeeds in applying, against them, the defense mechanism of denial by overcompensation. The cramped nature of the manifestations of mania is due to the fact that they are of a reaction-formation type, that they serve the purpose of denying opposite attitudes.[68] The mania is not a genuine freedom from depression but a cramped denial of dependencies.

The liberation frequently is a pretended one, repeating pretenses made by the child in his struggle against narcissistic shocks, using the primitive defense mechanisms of denial, and also other defense mechanisms. Projection is used by patients who in their mania feel themselves to be loved and admired by everybody, or even, in a more paranoid way, mistreated and therefore entitled to do whatever they like without consideration for anyone else.[69] Some maniacs persecute those very traits in others which, during their depression, they hated in themselves. In some cases the continued effectiveness of the superego is manifest; a manic behavior may be rationalized or idealized as fulfilling some ideal purpose. The liberation, then, is maintained by a denying countercathexis, and endangered by the possibility of the outbreak of another depression.

In a cramped sort of protest, stressing "I do not need any control any more," all or many impulses—aggressive, sensual, and tender ones—are discharged; the child is thrown out with the bath water; reason is overthrown with the superego. A state is created resembling the original pleasure principle under whose operation impulses were yielded to, whenever they arose, without any consideration of reality. A reasonable ego, once more, is overwhelmed, this time not by a punishing superego but rather by an abandonment of limiting reason altogether. In mania, what actually happens is the very thing neurotics with a fear of their own excitement are afraid of: a breakdown of the organization of the ego as a result of the instinctual impulses discharging in an uncontrolled way. The patients again become narcissistic, though in a form different from that during the depression; they re-enact the omnipotence of primary narcissism, not only of being a person without guilt feelings but also of being a suckling who, having obtained his food, thereby loses the concept of objects.

That the maniac does not fall into a peaceful sleep but into a state of tense and irresistible impulses is probably ascribable to two circumstances: (1) In contradistinction to the baby, he has dammed up many impulses for many years and has invested all of his mental energy in "tonic" intra-psychic cathexes which now become superfluous and need to be abreacted. (2) His actions are cramped and exaggerated because they are denials of contradictory attitudes still effective in the unconscious.

It has been mentioned that morbid impulses can protect against depressions inasmuch as they are different means for achieving the same ends. There is a definite relationship between specific morbid impulses and unspecific manic impulses, and many impulse neuroses are actually equivalents of mania.

The insight that the manic-depressive cycle can be traced back, in the last analysis, to the cycle of satiety and hunger once again brings up the problem of periodicity. Periodicity is a biological factor. It was first thought to be a mode of expression of a rhythm inherent in all vital processes. It was then supposed by Freud to be a biological necessity, correlated with a pressure that compels a periodic relinquishing of differentiations in the psychic apparatus.[70] But the relation that apparently obtains between states without a superego and the satiated infant and between the pangs of conscience and those of hunger revealed another type of biological alternation. The alternation of hunger and satiety recurs of necessity (provided the infant does not starve); and this is indelibly imprinted in memory. Each subsequent alternation of pleasure and pain is sensed as if it followed the pattern of this memory. According to this pattern, pleasure is expected after every pain, and pain after every pleasure; and the primitive idea is set up that any suffering bestows the privilege of some later compensating joy, and any punishment admits of a later sin. Punishment and the loss of parental love were perceived as analogous to hunger, and absolution as corresponding to satiety. After the parents have been introjected, the ego repeats intra-psychically the same pattern in relation to the superego. In depressions, the ego no longer feels loved by the superego; it has been deserted, its oral wishes unrealized. In mania, the forgiving oral love union with the superego is restored.[71]

The recognition of this relationship still leaves much that is puzzling in regard to periodicity, especially the chief question: why in some cases there must be an evident or concealed external precipitant to bring about the changes in phase, whereas in other cases this change corresponds to a regular, apparently biologically founded rhythm. For example, it is true that in menstrual depressions, analysis can demonstrate that menstruation is felt subjectively to be a frustration, meaning "I have neither child nor penis";[72] yet it is impossible to get rid of the impression that additional purely biological factors are involved.[73]

Historical Summary

The basic psychoanalytic knowledge about the manic-depressive disorders is contained in a few separate, mutually supplementary publications. The best method of summariz-ing will be a brief review of these papers. Two important essays by Abraham, 1911[74] and 1916,[75] were followed by Freud's essay, "Mourning and Melancholia," 1917,[76] which contained the formulation of fundamental concepts, which in turn were elaborated and extended by Abraham in 1924.[77]

Finally, a publication by Rado in 1927[78] brought the solutions to certain important and pertinent problems still unclarified.

Abraham's first-mentioned publication reported the fundamental discovery that ambivalence is the basic characteristic in the mental life of the depressed patient, the influence of which appears to be much greater than in compulsion neurosis. The quantities of love and hate that coexist are more nearly equal; depressed patients are unable to love because they hate whenever they love. Abraham further found the pregenital foundation of this ambivalence, and stated that the patient is as ambivalent toward himself as he is toward objects. The sadism with which the depressed person attacks himself arises from the turning inward of a sadism originally outwardly directed.

Abraham's second publication recorded his discovery that in depressed patients, oral eroticism is enormously increased. He showed that conflicts around oral eroticism were at work in the depressive inhibitions, in eating disturbances and in "oral" character traits. It became clear that the ambivalence and narcissism described in the first paper have an oral root.

Freud's paper, "Mourning and Melancholia," starting with the analysis of the depressive self-reproaches, stated that depressed persons, after the loss of an object, act as if they have lost their ego. Freud described the pathognomonic introjection. He then showed how the depressive states proved the existence of a superego, and that struggles between the superego and the ego, after the introjection, replace struggles originally carried on between the ego and its ambivalently loved object.

Abraham's book not only supplied a mass of convincing

clinical material that corroborated the view that Freud had set forth as theoretical formulations but also added several valuable points of theory. He introduced the two subdivisions of the oral and anal stages of libidinal organization; he showed that self-reproaches are not only internalized reproaches of the ego against the object but also internalized reproaches of the object against the ego. The book further introduced new formulations of the etiological prerequisites (the most important of which is represented in the discovery of the primal depression of childhood) and a study of mania, which was an elaboration of Freud's remarks on mania in "Group Psychology and the Analysis of the Ego."[79]

The paper by Rado unmasked the self-reproaches as an ambivalent ingratiation of (the object and) the superego. The connections between depression and self-esteem were clarified. The dual introjection of the object into the ego and into the superego was explained, and the differentiation of the "good" (i.e., protecting) and the "bad" (i.e., punishing) aspects of the superego was used for clarification of the aims of the depressive mechanisms. Besides, Rado explained the manic-depressive periodicity as a special case of the general periodicity of transgression and expiation, as an outcome, in the last analysis, of the fundamental biological periodicity of hunger and satiety in the infant. Later papers brought elaborations and clinical illustrations.[80]

Therapeutic Psychoanalysis in Manic-Depressive Disorders

The therapeutic outlook for psychoanalysis is very different in cases of neurotic depressions and in severe manic-depressive psychoses. As to neurotic depression, the mildest cases do not need any special treatment; the solution of the basic infantile conflicts in the course of the analysis of the main neurosis automatically brings a solution of neurotic inferiority feelings and a relative harmony with the superego. More severe cases in which depression dominates the clinical picture present the same difficulties as compulsion neuroses, since they are based on a similar pregenital fixation.

The difficulties encountered in the psychoanalytic treatment of manic-depressive psychoses are of quite another nature. The more "internalized" the pathogenic processes are, the more difficult it is to establish the transference contact necessary for analysis. In narcissistic states, the analyst has no other means than to use nonnarcissistic remainders in the personality in attempts to increase the patient's object relationships sufficiently to start the analytic work.

There are three special types of difficulties that analysis must overcome in the case of manic-depressive patients. A relatively slight problem is the first one, present also in neurotic depressions, namely, the oral fixation, that is, the remoteness of the crucial infantile experiences which the analysis must uncover (the history of the primal depression). Of greater severity is the second difficulty, consisting in the narcissistic nature of the illness and the consequent looseness of the transference relationship. Even where this relationship is established, it is persistently ambivalent, to a degree unknown in any other type of neurosis; and this relationship is constantly threatened by the tendency toward a sudden unaccountable narcissistic regression. The third difficulty is the most crucial one. In a severe depressive or manic condition the patient is inaccessible to analytic in-

fluence. The reasonable ego, which is supposed to learn to
face its conflicts by analysis, is simply nonexistent. However,
Abraham called attention to the fact, since confirmed by
many psychiatrists, that even inaccessible depressed patients, agitated anxious ones as well as monotonously complaining ones without apparent contact with the objective
world, are grateful to an attentive listener and may repay
kind patience with a sudden contact—which, however, is
no easy task with such patients.[81]

The manic-depressive patients offer one natural way
out of the last difficulty: the frequency of free intervals during which they are capable of object relationships. The free
interval is obviously the period of choice for analytic efforts.
Yet even in the free intervals the ambivalence and the narcissistic orientation remain as hindrances. Besides, there is
the potential danger that an analysis begun in the free interval may precipitate a new attack. Abraham, on the basis
of rich clinical experience, denies the seriousness of this
danger, and in fact reports that analysis carried out during
the free period tended to prolong the free interval.[82] He also
succeeded in effecting true cures, although only after very
long treatment, the more prolonged because of intervening
attacks of the illness.

Taking into consideration the apparent futility of most
other types of therapy and the hope that increasing progress
in practical experience will show what modifications in technique are needed, one should also not overlook the fact that
even if the analysis fails, the patient is temporarily relieved
through the opportunity of unburdening himself by talking.
On the basis of these considerations the manic-depressive
patient, after he or his relatives have been informed of the
doubtfulness of the prognosis, may be advised to undergo

analysis. But one thing must be borne in mind: the analyst may be deceived by the patient's dissimulation and by the abruptness with which things happen in depressions. In all severe depressions a grave danger of suicide is always present. Even though the analyst's contact with the patient is different from that of the nonanalytic psychiatrist, he must never disregard the caution that psychiatry teaches. The more extensive, planned psychoanalytic study of manic-depressive disorders, needed both for the benefit of the patients and for the benefit of science, must be undertaken within institutions.

The Mechanism
of Depression

EDWARD BIBRING

Our systematic understanding of the dynamic structure
of the depression began with Freud's first attempt at the
explanation of "Mourning and Melancholia,"[1] based on
Abraham's earlier work.[2] Freud points out that grief and
melancholic depression, though they have many clinical
features in common, differ in important aspects. In grief
there is an *actual* loss of an object, consequently a feeling
of the world being "poor and empty," but there is no fall
in self-esteem, no self-accusation. In melancholic depressions, there is usually an *emotional* loss of object due to disappointment or related factors. Consequently "the melancholic displays an extraordinary fall of self-esteem, a loss of
the ego: the ego itself seems poor and empty, and is inclined
to self-reproaches."

Freud offers various explanations for the difference. In
the first place, simple depression, as represented by the uncomplicated grief reaction, is of an object-libidinal origin,
in distinction from the narcissistic type of depression as
exemplified by the melancholic form which may "extend
beyond the clear case of a loss by death and include those

[1] See references in chapter notes at back of book.

situations of being wounded, hurt, neglected, out of favor, or disappointed, which can impart opposite feelings of love and hate." The disappointment by the (narcissistically chosen) object not only incurs a high degree of ambivalent feelings, but leads finally to a withdrawal of the libido from the object and to a reinforcing cathexis of the ego. This is achieved by the process of identification of the ego with the (emotionally) lost object. Freud accepted Abraham's proposition that the identification is carried out by the instinctual process of oral incorporation. This made it possible to trace the self-accusation back partly to feelings of guilt, to a need for self-punishment, partly and perhaps mainly to the aggressive feelings toward the object which had been turned against the patient's self as identified with the lost object.

Freud discusses among other problems that of the nature and origin of the *inhibition* so characteristic of the depressive states. According to him the inhibition is due to the "work of mourning" which absorbs nearly all libidinal energy, and which therefore accounts fully for the depressed person's loss of interest in the outside world. Freud extended this explanation also to the melancholic depression. The severe inhibition is explained by the fact that the "narcissistic wound" calls out for an unusually strong anticathexis which again results in the absorption of nearly all ego energy and consequently in an inhibition of functions including the interest in the external world.

Freud's explanations were further elaborated by various authors, particularly by Abraham and Rado. Abraham continued to explore his own and Freud's propositions within a detailed framework of the infantile libidinal development, particularly in regard to the oral and anal phases without

reference to the ego aspect.[3] He was the first to introduce
the concept of a primal depression which develops in early
childhood in reaction to a "severe injury of infantile narcissism through a combination of disappointments in love."
The primal disappointment was assumed to have occurred
in the later oral-cannibalistic stage of infantile development
and was conceived of as oral frustration. The subsequent
depressions follow the pattern established by the first.

Rado studied the influence of the varying phases and
vicissitudes of the nursing situation on the infantile ego.[4]
Severe frustration on the oral level lowers the feeling of
security and consequently the "self-esteem" of the infantile
ego. Rado saw in the change from hunger (which he considered the deepest point of fixation in depression) to satisfaction the earliest model for a series of ego attitudes ranging from rage to depression, to self-punishment, to craving
for affection, and finally to gratification and reconciliation,
as observed in the manic and depressive states. Rado's contribution, though written in 1928, seems still to a large extent influenced by the concepts developed prior to the
structural approach, which conceived of the ego as the
"agent" of the instinctual drives, whose functions were predominantly modeled by and after the drives.

It would lead too far afield to quote the important contributions of other authors. In general, one can say that
Freud's original distinction between simple (object-libidinal) and melancholic (narcissistic-ambivalent) depression
was somewhat leveled down. On the one hand, the grief
reaction frequently appeared complicated by ambivalence
toward the lost object. On the other hand, increased observations suggested that identification occurred as a very frequent, if not regular, reaction to the (actual or emotional)

loss of an object; that it was perhaps the only way of over-coming such a loss. Since identification (an ego function) was thought of as being closely linked up, if not identical, with oral incorporation (an instinctual process), it became a generally accepted proposition that the etiology of depres-sion was intimately connected on the one hand with oral frustration, on the other hand with aggression in general, and oral aggression in particular.*

Fenichel's systematic survey of the literature on the subject can be considered as representative of the current conceptions of the various aspects of depression.[5] He states that the simple as well as the melancholic forms of depres-sion have in common a decrease in self-esteem. The clinical differences are viewed as stages in the course of the struggle to regain the lost self-esteem by various recovery mecha-nisms. A *slightly sad person* needs consolation, "narcissistic" (predominantly oral) "supplies" from the (external) ob-jects. A *severe depression* represents the state into which "the orally dependent individual gets when the vital sup-plies are lacking." Such persistent lack usually leads to the familiar sequence of events: the libidinal withdraw from the disappointing and therefore hated external object is fol-lowed by the "fateful" regression to the oral point of fixation and subsequent "incorporation" of the object. The struggle for the restoration of the self-esteem is now continued on the intrapsychic level, partly as "desperate attempts" to get from the introjected object (or the superego) the vital nar-cissistic supplies which originally were demanded from the real object partly by turning the object-directed aggression

---

* It should be stressed at this point that the concept of identification is applied in the following paragraphs in terms of pure ego-function which may or may not have any connection with "oral incorporation."

toward oneself, particularly in the form of self-accusations and self-hatred.

Not all authors followed this line of thinking. Some maintained in principle Freud's original conception that the different clinical types of depression are based on essentially different mechanisms. Thus Edoardo Weiss separates clinically as well as theoretically a "simple" or "essential" type of depression from the "melancholic" type.[6] According to him, simple depression is characterized by a decrease in the intensity of self-experience of the individual; "he is *less awake* and the external world conveys to him much less intense meaning than it does to other persons." Applying Federn's ego-psychological approach,[7] Weiss states that the reason for the lowered ego feeling is to be found in the fact that "the libido is fixated to an object or goal which is rejected but cannot be relinquished," and that this continuous struggle finally exhausts the libido of the person to a degree which results in depression. Freud's explanation of the inhibition in depression by an absorption of ego energy is confined by Weiss to the "simple" depression.

In melancholic depression the patient's narcissism is "injured in the most obvious way." As a consequence, the main characteristics of melancholic depression are loss of self-esteem and the subsequent "development of self-hatred and self-accusations due to feelings of guilt and inferiority, irrespective of what the particular origin of such feelings might be." The "ego feeling" in melancholic depression is, in contrast to the simple type, not lowered but increased. In brief, simple depression results from exhaustion of ego libido due to an unsolvable conflict (the "ego" is "empty") whereas melancholic depression is due to self-hatred as a consequence of an extensive loss of self-esteem through rejection.

Edith Jacobson discusses the impact of early disappointments in the parental omnipotence and of the subsequent
devaluation of the parental images on the little child's ego
formation.[8] Such disappointment goes along with devaluation
and "destruction" of the infantile self and causes a primary
childhood depression which is repeated whenever in later
years a similar disillusionment takes place.

However, Jacobson describes briefly another form of
depression which she calls an "endogenous" or "a mild,
blank" type and which she characterizes in terms similar to
Edoardo Weiss, by a feebleness of the ego, "a feeling of
disillusionment in life, a general physical fatigue and exhaustion, emotional emptiness, lack of initiative, and hypochondriac fears." In this type of depression, the feeling of
guilt appears as a secondary formation, rather than as a
primary or essential, etiological factor. Fenichel states also
briefly that "many a simple neurotic depression" is due to
"the circumstance that since the greater percentage of the
available mental energy is used up in unconscious conflicts,
not enough is left to provide the normal enjoyment of life
and vitality."

This rather sketchy survey of the psychoanalytic literature on depression may suffice to demonstrate two major
trends in explaining the structure and genesis of depression.
According to one approach there exist at least two types of
depression which differ clinically as well as theoretically;
the first type (called simple, essential, endogenous, mild,
blank, etc.) is represented on the one hand by the uncomplicated grief reaction (Freud), on the other hand by the
depression primarily due to exhaustion of the "ego energy,"
for whatever reasons, and in whatever ways this may come
about. The second (severe or melancholic) type is characterized by the familiar etiological syndrome: narcissistic injury,

oral mechanisms of recovery, such as identification via incorporation and the concomitant turning of the aggression from the object against the self. According to the second approach, a loss of self-esteem is common to all types of depression. Consequently the clinical differences (ranging from simple sadness to the severe forms of melancholia) are explained by additional predominantly oral-aggressive etiological mechanisms which are employed in the course of the struggle for readjustment.

It is characteristic of the present state of affairs that Fenichel, notwithstanding the fact that he considers the existence of the exhaustion type of depression and occasionally hints at other possible types, nevertheless proceeds to define the general predisposition to depression in terms of an *"oral fixation which determines the later reaction to narcissistic shocks"* and "the narcissistic injury may create a depressive disposition because it *occurs early enough to be met by an orally oriented ego,"** by what apparently is meant an "ego" which is tuned to external oral-narcissistic supplies. Fenichel takes also into consideration the reverse possibility, namely that shocks to the "self-esteem" in early childhood may secondarily create the decisive oral fixation in the sense that the *ego may become fixated to oral defense mechanisms,* but he did not pursue this possibility any further. Be it as it may, the same holds true of the phenomenon of elation which is also considered as a "narcissistic neurosis" like depression. "It too has its roots in oral eroticism. Incorporation and identification play a large role in both states."[9]

In this article an attempt is made to approach the problem of depression from the ego-psychological point of view,

* My italics.

which may be formulated in the thesis that depression is an ego-psychological phenomenon, a "state of the ego," an affective state. This refers to all "normal" and "neurotic" depressions, and probably also to what is called "psychotic" depression.

Before entering the discussion of the basic mechanism of depression, I should like to quote some rather trivial instances of normal and neurotic depression, in order to elicit a primary model of depression.*

During the political crisis which preceded the recent war, many people felt depressed. Disregarding the specific ways in which the reaction was brought about in the various individuals, the common feeling was that the war, which they all did not want, seemed unavoidable, that it seemed impossible to do what they desired, namely to preserve peace.

Another example: a young girl fell into deep depression when general mobilization was ordered. She had the feeling that her old fear of merciless powers disrupting the peoples' lives had come true. The evidence of their existence undermined her former attempts to deny both the existence of the relentless powers and her fear of them. The fact that it was a power beyond her reach (the government, the world powers) made her feel completely helpless and depressed.

In the case of a man of about thirty, the persistent motive for the recurrent depression was not too easy to discover. He had a vivid feeling of his own existence whenever

---

* It may be helpful to make it clear at this point that any descriptive classification of the various clinical pictures of depression is at first of no significance for the particular approach intended here since the question as to whether there is a common denominator in terms of the ego cuts across all clinical distinctions.

he had to cope with complicated, usually professional problems. When forced by the circumstances to do plain routine work for a longer while, he regularly developed a depression. Analysis revealed among other factors that any routine performance made him feel insignificant, at a standstill, instead of proving his strength, or his growing stronger and more skillful by meeting the challenge of the complicated "test situation." His depression set in whenever he felt that his fear to remain weak and therefore unfit to meet "dangers" and "attackers," etc., seemed to come true.

One could quote many more trivial and complicated instances: the man who is depressed because he believes that he suffers from an inoperable cancer; the girl who finds herself alone on a weekend without a date; the patient who becomes depressed because he suffered an unexpected relapse into his neurosis, or because he felt that the warded-off "bad" impulses were still latently operative in him, or because he could not resist temptation; the man who develops a depression whenever he or his wife get sick or whenever he hears of people being tricked, people whom he considers as honest, but not a match for the "foxes," etc.

However trivial these instances may be, they seem to present a basic pattern which they have in common. In all these instances, the individuals either felt helplessly exposed to superior powers, fatal organic disease, or recurrent neurosis, or to the seemingly inescapable fate of being lonely, isolated, or unloved, or unavoidably confronted with the apparent evidence of being weak, inferior, or a failure. In all instances, the depression accompanied a feeling of being doomed, irrespective of what the conscious or unconscious background of this feeling may have been: in all of them a blow was dealt to the person's self-esteem, on whatever grounds such self-esteem may have been founded. From this point of view, depression can be defined as the emotional expression (indication) of a state of helplessness and powerlessness* of the ego, irrespective of what may have caused the breakdown of the mechanisms which established his self-esteem.

The feelings of helplessness are not the only characteristic of depression. On further analysis of the quoted and other instances one invariably finds the condition that certain narcissistically significant, i.e., for the self-esteem pertinent, goals and objects are strongly maintained. Irrespective of their unconscious implications, one may roughly distinguish between three groups of such persisting aspirations of the person: (1) the wish to be worthy, to be loved, to be appreciated, not to be inferior or unworthy; (2) the wish to be strong, superior, great, secure, not to be weak and insecure; and (3) the wish to be good, to be loving, not to be aggressive, hateful and destructive. It is exactly from the tension between these highly charged narcissistic aspirations on the one hand, and the ego's acute awareness of its (real and imaginary) helplessness and incapacity to live up to them on the other hand, that depression results.

In the first group the depression sets in whenever the fear of being inferior or defective seems to come true, whenever and in whatever way the person comes to feel that all effort was in vain, that he is definitely doomed to be a "failure." In the second group of persisting tensions (schematically described as the desire to be strong), the depression is due to the shocklike (actual or imaginary or symbolic)

---

* The term "powerlessness" is not used in any objective or realistic sense, but entirely in its subjective meaning. Just as inferiority feelings do not prove any real inferiority of the patient, so the feeling of being powerless does not imply any real lack of power.

evidence that this goal will never be achieved due to the ego's weakness, that one is doomed to be a "victim" (with regard to dangers, or merciless powers and their unconscious implications). In the third group of tensions (the desire to be loving, not to be aggressive, etc.), the narcissistic shock (blow to the self-esteem) is due to the unexpected awareness of the existence of latent aggressive tendencies within the self, with all the consequences involved, and this in spite of the fact that one had tried hard to be loving and not to hate, not to be "evil."

These three sets of conditions are, of course, not exclusive of each other but may, under certain circumstances, co-exist in varying combinations in the same individual and at the same time. Though the persisting aspirations are of a threefold nature, the *basic mechanism of the resulting depression appears to be essentially the same.* According to this view, depression is primarily not determined by a conflict between the ego on the one hand and the id, or the superego, or the environment on the other hand, but stems primarily from a tension within the ego itself, from an inner-systemic "conflict." Thus depression can be defined as the emotional correlate of a partial or complete collapse of the self-esteem of the ego, since it feels unable to live up to its aspirations (ego ideal, superego) while they are strongly maintained.

A suitable illustration of the intimate connection between the state of helplessness and depression is offered by the girl quoted above who reacted with depression to general mobilization. Her infantile (but "denied") fear that there are inaccessible merciless powers disrupting the peoples' lives seemed to be substantiated by the political events. The government and the international powers were so far beyond her reach that she felt utterly helpless and depressed. However, her reaction to various individuals who—in her opinion—threatened to disrupt her life was characteristically different: she did not develop any depression but a violent rage which sometimes led to physical attack. It is also characteristic that she felt relieved immediately after having succeeded in hurting (mostly verbally) the disappointing love object. This served as proof that she had at least as much power over the object as she was afraid the object might have over her, in brief, that she was not helpless, that she could "get even" with them. This feeling of power over the object made any rage as well as any depression unnecessary. She became depressed, however, when she found herself confronted with forces beyond her reach, that is, when the ego in all its relative power was made to feel helpless and consequently any attempt to cope with the situation meaningless.

One could ask at this point whether the simple, i.e., uncomplicated grief reaction fits in the proposed scheme. In the instance of an actual loss of love object, the resulting tension can be described as a longing for the lost object and love, and a wish to retrieve the loss (maintenance of object and goal). The depression, sometimes accompanied by a feeling of pain, appears to derive from the fact that here too the ego is confronted with an inescapable situation, since it does not have the power to undo the loss. Observation shows, e.g., that an exacerbation of the grief reaction occurs whenever certain conditions bring the loss and the inability to retrieve it acutely into awareness.

According to the conception exposed here, basic depression represents a state of the ego whose main characteristics are a decrease of self-esteem, a more or less intense state of helplessness, a more or less intensive and extensive inhibition of functions, and a more or less intensely felt particular emotion; in other words, depression represents an affective state, which indicates a state of the ego in terms of helplessness and inhibition of functions.

To clarify this further, I should like to compare depression with similar affective states, such as depersonalization and boredom. They seem to be phenomenologically related and it is sometimes difficult for the patients to keep them apart.

The main complaint of depersonalized persons refers to not having any feelings, to being blocked emotionally, being "frozen" which is often accompanied by feelings of unreality of the self, of behaving like automatons, etc. Clinical observations show that depersonalization often develops in place of an acute outburst of anger, and for that reason it has been classified as "defense mechanism," though it is difficult to define the actual process. One may describe it more generally as acute blocking in *statu nascendi* of overwhelming tensions (aggression and others) *within* the ego, which goes along with certain changes in the feeling function of the ego which are experienced as various forms of inhibition. A related type of "depersonalization" is represented by the well-known behavior in situations of danger. The persons involved describe a state of cold alertness and clarity of mind and a feeling of acting like an automaton, yet mostly in highly rational manner. When the danger has passed, many of these individuals show a delayed reaction in form of tremors, crying spells, sweating, palpitation, and other expressions or equivalents of anxiety. The anxiety which threatened to overwhelm the ego was blocked in *statu nascendi* or "bound" (anticathected) as long as the danger lasted, and liberated only when the danger subsided. In both instances of depersonalization, the ego protects itself actively against the danger of being overwhelmed by strong tensions by blocking their further development, as a measure of defense. In both instances a modification of the feeling function of the ego takes place which can be described under the category of inhibition.

The dynamic conditions of boredom, which too represent a state of particular mental inhibition, have been discussed by Fenichel[10] and others, most recently by Greenson.[11] According to the definition of Lipps (quoted by Fenichel) boredom is a painful feeling originating in a tension between a need for mental activity and the lack of adequate stimulation, or the ego's incapacity of being stimulated to such activity. Fenichel adds the hypothesis that this inability is the result of repression of the instinctual "aims." The need for activity is felt, but since the "aims are repressed," there is an incapacity to develop direction from within. This forces the person to seek a solution from external stimulation. He is, however, not capable of adequate stimulation from outside, because the gratifications offered are either too much removed from the (unconscious) aims to serve as substitutes, or because they come so close to the warded-off aims that they incur inhibition. A certain similarity with depression and a characteristic difference becomes obvious. The (unconscious) goals are maintained in depression as well as in boredom, but the ability to reach them is interfered with in boredom by the repression of the true goals and the rejection of substitutes because they are either inadequate or prohibited. The result is a lack of directions, the inability to bring about goal-directed behavior in spite of many attempts in this direction, and subsequently a feeling of emptiness and boredom. In depression the ego is shocked into passivity not because there is a conflict regarding the goals, but because of its own incapacity to live up to the undisputed narcissistic aspirations.

The conditions leading to boredom as well as to depression could be observed in the case of a female patient who passionately liked to travel and who was highly excited when she started to make arrangements for a journey to a "new" place. She was not interested in traveling to "civilized" countries, but preferred those which seemed "exotic" and therefore exciting to her, such as the oriental countries. She used to prepare for such travels, reading copious literature about them and particularly about the customs of the people. But she repeatedly went through the same experience: she was all enthusiastic at the beginning; after a while, however, she began to lose interest, felt bored and finally depressed. Analysis revealed that she had particular conceptions of the "noncivilized" peoples, that the customs and habits in which she was (unconsciously) interested were of sexual nature. Her conscious-unconscious hopes to find amorous adventures were predominantly concerned with perverted practices which she was eager to learn—mainly for narcissistic reasons. Since her repressed wishes could not be gratified by the various substitutes, her initial excitement subsided very soon and she felt disappointed and bored. The fact that she went through this same experience with a certain regularity made her feel increasingly depressed, i.e., helpless with regard to the fulfillment of her narcissistic expectations.

The same patient reacted with depression whenever she was told that a person had died in early years. It was one of her painful fears that she would die before her life finished its natural course, which meant before certain aspirations had been fulfilled. She felt that people should only die when they had lived their lives to a meaningful end. One unconscious meaning of this fear was that she could pass away before having learned to know what she wanted so badly, the sexual secrets of the "children of nature." Here too, the depression was due to a feeling of helplessness inevitably induced by the evidence that people did die young in age before their lives were "fulfilled," before they "knew all," before they could catch up with the grownups. Cases of involutionary melancholia often expose a similar psychology. The curtain falls before certain expectations are fulfilled, before the "happy end" is enacted.

Many patients whose main symptom consists in chronic boredom show a similar pattern. They get occasionally excited out of proportion about new impressions or new activities which seem to hold a promise in regard to unconscious narcissistic aspiration, but they lose interest very soon and fall back onto the chronic feelings of boredom, when the expected promising and "shattering" great event did not materialize. The feeling of boredom is finally followed by depression when a sense of helplessness and inescapability is added. These individuals show the same sequence of reactions in analysis, particularly at the beginning, since they transfer very soon the narcissistic fantasy of a great, all-pervasive, all-liberating experience onto the treatment situation. Disappointment, boredom, depression follow in quick succession to be repeated at similar constellations in the course of treatment.

To summarize: depersonalization, boredom, and depression represent affective states and states of mental inhibition. In *depersonalization,* usually aggressive tensions are acutely barred from emotional and motor expression by a—little understood—general blocking of the feeling functions as a measure of defense. In *boredom,* libidinal strivings are maintained but actively prevented from (substitute) gratification. The inhibition of functions in boredom refers to the blocking of the development of goal-directed (or need-directed) behavior. In boredom as well as in depersonalization the self-esteem of the person remains outside of the sphere of conflict. In *depression* the narcissistically important aims are perpetuated, but the narcissistic core of the ego, its self-esteem, is broken down, since the ego functions—which usually serve the gratification of the particular narcissistic strivings—appear to be highly inadequate, partly due to reality factors, partly due to internal reasons.

Freud defines inhibition as a "restriction of functions of the ego" and mentions two major causes for such restrictions: either they have been imposed upon the person as a measure of precaution, e.g., to prevent the development of anxiety or feelings of guilt, or brought about as a result of exhaustion of energy of the ego engaged in intense defensive activities.[12] He quotes as illustration of a general though transitory inhibition of ego function an obsessional patient, who "used to be overcome by a paralyzing fatigue which lasted for one or more days whenever something occurred which should obviously have thrown him into a rage." Freud adds: "We have here a point of departure from which we may hope to reach an understanding of the condition of general inhibition which characterizes states of depression, including the gravest form of them, melancholia."

The inhibition in depression as elaborated in this paper does not fall under either category; it is neither explained as due to a measure of precaution nor to a depletion of energy. It is rather due to the fact that certain strivings of the person become meaningless—since the ego appears incapable ever to gratify them.

This is further supported by a comparison of the state of depression with the state of fatigue. Is it apparently not by chance that depressions are so often subjectively experienced as fatigue, so much so that fatigue is considered to be an "equivalent" of depression. It is probably also not by chance that physical exhaustion through stress and strain, or disease, is frequently accompanied by feelings of depression. The depressed person, severely disappointed in himself, has lost his incentives and gives up, not the goals, but pursuing them, since this proves to be useless; he is "tired." The physically exhausted person is incapable of any effort; he is depressed. At least, one can formulate that in both cases vitality, the vigor in pursuing goals, is considerably lowered or nearly completely inhibited.

To clarify the status of depression still further, it may be helpful at this point to compare depression with the feeling of anxiety, particularly since the latter has been brought in close connection with the feeling of helplessness (Freud). Both are frequent—probably equally frequent—ego reactions, scaling from the mildest, practically insignificant forms to the most intensive, pathological structures. Since they cannot be reduced any further, it may be justified to call them basic ego reactions. From the point of view elaborated here, anxiety and depression represent diametrically opposed basic ego responses. Anxiety as a reaction to (external or internal) danger indicates the ego's desire to survive. The ego, challenged by the danger, mobilizes the signal of anxiety and prepares for fight or flight. In depression, the opposite takes place, the ego is paralyzed because it finds itself incapable to meet the "danger." In extreme situations the wish to live is replaced by the wish to die. (This does not mean, however, that anxiety and depression are exclusive of each other. A person may be anxious in one respect and depressed for other reasons, since the collapse of self-esteem is in many cases only a partial one. Or depression may follow anxiety, the mobilization of energy may be replaced by a decrease of self-reliance, etc.) *

It is hardly possible to discuss depression without taking into account the phenomenon of elation, which also extends from the mildest form to those of a very intense, pathological degree. Though elation frequently occurs as a compensatory reaction to states of anxiety as well as to states of depression, it nevertheless has to be considered as a basic (independent) state of mind in the ego's inventory of responses to internal or external stimuli. In contrast to depression, elation is the expression of an actual or imaginary fulfillment of the person's narcissistic aspirations.

Summarizing, one can say that there are four basic ego states: (1) the state of balanced narcissism (normal self-esteem), the secure and self-assured ego; (2) the state of excited or exhilarated self-esteem, the triumphant or elated ego; (3) the state of threatened narcissism, the anxious ego; and (4) the state of broken-down self-regard, the "inhibited" or paralyzed, the depressed ego. In other words, depression is on the same plane as anxiety and other reactive ego states. It is—essentially—"a human way of reacting to frustration

---

* Be it as it may, the very fact of depression, of the wish to die, or of "the ego letting itself die" (Freud) represents a problem to any biologically oriented psychology. Perhaps one could at this point venture the hypothesis that in cases of physical—and emotional—exhaustion, the feeling of fatigue as well as of depression serve as warning signals not to exert oneself any longer.

and misery" whenever the ego finds itself in a state of (real or imaginary) helplessness against "overwhelming odds."

It follows from the definition of depression that it is not warranted to define the predisposition to depression as exclusively consisting "in oral fixations which determine the later reaction to narcissistic shocks," or to generalize that the depressive predisposition is created by a narcissistic injury "met by an orally oriented ego." The "orally dependent type" which constantly needs "narcissistic supplies" from outside, represents perhaps the most frequent type of predisposition to depression, which is not surprising if one takes into consideration the fact that the infant has actually no power over its objects and the necessary supplies it has to receive from them, that it is entirely dependent on the benevolence of the environment for the gratification of his needs and maintenance of his life. Frequent frustrations of the infant's oral needs may mobilize at first anxiety and anger. If frustration is continued, however, in disregard of the "signals" produced by the infant, the anger will be replaced by feelings of exhaustion, of helplessness and depression. This early self-experience of the infantile ego's helplessness, of its lack of power to provide the vital supplies, is probably the most frequent factor predisposing to depression. I should like to stress the point that the emphasis is not on the oral frustration and subsequent oral fixation, but on the infant's or little child's shocklike experience of and fixation to the feeling of helplessness.

The narcissistic aspirations developed on the oral level, or subsequently built on it, may be generally defined as the need to get affection, to be loved, to be taken care of, to get the "supplies," or by the opposite defensive need: to be independent, self-supporting. Depression follows the painful discovery of not being loved or not being independent, whenever this discovery regressively evokes the primary feeling of helplessness with regard to the gratification of these narcissistic needs.

A strikingly different picture is offered by the anal-sadistic phase. In contrast to the child on the oral level, the child of the anal phase has often to defend certain of his strivings and cherished sources of gratification against the interference by the objects. The oral child is completely dependent on the objects; it is therefore easily made to feel helpless. The child of the anal phase usually has acquired a certain independent ego strength, a certain capacity to control his body and his instinctual interests as well as the objects. It has learned not only how to exert sphincter control but is also capable of saying "no," of defying grownups, of mobilizing various forms of aggression as a defense against the interfering objects. The narcissistic aspirations characteristic of this phase refer to mastery over the body as well as over the drives and the objects. When in reaction to the sometimes intense aggression, feelings of remorse and guilt are developed, together with a fear of punishment, the corresponding aspirations will consist of the wish to be good, not to be resentful, hostile, defiant, but to be loving, not to be dirty, but to be clean, etc. Depression, i.e., the feeling of relative powerlessness or helplessness, will refer to the lack of control over the libidinal as well as aggressive impulses or over the objects, to the feelings of weakness ("I am too weak ever to control the forbidden impulses or the interfering objects"), or to the feelings of guilt ("I shall never succeed in being good and loving, I am destined to be hateful, hostile and defiant, and therefore evil").

The phallic phase shows again a different type of ego

involvement. Competitive strivings within the oedipal situation are intimately linked up with exhibitionistic and sadistic needs to defeat the rival and to be admired by maternal images or substitutes. In the phallic stage, therefore, the narcissistic aspirations stem mainly from the competitive situation, the wish to be admired, to be center of attention, to be strong and victorious, not to be defeated, and so forth. Depression may result, e.g., when the fear of being defeated and ridiculed for one's shortcomings and defects, or the fear of retaliation, etc., seem to come true and the ego proves too weak to prevent the inevitable.

To summarize: what has been described as the basic mechanism of depression, the ego's shocking awareness of its helplessness in regard to its aspirations, is assumed to represent the core of normal, neurotic and probably also psychotic depression. It is further assumed on the basis of clinical material that such traumatic experiences usually occur in early childhood and establish a fixation of the ego to the state of helplessness. This state is later on regressively reactivated whenever situations arise which resemble the primary shock condition, i.e., when for external or internal reasons those particular functions which serve the fulfillment of the important aspiration, prove to be inadequate.

It has been mentioned above that as far as observations suggest the child of the oral phase is more frequently exposed to the traumatic impression of helplessness, particularly since it is actually helpless. Similar reactions may be established by any severe frustration of the little child's vital needs in and beyond the oral phase, e.g., of the child's needs for affection (Abraham), or by a failure in the child-mother relationship of mutuality[13] or by an early disappointment in the parental omnipotence,[14] etc.

It is finally assumed that all other factors which deter-

mine the different clinical pictures of depression represent
accelerating conditions or "complications" superimposed on
the basic mechanism by the oral defense mechanisms and
their sequelae. More precisely, one has to make a clearer distinction between: (1) the basic or essential mechanism of
depression (fall in self-esteem due to the awareness of one's
own real or imaginary, partial or total insufficiency or helplessness); (2) conditions which predispose to and help to
bring about depression; (3) the attempts at restitution associated with depression; (4) conditions which complicate
the basic type of depression such as aggression and orality;
and (5) the secondary use which may be made—consciously
or unconsciously—of an established depression (e.g., to get
attention and affection or other narcissistic gratification).

To discuss these points briefly: (1) According to the
viewpoint adopted here, *depression represents a basic reaction* to situations of narcissistic frustration which to prevent appears to be beyond the power of the ego, just as
anxiety represents a basic reaction of the ego to situations
of danger. Depression is defined as being primarily an ego
phenomenon, i.e., as being essentially independent of the
vicissitudes of aggression as well as of oral drives. Since depressions frequently appear to be linked up with self-reproaches, the concept of depression became synonymous
with self-accusation and self-destruction to such a degree
that nearly every depression was viewed as resulting from
the turning of originally object-directed aggression against
self. The same holds true of the relation between depression
and oral striving. Here, too, the frequent observation of oral
implications in depression led to the definition of the predisposition for depression in terms of oral fixation. It is true
that an "orally oriented person," who is dependent on ex-

ternal "supplies" for the maintenance of his self-esteem, is prone to narcissistic injuries and oral recovery mechanisms, but to reverse this statement is not justified.

It should be stressed that the conception of depression presented here does not invalidate the accepted theories of the role which orality and aggression play in the various types of depression. It implies, however, that the oral and aggressive strivings are not as universal in depression as is generally assumed and that consequently the theories built on them do not offer sufficient explanation, but require a certain modification: it is our contention, based on clinical observation, that it is the ego's awareness of its helplessness which in certain cases forces it to turn the aggression from the object against the self, thus aggravating and complicating the structure of depression.

If the conception presented here is correct, then any condition which forces a feeling of helplessness upon the infantile ego may create a predisposition to depression. The conception of the exhaustion type of depression comes very close to the viewpoint presented here with the difference that the emphasis is not on the exhaustion of libidinal energy but on the state of helplessness of the ego confronted with an insolvable situation.

(2) In general, one may say that everything that lowers or paralyzes the ego's self-esteem without changing the narcissistically important aims represents a condition of depression. External or internal, actual or symbolic factors may consciously or unconsciously refute the denial of weakness or defeat or danger, may dispel systems of self-deception, may destroy hope, may reveal lack of affection or respect or prove the existence in oneself of undesirable impulses or thoughts or attitudes, or offer evidence that dormant or neu-

tralized fears are actually "justified," and so forth; the subsequent results will be the same: the individual will regressively react with the feeling of powerlessness and helplessness with regard to his loneliness, isolation, weakness, inferiority, evilness or guilt. Whatever the external or internal objects or representations of the narcissistically important strivings may be, the mechanism of depression will be the same. The narcissistic shock may be mild or severe, focal or extensive, partial or complete, depending on whatever peripheral or central narcissistic aspirations are involved. These factors will contribute to the extent and intensity of the depression as well as the possibilities, the means, or the tempo of recovery.

Our scheme seems not only suitable to bring a certain order into the variety of configurations resulting in depression, but also permits a clearer conception of the therapeutic effort. From a theoretical as well as therapeutic point of view one has to pay attention not only to the dynamic and genetic basis of the persisting narcissistic aspirations, the frustrations of which the ego cannot tolerate, but also the dynamic and genetic conditions which forced the infantile ego to become fixated to feelings of helplessness. Its major importance in the therapy of depression is obvious.*

The same conditions which bring about depression, in reverse serve frequently the restitution from depression. Generally one can say that depression subsides either (a) when the narcissistically important goals and objects appear to be again within reach (which is frequently followed by a temporary elation), or (b) when they become sufficiently modi-

---

* This is to some degree in agreement with Karen Horney[15] who stressed the necessity of analyzing not only the "conflicts," but also the "hopelessness."

fied or reduced to become realizable; or (c) when they are altogether relinquished; or (d) when the ego recovers from the narcissistic shock by regaining its self-esteem with the help of various recovery mechanisms (with or without any change of object and goal). Finally (e) defense can be directed also against the affect of depression as such. This usually results in apathy or hypomania. Certain observations suggest that apathy is due to a "blocking" of the depressive emotion, to the mechanism of depersonalization in a (usually chronically) depressed person; whereas certain types of hypomania represent a reaction formation to depression, usually combined with a denial of the causes of depression.[16]

(4) The most frequent complication of the basic structure of depression can be found in the large group of orally dependent people who thrive on "oral-narcissistic supplies" and collapse when these are lacking, or who in reaction to severe frustration regress to the oral mechanism of restitution, the most fateful recovery mechanism consisting in the "incorporation" of the objects in cases of severely ambivalent attitudes toward it.

The correlation between depression and aggression on the one hand, mania and aggression on the other, can be observed in the fantasies as well as in the occasional acting out of depressive patients. On recovery from depression by regaining self-esteem and the feeling of strength, aggressive impulses are released and directed against the object world. Under such conditions, e.g., a female patient frequently had the fantasy of walking along the street, with a large sword in her hand and cutting off the heads of the people passing by to the right and left. The sequence of depression, self-accusation, hypomania, aggression against the outside world, could be clearly observed in the patient. But as much as her aggressive fantasies were secondary to her exaggerated self-esteem, so was the turning of aggression against the self—particularly in form of self-hatred—secondary to the lowering of self-esteem. On the basis of similar observations it seems justified to generalize that the turning of aggressive impulses against the self is secondary to a breakdown of the self-esteem. It is ultimately due to the feeling of powerlessness and helplessness (often combined with masochistic tendencies) that the ego "surrenders" to the superego and accepts punishment. We observe at least in certain instances the opposite tendencies of the ego, namely, to defy and "repress" the demands of the superego as long as the ego feels strong and powerful in its rebellion. There are cases where no feeling of guilt and no self-accusation developed (though one would normally expect it) because the "bad" deed was to a high degree narcissistically gratifying, whereas guilt and self-reproaches develop when the gratification subsides. However, there are depressions which are not accompanied by any self-aggression and there are cases of angry self-hatred which do not show any manifest signs of depression and which are not the result of a defensive action but demonstrate rather a hostile nonidentification with or "rejection" of a given weakness of the self. Such persons hate or resent certain features in themselves in the same way as they hate or resent the same traits in another person. Finally, there is a decisive difference between the "ego killing itself" and the "ego letting itself die." Only in the first case aggression is involved. Giving up the struggle because one is tired and feels helpless is not identical with self-destruction.

(5) It is hardly necessary to discuss the conscious and unconscious secondary gains which many patients derive

from a depression. This may proceed on the external as well as internal level. By demonstrating their sufferings they try to obtain the "narcissistic supplies" which they need, or they may exploit the depression for the justification of the various aggressive impulses toward external objects, thus closing the vicious circle.

A Contribution to the Psychogenesis of Manic-Depressive States

MELANIE KLEIN

My earlier writings contain the account of a phase of sadism at its zenith, through which children pass during the first year of life.* In the very first months of the baby's existence it has sadistic impulses directed, not only against its mother's breast, but also against the inside of her body: scooping it out, devouring the contents, destroying it by every means which sadism can suggest. The development of the infant is governed by the mechanisms of introjection and projection. From the beginning the ego introjects objects "good" and "bad," for both of which the mother's breast is the prototype—for good objects when the child obtains it, for bad ones when it fails him. But it is because the baby projects its own aggression on to these objects that it feels them to be "bad" and not only in that they frustrate its desires: the child conceives of them as actually dangerous —persectuors who it fears will devour it, scoop out the

* *The Psycho-Analysis of Children,* chapters viii and ix.

182

inside of its body, cut it to pieces, poison it—in short, com-
passing its destruction by all the means which sadism can
devise. These images, which are a fantastically distorted
picture of the real objects upon which they are based, become installed not only in the outside world but, by the
process of incorporation, also within the ego. Hence, quite
little children pass through anxiety-situations (and react to
them with defence-mechanisms), the content of which is
comparable to that of the psychoses of adults.

One of the earliest methods of defence against the
dread of persecutors, whether conceived of as existing in
the external world or internalized, is that of scotomization,
the *denial of psychic reality*; this may result in a considerable restriction of the mechanisms of introjection and projection and in the denial of external reality, and forms the basis
of the most severe psychoses. Very soon, too, the ego tries
to defend itself against internalized persecutors by the
processes of expulsion and projection. At the same time,
since the dread of internalized objects is by no means extinguished with their projection, the ego marshals against
the persecutors inside the body the same forces as it employs against those in the outside world. These anxiety-
contents and defence-mechanisms form the basis of paranoia. In the infantile dread of magicians, witches, evil beasts,
etc., we detect something of this same anxiety, but here it
has already undergone projection and modification. One of
my conclusions, moreover, was that infantile psychotic
anxiety, in particular paranoid anxiety, is bound and modified by the obsessional mechanisms which make their appearance very early.

In the present paper I propose to deal with depressive
states in their relation to paranoia on the one hand and to
mania on the other. I have acquired the material upon which

my conclusions are based from the analysis of depressive states in cases of severe neurosis, border-line cases and in patients, both adults and children, who displayed mixed paranoiac and depressive trends.

I have studied manic states in various degrees and forms, including the slightly hypomanic states which occur in normal persons. The analysis of depressive and manic features in normal children and adults also proved very instructive.

According to Freud and Abraham, the fundamental process in melancholia is the loss of the loved object. The real loss of a real object, or some similar situation having the same significance, results in the object becoming installed within the ego. Owing, however, to an excess of cannibalistic impulses in the subject, this introjection miscarries and the consequence is illness.

Now, why is it that the process of introjection is so specific for melancholia? I believe that the main difference between incorporation in paranoia and in melancholia is connected with changes in the relation of the subject to the object, though it is also a question of a change in the constitution of the introjecting ego. According to Edward Glover, the ego, at first but loosely organized, consists of a considerable number of ego-nuclei. In his view, in the first place an oral ego-nucleus and later an anal ego-nucleus predominates over the others.[1] In this very early phase, in which oral sadism plays a prominent part and which in my view is the basis of schizophrenia,* the ego's power of iden-

---

[1] See references in chapter notes at back of book.

* I would refer the reader to my account of the phase in which the child makes onslaughts on the mother's body. This phase is initiated by the onset of oral sadism and in my view it is the basis of paranoia (cf. *The Psycho-Analysis of Children,* chapter viii).

tifying itself with its objects is as yet small, partly because it is itself still unco-ordinated and partly because the introjected objects are still mainly partial objects, which it equates wtih faeces.

In paranoia the characteristic defences are chiefly aimed at annihilating the "persecutors," while anxiety on the ego's account occupies a prominent place in the picture. As the ego becomes more fully organized, the internalized imagos will approximate more closely to reality and the ego will identify itself more fully with "good" objects. The dread of persecution, which was at first felt on the ego's account, now relates to the good object as well and from now on preservation of the good object is regarded as synonymous with the survival of the ego.

Hand in hand with this development goes a change of the highest importance; namely, from a partial object-relation to the relation to a complete object. Through this step the ego arrives at a new position, which forms the foundation of the situation called the loss of the loved object. Not until the object is loved *as a whole* can its loss be felt as a whole.

With this change in the relation to the object, new anxiety-contents make their appearance and a change takes place in the mechanisms of defence. The development of the libido also is decisively influenced. Paranoid anxiety lest the objects sadistically destroyed should themselves be a source of poison and danger inside the subject's body causes him, in spite of the vehemence of his oral-sadistic onslaughts, at the same time to be profoundly mistrustful of the objects while yet incorporating them.

This leads to a weakening of oral desires. One manifestation of this may be observed in the difficulties very

young children often have in taking food; these difficulties
I think have a paranoid root. As a child (or an adult) identifies himself more fully with a good object, the libidinal
urges increase; he develops a greedy love and desire to
devour this object and the mechanism of introjection is reinforced. Besides, he finds himself constantly impelled to
repeat the incorporation of a good object—*i.e.*, the repetition
of the act is designed to test the reality of his fears and
disprove them—partly because he dreads that he has for-
feited it by his cannibalism and partly because he fears internalized persecutors against whom he requires a good
object to help him. In this stage the ego is more than ever
driven both by love and by need to introject the object.

Another stimulus for an increase of introjection is the
phantasy that the loved object may be preserved in safety
inside oneself. In this case the dangers of the inside are
projected on to the external world.

If, however, consideration for the object increases, and
a better acknowledgement of psychic reality sets in, the
anxiety lest the object should be destroyed in the process
of introjecting it leads—as Abraham has described—to various disturbances of the function of introjection.

In my experience there is, furthermore, a deep anxiety
as to the dangers which await the object inside the ego. It
cannot be safely maintained there, as the inside is felt to
be a dangerous and poisonous place in which the loved
object would perish. Here we see one of the situations which
I described above as being fundamental for "the loss of the
loved object"; the situation, namely, when the ego becomes
fully identified with its good internalized objects, and at the
same time becomes aware of its own incapacity to protect
and preserve them against the internalized persecuting ob-

jects and the id. This anxiety is psychologically justified.

For the ego, when it becomes fully identified with the object, does not abandon its earlier defence-mechanisms. According to Abraham's hypothesis, the annihilation and expulsion of the object—processes characteristic of the earlier anal level—initiate the depressive mechanism. If this be so, it confirms my concept of the genetic connection between paranoia and melancholia. In my opinion, the paranoiac mechanism of destroying the objects (whether inside the body or in the outside world) by every means derived from oral, urethral and anal sadism persists, but still in a lesser degree and with a certain modification due to the change in the subject's relation to his objects. As I have said, the dread lest the *good* object should be expelled along with the *bad* causes the mechanisms of expulsion and projection to lose value. We know that, at this stage, the ego makes a greater use of introjection of the *good* object as a mechanism of defence. This is associated with another important mechanism: that of making reparation to the object. In certain of my earlier works* I discussed in detail the concept of restoration and showed that it is far more than a mere reaction-formation. The ego feels impelled (and I can now add, impelled by its identification with the good object) to make restitution for all the sadistic attacks that it has launched on that object. When a well-marked cleavage between good and bad objects has been attained, the subject attempts to restore the former, making good in the restoration every detail of his sadistic attacks. But the ego cannot as yet believe enough in the benevolence of the object and in its own capacity to make restitution. On the

---

* "Infantile Anxiety-Situations Reflected in a Work of Art and in the Creative Impulse," p. 227; also *The Psycho-Analysis of Children*.

other hand, through its identification with a good object and through the other mental advances which this implies, the ego finds itself forced to a fuller recognition of psychic reality, and this exposes it to fierce conflicts. Some of its objects (an indefinite number) are persectuors to it, ready to devour it and do violence to it. In all sorts of ways they endanger both the ego and the good object. Every injury inflicted in phantasy by the child upon its parents (primarily from hate and secondarily in self-defence), every act of violence committed by one object upon another (in particular the destructive, sadistic coitus of the parents, which the child regards as yet another result of its own sadistic wishes) —all this is played out, both in the outside world and, since the ego is constantly absorbing into itself the whole external world, within the ego as well. Now, however, all these processes are viewed as a perpetual source of danger both to the good object and to the ego.

It is true that, now that good and bad objects are more clearly differentiated, the subject's hate is directed rather against the latter, while his love and his attempts at reparation are more focused on the former; but the excess of his sadism and anxiety acts as a check to this advance in his mental development. Every internal or external stimulus (*e.g.* every real frustration) is fraught with the utmost danger: not only bad objects but also the good ones are thus menaced by the id, for every access of hate or anxiety may temporarily abolish the differentiation and thus result in a "loss of the loved object." And it is not only the vehemence of the subject's uncontrollable hatred but that of his love too which imperils the object. For at this stage of his development loving an object and devouring it are very closely connected. A little child which believes, when its mother disappears, that it has eaten her up and destroyed her (whether from motives of love or of hate) is tormented by anxiety both for her and for the good mother which it has absorbed into itself.

It now becomes plain why, at this phase of development, the ego feels itself constantly menaced in its possession of internalized good objects. It is full of anxiety lest such objects should die. Both in children and adults suffering from depression, I have discovered the dread of harbouring dying or dead objects (especially the parents) inside one and an identification of the ego with objects in this condition.

From the very beginning of psychic development there is a constant correlation of real objects with those installed within the ego. It is for this reason that the anxiety which I have just described manifests itself in a child's exaggerated fixation to its mother or whoever looks after it.* The absence of the mother arouses in the child anxiety lest it should be handed over to bad objects, external and internalized, either because of her *death* or because of her return in the guise of a "*bad*" mother.

Both cases mean to the child the loss of the loved mother, and I would particularly draw attention to the fact that dread of the loss of the "good," internalized object becomes a perpetual source of anxiety lest the real mother should die. On the other hand, every experience which suggests the loss of the real loved object stimulates the dread of losing the internalized one too.

I have already stated that my experience has led me

* For many years now I have supported the view that the source of a child's fixation to its mother is not simply its dependence on her, but also its anxiety and sense of guilt, and that these feelings are connected with its early aggression against her.

to conclude that the loss of the loved object takes place during that phase of development in which the ego makes the transition from partial to total incorporation of the object. Having now described the situation of the ego in that phase, I can express myself with greater precision on this point. The processes which subsequently become clear as the "loss of the loved object" are determined by the subject's sense of failure (during weaning and in the periods which precede and follow it) to secure his *good, internalized* object, *i.e.* to possess himself of it. One reason for his failure is that he has been unable to overcome his paranoid dread of internalized persecutors.

At this point we are confronted with a question of importance for our whole theory. My own observations and those of a number of my English colleagues have led us to conclude that the direct influence of the early processes of introjection upon both normal and pathological development is very much more momentous, and in some ways differs from what has hitherto commonly been accepted in psycho-analytical circles.

According to our views, even the earliest incorporated objects form the basis of the super-ego and enter into its structure. The question is by no means a merely theoretical one. As we study the relations of the early infantile ego to its internalized objects and to the id, and come to understand the gradual changes these relations undergo, we obtain a deeper insight into the specific anxiety-situations through which the ego passes and the specific defence-mechanisms which it develops as it becomes more highly organized. Viewed from this standpoint in our experience we find that we arrive at a more complete understanding of the earliest phases of psychic development, of the structure of the super-ego and of the genesis of psychotic diseases. For where we deal with aetiology it seems essential to regard the libido-disposition not merely as such, but also to consider it in connection with the subject's earliest relations to his internalized and external objects, a consideration which implies an understanding of the defence-mechanisms developed by the ego gradually in dealing with its varying anxiety-situations.

If we accept this view of the formation of the super-ego, its relentless severity in the case of the melancholic becomes more intelligible. The persecutions and demands of bad internalized objects; the attacks of such objects upon one another (especially that represented by the sadistic coitus of the parents); the urgent necessity to fulfil the very strict demands of the "good objects" and to protect and placate them within the ego, with the resultant hatred of the id; the constant uncertainty as to the "goodness" of a good object, which causes it so readily to become transformed into a bad one—all these factors combine to produce in the ego a sense of being a prey to contradictory and impossible claims from within, a condition which is felt as a bad conscience. That is to say: the earliest utterances of conscience are associated with persecution by bad objects. The very word "gnawing of conscience" (*Gewissensbisse*) testifies to the relentless "persecution" by conscience and to the fact that it is originally conceived of as devouring its victim.

Among the various internal demands which go to make up the severity of the super-ego in the melancholic, I have mentioned his urgent need to comply with the very strict demands of the "good" objects. It is this part of the picture only—namely, the cruelty of the "good," *i.e.* loved, objects within—which has been recognized by general analytic opinion; it became clear in the relentless severity of the super-ego in the melancholic. But in my view it is only by looking at the whole relation of the ego to its phantastically bad objects as well as to its good objects, only by looking at the whole picture of the internal situation which I have tried to outline in this paper, that we can understand the slavery to which the ego submits when complying with the extremely cruel demands and admonitions of its loved object which has become installed within the ego. As I have mentioned before, the ego endeavours to keep the good apart from the bad, and the real from the phantastic objects. The result is a conception of extremely bad and *extremely perfect* objects, that is to say, its loved objects are in many ways intensely moral and exacting. At the same time, as the infant cannot fully keep his good and bad objects apart in his mind,* some of the cruelty of the bad objects and of the id becomes attached to the good objects and this then again increases the severity of their demands.† These strict demands serve the purpose of supporting the ego in its fight against its uncontrollable hatred and its bad attacking objects, with whom the ego is partly identified.‡ The stronger the anxiety is of losing the loved objects, the more the ego strives to save them, and the harder the task of

* I have explained that, gradually, by unifying and then splitting up the good and bad, the phantastic and the real, the external and the internal objects, the ego makes its way towards a more realistic conception both of the external and the internal objects and thus obtains a satisfactory relation to both. (Cf. *Psycho-Analysis of Children.*)

† In *The Ego and the Id,* Freud has shown that in melancholia the destructive component has become concentrated in the super-ego and is directed against the ego.

‡ It is well known that some children display an urgent need to be kept under strict discipline and thus to be stopped by an external agency from doing wrong.

restoration becomes, the stricter will grow the demands which are associated with the super-ego.

I have tried to show that the difficulties which the ego experiences when it passes on to the incorporation of whole objects proceed from its as yet imperfect capacity for mastering, by means of its new defence-mechanisms, the fresh anxiety-contents arising out of this advance in its development.

I am aware how difficult it is to draw a sharp line between the anxiety-contents and feelings of the paranoiac and those of the depressive since they are so closely linked up with each other. But they can be distinguished one from the other if, as a criterion of differentiation, one considers whether the persecution-anxiety is mainly related to the preservation of the ego—in which case it is paranoiac—or to the preservation of the good internalized objects with whom the ego is identified as a whole. In the latter case—which is the case of the depressive—the anxiety and feelings of suffering are of a much more complex nature. The anxiety lest the good objects and with them the ego should be destroyed, or that they are in a state of disintegration, is interwoven with continuous and desperate efforts to save the good objects both internalized and external.

It seems to me that only when the ego has introjected the object as a whole, and has established a better relationship to the external world and to real people, is it able fully to realize the disaster created through its sadism and especially through its cannibalism, and to feel distressed about it. This distress is related not only to the past but to the present as well, since at this early stage of development sadism is at its height. It requires a fuller identification with the loved object, and a fuller recognition of its value, for the ego to become aware of the state of disintegration to which it has reduced and is continuing to reduce its loved object. The ego then finds itself confronted with the psychic reality that its loved objects are in a state of dissolution—in bits—and the despair, remorse and anxiety deriving from this recognition are at the bottom of numerous anxiety-situations. To quote only a few of them: there is anxiety how to put the bits together in the right way and at the right time; how to pick out the good bits and do away with the bad ones; how to bring the object to life when it has been put together; and there is the anxiety of being inter-fered with in this task by bad objects and by one's own hatred, etc.

Anxiety-situations of this kind I have found to be at the bottom not only of depression, but of all inhibitions of work. The attempts to save the loved object, to repair and restore it, attempts which in the state of depression are coupled with despair, since the ego doubts its capacity to achieve this restoration, are determining factors for all sublimations and the whole of the ego-development. In this connection I shall only mention the specific importance for sublimation of the bits to which the loved object has been reduced and the effort to put them together. It is a "perfect" object which is in pieces; thus the effort to undo the state of disintegration to which it has been reduced presupposes the necessity to make it beautiful and "perfect." The idea of perfection is, moreover, so compelling because it disproves the idea of dis-integration. In some patients who had turned away from their mother in dislike or hate, or used other mechanisms to get away from her, I have found that there existed in their minds nevertheless a beautiful picture of the mother, but one which was felt to be a *picture* of her only, not her real self. The real object was felt to be unattractive—really an injured, incurable and therefore dreaded person. The beautiful picture had been dissociated from the real object but had never been given up, and played a great part in the specific ways of their sublimations.

It appears that the desire for perfection is rooted in the depressive anxiety of disintegration, which is thus of great importance in all sublimations.

As I have pointed out before, the ego comes to a realization of its love for a good object, a whole object and in addition a real object, together with an overwhelming feeling of guilt towards it. Full identification with the object based on the libidinal attachment, first to the breast, then to the whole person, goes hand in hand with anxiety for it (of its disintegration), with guilt and remorse, with a sense of responsibility for preserving it intact against persecutors and the id, and with sadness relating to expectations of the impending loss of it. These emotions, whether conscious or unconscious, are in my view among the essential and fundamental elements of the feelings we call love.

In this connection I may say we are familiar with the self-reproaches of the depressive which represent reproaches against the introjected object. But the ego's hate of the id, which is paramount in this phase, accounts even more for its feelings of unworthiness and despair than do its reproaches against the object. I have often found that these reproaches and the hatred against bad objects are secondarily increased as a defense against the hatred of the id, which is even more unbearable. In the last analysis it is the ego's unconscious knowledge that the hate is indeed also there, as well as the love, and that it may at any time get the upper hand (the ego's anxiety of being carried away by the id and so destroying the loved object), which brings about the sorrow, feelings of guilt and the despair which underlie grief. This anxiety is also responsible for the doubt in the goodness of the loved object. As Freud has pointed out, doubt is in reality a doubt of one's own love and "a man who doubts his own love may, or rather *must*, doubt every lesser thing."[2]

The paranoiac, I should say, has also introjected a whole and real object, but has not been able to achieve a full identification with it, or, if he has got as far as this, he has not been able to maintain it. To mention a few of the reasons which are responsible for this failure: the persecution-anxiety is too great; suspicions and anxieties of a phantastic nature stand in the way of a full and stable introjection of a good object and a real one. In so far as it has been introjected, there is little capacity to maintain it as a good object, since doubts and suspicions of all kinds will soon turn the loved object again into a persecutor. Thus his relationship to whole objects and to the real world is still influenced by his early relation to internalized part-objects and faeces as persecutors and may again give way to the latter.

It seems to me characteristic of the paranoiac that, though, on account of his persecution-anxiety and his suspicions, he develops a very strong and acute power of observation of the external world and of real objects, this observation and his sense of reality are nevertheless distorted, since his persecution-anxiety makes him look at people mainly from the point of view of whether they are persecutors or not. Where the persecution-anxiety for the ego is in the ascendant, a full and stable identification with another object, in the sense of looking at it and understanding it as it really is, and a full capacity for love, are not possible.

Another important reason why the paranoiac cannot maintain his whole-object relation is that while the persecution-anxieties and the anxiety for himself are still so strongly in operation he cannot endure the additional burden of anxieties for a loved object, and, besides, the feelings of guilt and remorse which accompany this depressive position. Moreover, in this position he can make far less use of projection, for fear of expelling his good objects and so losing them, and, on the other hand, for fear of injuring good external objects by expelling what is bad from within himself.

Thus we see that the sufferings connected with the depressive position thrust him back to the paranoiac position. Nevertheless, though he has retreated from it, the depressive position has been reached and therefore the liability to depression is always there. This accounts, in my opinion, for the fact that we frequently meet depression along with severe paranoia as well as in milder cases.

If we compare the feelings of the paranoiac with those of the depressive in regard to disintegration, one can see that characteristically the depressive is filled with sorrow and anxiety for the object, which he would strive to unite again into a whole, while to the paranoiac the disintegrated object is mainly a mulititude of persecutors, since each piece is growing again into a persecutor.[3] This conception of the dangerous fragments to which the object is reduced seems to me to be in keeping with the introjection of part-objects which are equated with faeces (Abraham), and with the anxiety of a multitude of internal persecutors to which, in my view, the introjection of many part-objects and the multitude of dangerous faeces gives rise.

I have already considered the distinctions between the paranoiac and the depressive from the point of view of their different relations to loved objects. Let us take inhibitions and anxieties about food in this connection. The anxiety of absorbing dangerous substances destructive to one's inside will thus be paranoiac, while the anxiety of destroying the external good objects by biting and chewing, or of endangering the internal good object by introducing bad substances from outside into it, well be depressive. Again, the anxiety of leading an external good object into danger within oneself by incorporating it is a depressive one. On the other hand, in cases with strong paranoiac features I have met phantasies of luring an external object into one's inside, which was regarded as a cave full of dangerous monsters, etc. Here we can see the paranoiac reasons for an intensification of the introjection-mechanism, while the depressive employs this mechanism so characteristically, as we know, for the purpose of incorporating a *good* object.

Considering now hypochondriacal symtoms in this comparative way, the pains and other manifestations which in phantasy result from the attacks of persecuting objects within against the ego are typically paranoid.[*] The symptoms which derive, on the other hand, from the attacks of bad internal objects and the id against good ones, *i.e.*, and internal warfare in which *the ego is identified with the sufferings of the good objects,* are typically depressive.

For instance, patient X, who had been told as a child that he had tapeworms (which he himself never saw) connected the tapeworms inside him with his greediness. In his analysis he had phantasies that a tapeworm was eating its

[*] Dr. Clifford Scott mentioned in his course of lectures on Psychoses, at the Institute of Psycho-Analysis, in the autumn of 1934, that in his experience, in schizophrenia clinically the hypochondriacal symptoms are more manifold and bizarre and are linked to persecutions and part-object functions. This may be seen even after a short examination. In depressive reactions clinically the hypochondriacal symptoms are less varied and more related in their expression to ego-functions.

way through his body and a strong anxiety of cancer came to the fore. The patient, who suffered from hypochondriacal and paranoid anxieties, was very suspicious of me, and, among other things, suspected me of being allied with people who were hostile towards him. At this time he dreamt that a detective was arresting a hostile and persecuting person and putting this person in prison. But then the detective proved unreliable and became the accomplice of the enemy. The detective stood for myself and the whole anxiety was internalized and was also connected with the tapeworm-phantasy. The prison in which the enemy was kept was his own inside—actually the special part of his inside where the persecutor was to be confined. It became clear that the dangerous tapeworm (one of his associations was that the tapeworm is bisexual) represented the two parents in a hostile alliance (actually in intercourse) against him.

At the time when the tapeworm-phantasies were being analysed the patient developed diarrhoea which—as X wrongly thought—was mixed with blood. This frightened him very much; he felt it as a confirmation of dangerous processes going on inside him. This feeling was founded on phantasies in which he attacked his bad united parents in his inside with poisonous excreta. The diarrhoea meant to him poisonous excreta, as well as the bad penis of his father. The blood which he thought was in his faeces represented me (this was shown by associations in which I was connected with blood). Thus the diarrhoea was felt to represent dangerous weapons with which he was fighting his bad internalized parents, as well as his poisoned and broken-up parents themselves—the tapeworm. In his early childhood he had in phantasy attacked his real parents with poisonous excreta and actually disturbed them in intercourse by defaecating. Diarrhoea had always been something very frightening to him. Along with these attacks on his real parents this whole warfare became internalized and threatened his ego with destruction. I may mention that this patient remembered during his analysis that at about ten years of age he had definitely felt that he had a little man inside his stomach who controlled him and gave him orders, which he, the patient, had to execute, although they were always perverse and wrong (he had had similar feelings about his real father's requests).

When the analysis progressed and distrust in me had diminished, the patient became very much concerned about me. X had always worried about his mother's health; but he had not been able to develop real love towards her, though he did his best to please her. Now, together with the concern for me, strong feelings of love and gratitude came to the fore, together with feelings of unworthiness, sorrow and depression. The patient had never felt really happy, his depression had been spread out, one might say, over his whole life, but he had not suffered from actual depressed states. In his analysis he went through phases of deep depression with all the symptoms characteristic of this state of mind. At the same time the feelings and phantasies connected with his hypochondriacal pains changed. For instance, the patient felt anxiety that the cancer would make its way through the lining of his stomach; but now it appeared that, while he feared for his stomach, he really wanted to protect "me" inside him—actually the internalized mother—who he felt was being attacked by the father's penis and by his own id (the cancer). Another time the patient had phantasies (connected with physical discomfort) about an internal haemorrhage from which he would die. It became clear that I was identified with the haemorrhage, the good blood representing me. We must remember that, when the paranoid anxieties dominated and I was mainly felt as a persecutor, I had been identified with the *bad* blood which was mixed with the diarrhoea (with the bad father). Now the precious *good* blood represented me—losing it meant my death, which would imply his death. It became clear now that the cancer which he made responsible for the death of his loved object, as well as for his own, and which stood for the bad father's penis, was even more felt to be his own sadism, especially his greed. That is why he felt so unworthy and so much in despair.

While the paranoid anxieties predominated and the anxiety of his bad united objects prevailed, X felt only hypochondriacal anxieties for his own body. When depression and sorrow had set in, the love and the concern for the good object came to the fore and the anxiety-contents as well as the whole feelings and defences altered. In this case, as well as in others, I have found that *paranoid fears and suspicions were reinforced as a defence against the depressive position* which was overlaid by them. I shall now quote another case, Y, with strong paranoiac and depressive features (paranoia predominating) and with hypochondria. His complaints about manifold physical troubles, which occupied a large part of the hours, alternated with strong feelings of suspicion about people in his environment and often became directly related to them, since he made them responsible for his physical troubles in one way or another. When, after hard analytic work, distrust and suspicion diminished, his relation to me improved more and more. It became clear that, buried under the continuous paranoid accusations, complaints and criticisms of others, there existed a very profound love for his mother and concern for his parents as well as for other people. At the same time sorrow and severe depression came more and more to the fore. During this phase the hypochondriacal complaints altered, both in the way they were presented to me and in the content which underlay them. For instance, the patient complained about different physical troubles and then went on to say what medicines he had taken—enumerating what he had done for his chest, his throat, his nose, his ears, his intestines, etc. It sounded rather as if he were nursing these parts of his body and his organs. He went on to speak about his concern for some young people under his care (he is a teacher) and then about the worry he was feeling for some members of his family. It became quite clear that the different organs he was trying to cure were identified with his internalized brothers and sisters, about whom he felt guilty and whom he had to be perpetually keeping alive. It was his *over-anxiousness* to put them right, because he had damaged them in phantasy, and his *excessive* sorrow and despair about it, which had led to such an increase of the paranoid anxieties and defences that love and concern for people and identification with them became buried under hate. In this case, too, when depression came to the fore in full force and the paranoid anxieties diminished, the hypochondriacal anxieties became related to the internalized loved objects and thus to the ego, while before they had been experienced in reference to the ego only.

After having attempted to differentiate between the anxiety-contents, feelings and defences at work in paranoia and those in the depressive states, I must again make clear that in my view the depressive state is based on the paranoid state and genetically derived from it. I consider the depressive state as being the result of a mixture of paranoid anxiety and of those anxiety-contents, distressed feelings and defences which are connected with the impending loss of the whole loved object. It seems to me that to introduce a term for those specific anxieties and defences might further the understanding of the structure and nature of paranoia as well as of the manic-depressive states.*

In my view, wherever a state of depression exists, be it in the normal, the neurotic, in manic-depressives or in mixed cases, there is always in it this specific grouping of anxieties, distressed feelings and different varieties of these defences, which I have here described and called the depressive position.

If this point of view proves correct, we should be able to understand those very frequent cases where we are presented with a picture of mixed paranoiac and depressive trends, since we could then isolate the various elements of which it is composed.

The considerations that I have brought forward in this paper about depressive states may lead us, in my opinion,

---

* This brings me to another question of terminology. In my former work I have described the psychotic anxieties and mechanisms of the child in terms of phases of development. The genetic connection between them, it is true, is given full justice by this description, and so is the fluctuation which goes on between them under the pressure of anxiety until more stability is reached; but since in normal development the psychotic anxieties and mechanisms never solely predominate (a fact which, of course, I have emphasized) the term psychotic phases is not really satisfactory. I am now using the term "position" in relation to the child's early developmental psychotic anxieties and defences. It seems to me easier to associate with this term, than with the words "mechanisms" or "phases," the differences between the developmental psychotic anxieties of the child and the psychoses of the adult: *e.g.*, the quick change-over that occurs from a persecution-anxiety or depressed feeling to a normal attitude—a change-over that is so characteristic for the child.

to a better understanding of the still rather enigmatic reaction of suicide. According to the findings of Abraham and James Glover, a suicide is directed against the introjected object. But, while in committing suicide the ego intends to murder its bad objects, in my view at the same time it also always aims at saving its loved objects, internal or external. To put it shortly: in some cases the phantasies underlying suicide aim at preserving the internalized good objects and that part of the ego which is identified with good objects, and also at destroying the other part of the ego which is identified with the bad objects and the id. Thus the ego is enabled to become united with its loved objects.

In other cases, suicide seems to be determined by the same type of phantasies, but here they relate to the external world and real objects, partly as substitutes for the internalized ones. As already stated, the subject hates not only his "bad" objects, but his id as well and that vehemently. In committing suicide, his purpose may be to make a clean breach in his relation to the outside world because he desires to rid some real object—or the "good" object which that whole world represents and which the ego is identified with —of himself, or of that part of his ego which is identified with his bad objects and his id.* At bottom we perceive in such a step his reaction to his own sadistic attacks on his mother's body, which to a little child is the first representative of the outside world. Hatred and revenge against the real (good) objects also always play an important part in such a step, but it is precisely the uncontrollable dangerous hatred, which is perpetually welling up in him, from which the melancholic by his suicide is in part struggling to preserve his real objects.

* These reasons are largely responsible for that state of mind in the melancholic in which he breaks off all relations with the external world.

Freud has stated that mania has for its basis the same contents as melancholia and is, in fact, a way of escape from that state. I would suggest that in mania the ego seeks refuge not only from melancholia but also from a paranoiac condition which it is unable to master. Its torturing and perilous dependence on its loved objects drives the ego to find freedom. But its identification with these objects is too profound to be renounced. On the other hand, the ego is pursued by its dread of bad objects and of the id and, in its effort to escape from all these miseries, it has recourse to many different mechanisms, some of which, since they belong to different phases of development, are mutually incompatible.

The *sense of omnipotence,* in my opinion, is what first and foremost characterizes mania and, further (as Helene Deutsch has stated[4]) mania is based on the mechanism of *denial.* I differ, however, from Helene Deutsch in the following point. She holds that this "denial" is connected with the phallic phase and the castration complex (in girls it is a denial of the lack of the penis); while my observations have led me to conclude that this mechanism of denial originates in that very early phase in which the undeveloped ego endeavours to defend itself from the most overpowering and profound anxiety of all, namely, its dread of internalized persecutors and of the id. That is to say, that which is *first of all denied is psychic reality* and the ego may then go on to deny a great deal of external reality.

We know that scotomization may lead to the subject's becoming entirely cut off from reality, and to his complete inactivity. In mania, however, denial is associated with an overactivity, although this excess of activity, as Helene Deutsch points out, often bears no relation to any actual results achieved. I have explained that in this state the source of the conflict is that the ego is unwilling and unable to renounce its good internal objects and yet endeavours to escape from the perils of dependence on them as well as from its bad objects. Its attempt to detach itself from an object without at the same time completely renouncing it seems to be conditioned by an increase in the ego's own strength. It succeeds in this compromise by *denying the importance* of its good objects and also of the dangers with which it is menaced from its bad objects and the id. At the same time, however, it endeavours ceaselessly to *master and control* all its objects, and the evidence of this effort is its hyperactivity.

What to my view is quite specific for mania is the *utilization of the sense of omnipotence* for the purpose of *controlling and mastering* objects. This is necessary for two reasons: (*a*) in order to deny the dread of them which is being experienced, and (*b*) so that the mechanism (acquired in the previous—the depressive—position) of making reparation to the object may be carried through.* By mastering his objects the manic person imagines he will prevent them not only from injuring himself but from being a danger to one another. His mastery is to enable him particularly to prevent dangerous coitus between the parents he has internalized and their death within him.† The manic defence assumes so many forms that it is, of course, not easy to postulate a general mechanism. But I believe that we really have such a mechanism (though its varieties are infinite) in this mastery of the internalized parents, while

---

* This "reparation," in accordance with the phantastic character of the whole position, is nearly always of a quite unpractical and unrealizable nature.

† Bertram Lewin reported about an acute manic patient who identified herself with both parents in intercourse (*Psycho-Analytic Quarterly*, 1933).

at the same time the existence of this internal world is being depreciated and denied. Both in children and in adults I have found that, where obsessional neurosis was the most powerful factor in the case, such mastery betokened a forcible separation of two (or more) objects; whereas, where mania was in the ascendant, the patient had recourse to methods more violent. That is to say, the objects were killed but, since the subject was omnipotent, he supposed he could also immediately call them to life again. One of my patients spoke of this process as "keeping them in suspended animation." The killing corresponds to the defence-mechanism (retained from the earliest phase) of destruction of the object; the resuscitation corresponds to the reparation made to the object. In this position the ego effects a similar compromise in its relation to real objects. The hunger for objects, so characteristic of mania, indicates that the ego has retained one defence-mechanism of the depressive position: the introjection of good objects. The manic subject *denies* the different forms of anxiety associated with this introjection (anxiety, that is to say, lest either he should introject bad objects or else destroy his good objects by the process of introjection); his denial relates not merely to the impulses of the id but to his own concern for the object's safety. Thus we may suppose that the process by which ego and ego-ideal come to coincide (as Freud has shown that they do in mania) is as follows. The ego incorporates the object in a cannibalistic way (the "feast," as Freud calls it in his account of mania) but denies that it feels any concern for it. "Surely," argues the ego, "it is not a matter of such great importance if this particular object is destroyed. There are so many others to be incorporated." This *disparagement of the object's importance and the contempt for it* is, I think, a specific characteristic of mania and enables the ego to effect that partial detachment which we observe side by side with its hunger for objects. Such detachment, which the ego cannot achieve in the depressive position, represents an advance, a fortifying of the ego in relation to its objects. But this advance is counteracted by those earlier mechanisms described which the ego at the same time employs in mania.

Before I go on to make a few suggestions about the part which the paranoid, depressive and manic positions play in normal development, I shall speak about two dreams of a patient which illustrate some of the points I have put forward in connection with the psychotic positions. Various symptoms of which I shall here only mention severe states of depression and paranoid and hypochondriacal anxieties, had induced the patient C to come for analysis. At the time he dreamt these dreams his analysis was well advanced. He dreamt that he was travelling with his parents in a railway-carriage, probably without a roof, since they were in the open air. The patient felt that he was "managing the whole thing," taking care of the parents, who were much older and more in need of his care than in reality. The parents were lying in bed, not side by side, as they usually did, but with the ends of the beds joined together. The patient found it difficult to keep them warm. Then the patient urinated, while his parents were watching him, into a basin in the middle of which there was a cylindrical object. The urination seemed complicated, since he had to take special care not to urinate into the cylindrical part. He felt this would not have mattered had he been able to aim exactly into the cylinder and not splash anything about. When he had finished urinating he noticed that the basin was overflowing and felt this as unsatisfactory. While urinating he noticed that his penis was very large and he had an uncomfortable feeling about this—as if his father ought not to see it, since he would feel beaten by him and he did not want to humiliate his father. At the same time he felt that by urinating he was sparing his father the trouble of getting out of bed and urinating himself. Here the patient stopped, and then said that he really felt as if his parents were a part of himself. In the dream the basin with the cylinder was supposed to be a Chinese vase, but it was not right, because the stem was not underneath the basin, as it should have been, it was "in the wrong place," since it was above the basin—really inside it. The patient then associated the basin to a glass bowl, as used for gas-burners in his grandmother's house, and the cylindrical part reminded him of a gas-mantle. He then thought of a dark passage, at the end of which there was a low-burning gas-light, and said that this picture evoked in him sad feelings. It made him think of poor and dilapidated houses, where there seemed to be nothing alive but this low-burning gas-light. It is true, one had only to pull the string and then the light would burn fully. This reminded him that he had always been frightened of gas and that the flames of a gas-ring made him feel that they were jumping out at him, biting him, as if they were a lion's head. Another thing which frightened him about gas was the "pop" noise it made, when it was put out. After my interpretation that the cylindrical part in the basin and the gas-mantle were the same thing and that he was afraid to urinate into it because he did not want for some reason to put the flame out, he replied that of course one cannot extinguish a gas-flame in this way, as then poison remains behind—it is not like a candle which one can simply blow out.

The night after this the patient had the following

dream: he heard the frizzling sound of something which was frying in an oven. He could not see what it was, but he thought of something brown, probably a kidney which was frying in a pan. The noise he heard was like the squeaking or crying of a tiny voice and his feeling was that a live creature was being fried. His mother was there and he tried to draw her attention to this, and to make her understand that to fry something alive was much the worst thing to do, worse than boiling or cooking it. It was more torturing since the hot fat prevented it from burning altogether and kept it alive while skinning it. He could not make his mother understand this and she did not seem to mind. This worried him, but in a way it reassured him, as he thought it could not be so bad after all if she did not mind. The oven, which he did not open in the dream—he never saw the kidney and the pan—reminded him of a refrigerator. In a friend's flat he had repeatedly mixed up the refrigerator door with the oven door. He wonders whether heat and cold are, in a way, the same thing for him. The torturing hot fat in the pan reminds him of a book about tortures which he had read as a child; he was especially excited by beheadings and by tortures with hot oil. Beheading reminded him of King Charles. He had been very excited over the story of his execution and later on developed a sort of devotion towards him. As regards tortures with hot oil, he used to think a great deal about them, imagining himself in such a situation (especially his legs being burnt), and trying to find out how, if it had to be done, it could be done so as to cause the least possible pain.

On the day the patient told me this second dream, he had first remarked on the way I struck my match for lighting a cigarette. He said it was obvious that I did not strike the match in the right way as a bit of the top had flown towards him. He meant I did not strike it at the right angle, and then went on to say, "like his father, who served the balls the wrong way at tennis." He wondered how often it had happened before in his analysis that the top of the match had flown towards him. (He had remarked once or twice before that I must have silly matches, but now the criticism applied to my way of striking them.) He did not feel inclined to talk, complaining that he had developed a heavy cold in the last two days; his head felt very heavy and his ears were blocked up, the mucus was thicker than it had been at other times when he had a cold. Then he told me the dream which I have already given, and in the course of the associations once again mentioned the cold and that it made him so disinclined to do anything.

Through the analysis of these dreams a new light was thrown on some fundamental points in the patient's development. These had already come out and been worked through before in his analysis, but now they appeared in new connections and then became fully clear and convincing to him. I shall now single out only the points bearing on the conclusions arrived at in this paper; I may mention that I have no space to quote all the important associations given.

The urination in the dream led on to the early aggressive phantasies of the patient towards his parents, especially directed against their sexual intercourse. He had phantasied biting them and eating them up, and, among other attacks, urinating on and into his father's penis, in order to skin and burn it and to make his father set his mother's inside on fire in their intercourse (the torturing with hot oil). These phantasies extended to babies inside his mother's body, which were to be killed (burnt). The kidney burnt

alive stood both for his father's penis—equated to faeces—
and for the babies inside his mother's body (the stove which
he did not open). Castration of the father is expressed by
the associations about beheading. Appropriation of the
father's penis was shown by the feeling that his penis was
so large and that he urinated both for himself and for his
father (phantasies of having his father's penis inside his
own or joined on to his own had come out a great deal in
his analysis). The patient's urinating into the bowl meant
also his sexual intercourse with his mother (whereby the
bowl and the mother in the dream represented both her
as a real and as an internalized figure). The impotent and
castrated father was made to look on at the patient's intercourse with his mother—the reverse of the situation the
patient had gone through in phantasy in his childhood. The
wish to humiliate his father is expressed by his feeling that
he ought not to do so. These (and other) sadistic phantasies
had given rise to different anxiety-contents: the mother
could not be made to understand that she was endangered
by the burning and biting penis inside her (the burning and
biting lion's head, the gas-ring which he had lit), and that
her babies were in danger of being burnt, at the same time
being a danger to herself (the kidney in the oven). The
patient's feeling that the cylindrical stem was "in the wrong
place" (inside the bowl instead of outside) expressed not
only his early hate and jealousy that his mother took his
father's penis into herself, but also his anxiety about this
dangerous happening. The phantasy of keeping the kidney
and the penis alive while they were being tortured expressed
both the destructive tendencies against the father and the
babies, and, to a certain degree the wish to preserve them.
The special position of the beds—different from the one in
the actual bedroom—in which the parents were lying,

showed not only the primary aggressive and jealous drive to separate them in their intercourse, but also the anxiety lest they should be injured or killed by intercourse which in his phantasies the son had arranged to be so dangerous. The death-wishes against the parents had led to an overwhelming anxiety about their death. This is shown by associations and feelings about the low-burning gas-light, the advanced age of the parents in the dream (older than in reality), their helplessness and the necessity for the patient to keep them warm.

One of the defences against his feelings of guilt and his responsibility for the disaster he had arranged was brought out by the association of the patient that I am striking the matches, and that his father serves tennis balls, in the wrong way. Thus he makes the parents responsible for their own wrong and dangerous intercourse, but the fear of retaliation based on projection (my burning him) is expressed by his remark that he wondered how often during his analysis tops of my matches had flown towards him, and all the other anxiety-contents related to attacks against him (the lion's head, the burning oil).

The fact that he had internalized (introjected) his parents is shown in the following: (1) the railway-carriage, in which he was travelling with his parents, continuously taking care of them, "managing the whole thing," represented his own body; (2) the carriage was open, in contrast to his feeling, representing their internalization, that he could not free himself from his internalized objects, but its being open was a denial of this; (3) that he had to do everything for his parents, even to urinate for his father; (4) the definite expression of a feeling that they were a part of himself.

But through the internalization of his parents all the

anxiety-situations which I have mentioned before in regard to the real parents became internalized and thus multiplied, intensified and, partly, altered in character. His mother containing the burning penis and the dying children (the oven with frying pan) is inside him. Furthermore there are his parents having dangerous intercourse inside him and the necessity to keep them separated. This necessity became the source of many anxiety-situations and was found in his analysis to be at the bottom of his obsessional symptoms. At any time the parents may have dangerous intercourse, burn and eat each other and, since his ego has become the place where all these danger-situations are acted out, destroy him as well. Thus he has at the same time to bear great anxiety both for them and for himself. He is full of sorrow about the impending death of the internalized parents, but at the same time he dare not bring them back to full life (he dare not pull the string of the gas-burner), since intercourse would be implied in their coming fully to life and this would then result in their death and his.

Then there are the dangers threatening from the id. If jealousy and hate stirred by some real frustration are welling up in him, he will again in his phantasy attack the internalized father with his burning excreta, disturbing the parents' intercourse, which gives rise to renewed anxiety. Either external or internal stimuli may increase his paranoid anxieties of internalized persecutors. If he then kills his father inside him altogether, the dead father becomes a persecutor of a special kind. We see this from the patient's remark (and his subsequent associations) that if the gas is extinguished by liquid, poison remains behind. Here the paranoid position comes to the fore and the dead object within becomes equated with faeces and flatus.* However, the paranoid position, which had been very strong in the patient at the beginning of his analysis, but was then greatly diminished, did not appear much in the dreams.

What dominates the dreams are the distressed feelings which are connected with anxiety for his loved objects and, as I have pointed out before, are characteristic for the depressive position. In the dreams the patient deals with the depressive position in different ways. He uses the sadistic manic control over his parents by keeping them separated from each other and thus stopping them in pleasurable as well as in dangerous intercourse. At the same time, the way in which he takes care of them is indicative of obsessional mechanisms. But his main way of overcoming the depressive position is reparation. In the dream he devotes himself entirely to his parents in order to keep them alive and comfortable. His concern for his mother goes back to his earliest childhood, and the drive to put her right and to restore her as well as his father, and to make babies grow, plays an important part in all his sublimations. The connection between the dangerous happenings in his inside and his hypochondriacal anxieties is shown by the patient's remarks about the cold he had developed at the time he had the dreams. It appeared that the mucus, which was so extraordinarily thick, was identified with the urine in the bowl—with the fat in the pan—at the same time with his semen, and that in his head which he felt so heavy, he carried the genitals of his parents (the pan with the kidney). The

* In my experience the paranoiac conception of a dead object within is one of a secret and uncanny persecutor. He is felt as not being fully dead and may reappear at any time in cunning and plotting ways, and seems all the more dangerous and hostile because the subject tried to do away with him by killing him (the conception of a dangerous ghost).

mucus was supposed to preserve his mother's genital from contact with that of his father and at the same time it implied sexual intercourse with his mother within. The feeling which he had in his head was that of its being blocked up, a feeling which corresponded to the blocking off of one parent's genital from the other, and so separating his internal objects. One stimulus for the dream had been a real frustration which the patient experienced shortly before he had these dreams, though this experience did not lead to a depression, but it influenced his emotional balance unconsciously; this became evident from the dreams. In the dreams the strength of the depressive position appears increased and the effectiveness of the patient's strong defences is, to a certain amount, reduced. This was not so in his actual life. It is interesting that another stimulus for the dreams was of a very different kind. It happened after this painful experience that he went recently with his parents on a short journey which he very much enjoyed. Actually the dream started in a way which reminded him of this pleasant journey, but then the depressive feelings overshadowed the gratifying ones. As I pointed out before, the patient used formerly to worry a great deal about his mother, but this attitude has changed during his analysis, and he has now quite a happy and care-free relation to his parents.

The points which I stressed in connection with the dreams seem to me to show that the process of internalization, which sets in in the earliest stage of infancy, is instrumental for the development of the psychotic positions. We see how, as soon as the parents become internalized, the early aggressive phantasies against them lead to the paranoid fear of external and, still more, internal persecutions, produce sorrow and distress about the impending death of the incorporated objects, together with hypchondriacal anxieties, and give rise to an attempt to master in an omnipotent, manic way the unbearable sufferings within, which are imposed on the ego. We also see how the masterful and sadistic control of the internalized parents becomes modified as the tendencies to restoration increases.

Space does not permit me to deal here in detail with the ways in which the normal child works through the depressive and manic positions, which in my view make up a part of normal development.* I shall confine myself therefore to a few remarks of a general nature.

In my former work I have brought forward the view which I referred to at the beginning of this paper, that in the first few months of its life the child goes through paranoid anxieties related to the "bad" denying breasts, which are felt as external and internalized persecutors.† From this relation to part-objects, and from their equation with faeces, springs at this stage the phantastic and unrealistic nature of the child's relation to all objects; to parts of its own body, people and things around it, which are at first but dimly perceived. The object-world of the child in the first two or three months of its life could be described as consisting of hostile and persecuting, or else of gratifying parts and portions of the real world. Before long the child perceives

---

* Edward Glover makes the suggestion that the child in its development goes through phases which provide the foundation for the psychotic disorders of melancholia and mania.[5]

† Dr. Susan Isaac has suggested in her remarks on "Anxiety in the First Year of Life" (to the British Psycho-Analytical Society, January, 1934), that the child's earliest experiences of painful external and internal stimuli provide a basis for phantasies about hostile external and internal objects and that they largely contribute to the building up of such phantasies. It seems that in the very earliest stage every unpleasant stimulus is related to the "bad," denying, persecuting breasts, every pleasant stimulus to the "good," gratifying breasts.

more and more of the whole person of the mother, and this more realistic perception extends to the world beyond the mother. (The fact that a good relation to its mother and to the external world helps the baby to overcome its early paranoid anxieties throws a new light on the importance of its earliest experiences. From its inception analysis has always laid stress on the importance of the child's early experiences, but it seems to me that only since we knew more about the nature and contents of its early anxieties, and the continuous interplay between its actual experiences and its phantasy-life, are we able fully to understand *why* the external factor is so important.) But when this happens its sadistic phantasies and feelings, especially its cannibalistic ones, are at their height. At the same time the child now experiences a change in its emotional attitude towards its mother. Its libidinal fixation to the breast develops into feelings towards her as a person. Thus feelings both of a destructive and of a loving nature are experienced towards one and the same object and this gives rise to deep and disturbing conflicts in the child's mind.

In the normal course of events the ego is faced at this point of its development—roughly between four to five months of age—with the necessity to acknowledge psychic reality as well as the external reality to a certain degree. It is thus made to realize that the loved object is at the same time the hated one; and, in addition to this, that the real objects and the imaginary figures, both external and internal, are bound up with each other. I have pointed out elsewhere that in the very young child there exists, side by side with its relations to real objects—but on a different plane, as it were—relations to its unreal imagos, both as excessively good and excessively bad figures,[6] and that these two kinds of object-relations intermingle and colour each other to an ever-increasing degree in the course of development.[7] The first important steps in this direction occur, in my view, when the child comes to know its mother as a whole person and becomes identified with her as a whole, real and loved person. It is then that the depressive position —the characteristics of which I have described in this paper —come to the fore. This position is stimulated and reinforced by the "loss of the loved object" which the baby experiences over and over again when the mother's breast is taken away from it, and this loss reaches its climax during weaning. Sandor Rado has pointed out that "the deepest fixation-point in the depressive disposition is to be found in the situation of threatened loss of love (Freud), more especially in the hunger situation of the suckling baby."[8] Referring to Freud's statement that in mania the ego is once more merged with the super-ego in unity, Rado comes to the conclusion that "this process is the faithful intrapsychic repetition of the experience of that fusing with the mother that takes place during drinking at her breast." I agree with these statements, but my views differ in important points from the conclusions which Rado arrives at, especially about the indirect and circuitous way in which he thinks that guilt becomes connected with these early experiences. I have pointed out before that, in my view, already during the suckling period, when it comes to know its mother as a whole person and when it progresses from the introjection of part-objects to the introjection of the whole object, the infant experiences some of the feelings of guilt and remorse, some of the pain which results from the conflict between love and uncontrollable hatred, some of the anxieties of the impending death of the loved internalized and external objects—that is to say, in a lesser and milder degree the sufferings and feelings which we find fully developed in the adult melancholic. Of course these feelings are experienced in a different setting. The whole situation and the defences of the baby, who obtains reassurance over and over again in the love of the mother, differ greatly from those in the adult melancholic. But the important point is that these sufferings, conflicts, and feelings of remorse and guilt, resulting from the relation of the ego to its internalized object, are already active in the baby. The same applies, as I suggested, to paranoid and manic positions. If the infant at this period of life fails to establish its loved object within— if the introjection of the "good" object miscarries—then the situation of the "loss of the loved object" arises already in the same sense as it is found in the adult melancholic. This first and fundamental external loss of a real loved object, which is experienced through the loss of the breast before and during weaning, will only result in later life in a depressive state if at this early period of development the infant has failed to establish its loved object within its ego. In my view it is also at this early stage of development that the manic phantasies, first of controlling the breast and, very soon after, of controlling the internalized parents as well as the external ones, set in with all the characteristics of the manic position which I have described, and are made use of to combat the depressive position. At any time that the child finds the breast again, after having lost it, the manic process by which the ego and ego-ideal come to coincide (Freud) is set going; for the child's gratification of being fed is not only felt to be a cannibalistic incorporation of external objects (the "feast" in mania, Freud calls it), but also sets going cannibalistic phantasies relating to the internalized loved objects and connects with the control over these objects. No doubt, the more the child can at this stage develop a happy relationship to its real mother, the more will it be able to overcome the depressive position. But all depends on how it is able to find its way out of the conflict between love and uncontrollable hatred and sadism. As I have pointed out before, in the earliest phase the persecuting and the good objects (breasts) are kept wide apart in the child's mind. When, along with the introjection of the whole and real object, they come closer together, the ego has over and over again recourse to that mechanism—so important for the development of the relations to objects— namely, a splitting of its imagos into loved and hated, that is to say, into good and dangerous ones.

One might think that it is actually at this point that ambivalence which, after all, refers to object-relations—that is to say, to whole and real objects—sets in. Ambivalence, carried out in a splitting of the imagos, enables the young child to gain more trust and belief in its real objects and thus in its internalized ones—to love them more and to carry out in an increasing degree its phantasies of restoration of the loved object. At the same time the paranoid anxieties and defences are directed towards the "bad" objects. The support which the ego gets from a real "good" object is increased by a flight-mechanism, which alternates between its external and internal good objects.

It seems that at this stage of development the unification of external and internal, loved and hated, real and imaginary objects is carried out in such a way that each step in the unification leads again to a renewed splitting of the imagos. But, as the adaptation to the external world increases, this splitting is carried out on planes which gradually become increasingly nearer and nearer to reality. This goes on until love for the real and the internalized objects and trust in them are well established. Then ambivalence, which is partly a safeguard against one's own hate and against the hated and terrifying objects, will in normal development again diminish in varying degrees.

Along with the increase in love for one's good and real objects goes a greater trust in one's capacity to love and a lessening of the paranoid anxiety of the bad objects—changes which lead to a decrease of sadism and again to better ways of mastering aggression and working it off. The reparation-tendencies which play an all-important part in the normal process of overcoming the infantile depressive position are set going by different methods, of which I shall just mention two fundamental ones: the manic and the obsessional defences and mechanisms.

It would appear that the step from the introjection of part-objects to whole loved objects with all its implications is of the most crucial importance in development. Its success —it is true—depends largely on how the ego has been able to deal with its sadism and its anxiety in the preceding stage of development and whether or not it has developed a strong libidinal relation to part-objects. But once the ego has made this step it has, as it were, arrived at a cross-road from which the ways determining the whole mental make-up radiate in different directions.

I have already considered at some length how a failure to maintain the identification with both internalized and real loved objects may result in psychotic disorders, such as depressive states, mania, or paranoia.

I shall now mention one or two other ways by which the ego attempts to make an end to all the sufferings which are connected with the depressive position, namely: (a) by a "flight to the 'good,' internalized object," a mechanism to which Melitta Schmideberg has drawn attention in connection with schizophrenia.[9] The ego has introjected a whole loved object, but owing to its immoderate dread of internalized persecutors, which are projected on to the external world, the ego takes refuge in an extravagant belief in the benevolence of his internalized objects. The result of such a flight may be denial of psychic and external reality and the deepest psychosis.

(b) By a flight to external "good" objects as a means to disprove all anxieties—internal as well as external. This is a mechanism which is characteristic for neurosis and may lead to a slavish dependence on objects and to a weakness of the ego.

These defence-mechanisms, as I pointed out before, play their part in the normal working-through of the infantile depressive position. Failure to work successfully through this position may lead to the predominance of one or another of the flight-mechanisms referred to and thus to a severe psychosis or a neurosis.

I have emphasized in this paper that, in my view, the infantile depressive position is the central position in the child's development. The normal development of the child and its capacity for love would seem to rest largely on how the ego works through this nodal position. This again depends on the modification undergone by the earliest mechanisms (which remain at work in normal persons) in accordance with the changes in the ego's relations to its objects, and especially on a successful interplay between the depressive, the manic and the obsessional positions and mechanisms.

THE THEORY
IN CONTEMPORARY
PRACTICE
AND RESEARCH

Anaclitic Depression

An Inquiry into the Genesis of Psychiatric Conditions in Early Childhood

RENÉ A. SPITZ

with the assistance of KATHERINE M. WOLF

Observation

A CIRCUMSCRIBED PSYCHIATIRIC SYNDROME. In the course of a long-term study of infant behavior in a nursery where we observed 123 unselected infants, each for a period of twelve to eighteen months, we encountered a striking syndrome. In the second half of the first year, a few of these infants developed a weepy behavior that was in marked contrast to their previously happy and outgoing behavior. After a time this weepiness gave way to withdrawal. The children in question would lie in their cots with averted faces, refusing to take part in the life of their surroundings. When we approached them we were ignored. Some of these children would watch us with a searching expression. If we were insistent enough, weeping would ensue and, in some cases, screaming. The sex of the approaching experimenter made no difference in the reaction in the majority of cases. Such behavior would persist for two to three months. During this period some of these children lost weight instead of gaining; the nursing personnel reported that some suffered from insomnia, which in one case led to segregation of the child. All showed a greater susceptibility to intercurrent colds or eczema. A gradual decline in the developmental quotient was observed in these cases.

This behavior syndrome lasted three months. Then the weepiness subsided, and stronger provocation became necessary to provoke it. A sort of frozen rigidity of expression appeared instead. These children would lie or sit with wide-open, expressionless eyes, frozen immobile face, and a far-away expression as if in a daze, apparently not perceiving what went on in their environment. This behavior was in some cases accompanied by autoerotic activities in the oral, anal, and genital zones. Contact with children who arrived at this stage became increasingly difficult and finally impossible. At best, screaming was elicited.

Among the 123 unselected children observed during the whole of the first year of their life we found this clear-cut syndrome in 19 cases. The gross picture of these cases showed many, if not all, of these traits. Individual differences were partly quantitative: i.e., one or the other trait, as for instance weeping, would for a period dominate the picture, and thus would impress the casual observer as the only one present; and partly qualitative: i.e., there was an attitude of complete withdrawal in some cases, as against others in which, when we succeeded in breaking through the rejection of any approach, we found a desperate clinging to the grown-up.

But apart from such individual differences the clinical picture was so distinctive that once we had called attention to it, it was easily recognizable by even untrained observers. It led us to assume that we were confronted with a psychiatric syndrome, which we illustrate in the three case histories following:

Case Histories

CASE 1.

Colored female. No significant events or behavior during the first half year. She is a particularly friendly child who smiles brilliantly at the approach of the experimenter.

When she was 7½ months old we noticed that her radiant smiling behavior had ceased. During the following two weeks it was impossible to approach her, as she slept heavily during the total of 12 hours we were there. After this period a change of behavior took place, which was protocolled as follows:

"She lay immobile in her crib. When approached she did not lift her shoulders, barely her head, to look at the experimenter with an expression of profound suffering sometimes seen in sick animals. With this expression she examined the observer. As soon as the observer started to speak to her or to touch her she began to weep. This was not the usual crying of babies which is always accompanied by a certain amount of vocalization going into screaming. It was a soundless weeping, tears running down her face. Speaking to her in soft comforting tones only resulted in the weeping becoming more intense, intermingled with moans and sobs, shaking her whole body.

"In the course of a two months' observation it was found that this reaction deepened. It was more and more difficult to make contact with the child. In our protocols there is a note seven weeks later to the effect that it took us almost an hour to achieve contact with her. In this period she lost weight and developed a serious feeding disturbance, having great difficulties in taking any food and in keeping it down."

After two months a certain measure was taken. The syndrome disappeared.

CASE 2.

White female. Intelligent, friendly child who smiles easily and ecstatically at the approaching observer. No notable event in the course of the first seven months. At this time a change occurred in the child. The observers got the feeling that the child was apprehensive. A week or two later the change was accentuated. The temper of the child had become unequal. She still was most friendly to the observer, but as often as not broke out crying when the observer approached closer. After another two weeks she could no longer be approached. No amount of persuasion helped. Whenever approached she sat up and wailed. Two weeks later, she would lie on her face, indifferent to the outside world, not interested in the other children living in the same room. Only strong stimulation could get her out of her apathy. She would then sit up and stare at the observer wide-eyed, a tragic expression on her face, silent. She would not accept toys, in fact she withdrew from them into the farthest corner of her bed. If the approach was pressed she would break into tears. This went on until the child was nine months old.

At this point a certain measure was taken. The syndrome disappeared.

CASE 3.

White female. This is a moderately intelligent, unusually beautiful child with enormously big blue eyes and golden curls. At the end of the eleventh month the child, who never had been very active, began to lose interest in playing with the experimenter, so that testing became difficult. In the following two weeks this behavior was more marked. The child was not only passive, but refused to touch any toys offered to her. She sat in a sort of daze, by the hour, staring silently into space. She did not even show the apprehensiveness in the presence of the approaching observer that was shown by other children. If a toy was put into contact with her she would withdraw into the farthest corner of her bed and there sit wide-eyed, absent, and without contact, with an immobile rigid expression on her beautiful face. When the toys were left with her she did not touch them until the experimenter had left the room. Then she immediately threw them out of her bed, where one would find them five or ten minutes later, forming a half-circle around the child, who would be sitting again in the same posture as before, or lying on her face. At 11 months 25 days (O; 11+25) she was observed to alternate playing with her feces, with genital masturbation, still in the same position described above. The fecal play would consist in her pulling a small pellet of feces the size of a very small pea out of her soiled diaper. With the same rigid immobile expression and rigid immobile body, she would roll this pellet on the sheet, pick it up, roll it between thumb and forefinger without looking at it, lose it from her fingers, and eagerly seek it again on the sheet. The time when she was seeking it on the sheet was the only moment when the rigid expression disappeared: and a near smile appeared when she had found it again. Alternately, she would rub her genitals.

As in the other case, a certain measure was taken, in this case when the child was eleven months thirty days (0; 11+30). The syndrome disappeared.

In all three cases the measure taken was the restitution of the mother, from whom the child had been separated approximately three to four months earlier.

Discussion of the Syndrome

In the three case histories the principal symptoms composing the syndrome are manifest. These symptoms fall into several categories; within each category we have grouped them on a scale of increasing severity. They are not all necessarily present at the same time, but most of them show up at one point or another in the clinical picture. They are:

Apprehension, sadness, weepiness.
Lack of contact, rejection of environment, withdrawal.
Retardation of development, retardation of reaction to stimuli,
slowness of movement, dejection, stupor.
Loss of appetite, refusal to eat, loss of weight.
Insomnia.

To this symptomatology should be added the physiognomic expression in these cases, which is difficult to describe.
This expression would in an adult be described as depression.

ETIOLOGY.

1) General environment.

The following table shows the sex and race distribution
of our sample.

Table 1.   Sex and Race Distribution

	White	Colored	Totals
Male	37	24	61
Female	40	22	62
Totals	77	46	123

These 123 infants stayed in the nursery from their four-
teenth day to the end of their first year and in a few cases
up to their eighteenth month. No selection was made in
the infants observed. We invariably tested and followed
each child admitted to the nursery up to the day when it
left. The observations took place at weekly intervals, and
totalled approximately 400 hours for each child. All these
infants shared the same environment, the same care, food,
and hygiene.

An apparently milder form of the syndrome presented in our three cases histories, with a similar drop in developmental quotient, was observed in 26 cases.

We shall now proceed to investigate the factors in the background and in the enviroment of these cases in order to isolate those that are etiologically significant.

2) Factors without demonstrable influence on the causation of the syndrome.

a.   Race and Sex.

The following two tables show the distribution of the different degrees of depression according to color and sex.

Table 2. Distribution According to Race

	White	Colored	Totals
Severe depression	7	12	19
Mild depression	17	9	26
No depression	32	18	50
No diagnosis*	21	7	28
Totals	77	46	123

Table 3.   Distribution According to Sex

	Male	Female	Totals
Severe depression	9	10	19
Mild depression	13	13	26
No depression	26	24	50
No diagnosis	13	15	28
Totals	61	62	123

* As in any psychiatric study, no exact diagnosis could be made in a certain number of cases. We include them in our tables for the purpose of showing the proportion of such undiagnosed cases within unselected total of observed children.

The factors of color and of sex do not appear to exert demonstrable influence on the incidence of the syndrome.

b.   Chronological age.

The youngest age at which the syndrome was manifested in our series was around the turn of the sixth month; the oldest was the eleventh month. The syndrome therefore seems to be independent of chronological age, within certain limits.

c.   Developmental and intellectual level.

It might be objected that in early childhood the developmental age is more significant than the chronological age. A hypothesis might state that a certain level of intelligence is prerequisite for any psychiatric syndrome. However, we have found the syndrome in question in children whose development was advanced by two months beyond their chronological age, just as well as in children whose development was one month retarded, as compared to their chronological age: the developmental quotients of the children affected would vary from 91 to 133; nor did the syndrome appear earlier in the children with the higher developmental quotient. So it would seem that within reasonable limits these factors play no significant role in the formation of the syndrome. The following table shows the average of the developmental quotients of the children with no dis-

Table 4.   Average Developmental Quotient

	Average developmental quotient
Severe depression	110
Mild depression	109
Others	109

turbance, with mild disturbance, and with severe disturbance.

3)   An etiologically significant factor.

There is one factor which all cases that developed the syndrome had in common. In all of them the mother was removed from the child somewhere between the sixth and eighth month for a practically unbroken period of three months, during which the child either did not see its mother at all, or at best once a week. This removal took place for unavoidable external reasons. Before the separation the mother had the full care of the infant, and as a result of special circumstances spent more time with the child than is usual in a private home. In each case a striking change in the child's behavior could be observed in the course of the four to six weeks following the mother's removal. The syndrome described above would then develop. *No* child developed the syndrome in question whose mother was *not* removed. Our proposition is that the syndrome observed developed only in children who were deprived of their love object for an appreciable period of time during their first year of life.

On the other hand, not all children whose mothers were removed developed the same syndrome. Hence, mother separation is a necessary, but not a sufficient cause for the development of the syndrome. The additional etiological factors which are required to make it effective in producing a depression will be touched upon in a later part of this paper, and discussed at length in a paper in preparation.

4)   Reactions to the loss of the love object.

The syndrome in question is extremely similar to that which is familiar to us from Abraham's[1] and Freud's[2] classi-

[1] See references in chapter notes at back of book.

cal descriptions of mourning, pathological mourning, and melancholia. The factor which appears to be of decisive etiological significance in our cases is the loss of the love object; this brings the syndrome closer to the consequences of the loss of the love object, as described by these authors. In melancholia there is added the feeling of being unloved, along with an incapacity to love, self-reproach, and suicidal tendencies. The absence of these symptoms in the child can be attributed to two reasons:

1) The child's fewer resources,
2) the difference in psychic structure between adult and infant.

As regards the greater resources of the adult: an adult suffering from melancholia is capable of expressing verbally that he feels unloved and that he is incapable of feeling love for anybody. We suspect that a child who up to a certain point was outgoing and friendly, but who now withdraws from every friendly approach, is expressing the same thing with the equipment at his disposal. We have of course no way of verifying this suspicion, just as we have no way of knowing whether anything like self-reproach can exist in a ten-month-old baby, even though it deprives itself of its usual enjoyment of toys or food. Nor can the infant enact a suicide; but it is striking that these cases one and all show a great susceptibility to intercurrent sickness.*

The difference in psychic structure between child and adult is far-reaching in its consequences. In the adult we have a well-established organization consisting of id, ego,

---

* This is strongly borne out in another series of cases observed in another institution. These were of a more severe nature—the resulting mortality among the children involved took on the aspect of a major catastrophe. See "Hospitalism."[3]

and superego. Particularly the manifestations of the superego are conspicuous in melancholia.

In the infant, during the first year, only an id and a
still weak—one might nearly say nascent—ego are available.
The weakness of the ego makes it especially vulnerable to
such a trauma as the loss of the love object is to the adult.
On the other hand, we may expect that just because the
infantile ego is not yet well-knit nor firmly established, it
may be more amenable than that of the adult in accepting
a substitute love object. Severe traumata in the case of the
adult impinge on a solid, complete ego organization, and
force it into a regression to an earlier fixation point. Not so
in the case of the infant. Here the injury will be manifested
in the form of a disturbance of the ego development. This
can take the form of a retardation, or a deformation, or
even of a destructive paralysis of ego development, dependent on the severity and the duration of the trauma.

Accordingly, clinical pictures vary in severity from temporary development arrest to loss or inhibition of already
acquired functions (one of the children observed by us was
already able to stand alone when he lost his mother; for the
following three months he stayed supine or at best stayed
in his cot), and in extreme cases result in irreversible progressive personality distortion. On the other hand, since the
infant's ego organization is in the process of development,
recovery from damage that is not irreparable is swifter, more
dramatic than in the case of the adult.

The clinical picture of the consequences of the loss of
the love object will be as varied in the infant as in the adult.
In the adult we encounter mourning, pathological mourning,
depression, melancholia. We cannot yet distinguish the
phenomena observed in infants in such detail. For the time

being and for the purposes of the present paper, we discuss that form of the clinical picture which in our belief comes closest to what Fenichel described as "simple depression," in his elaboration of the earlier findings on pre-oedipal infantile depression, called by Abraham "primal parathymia."[4] In view of the etiological factors which appeared in our findings, we prefer to follow a suggestion of R. M. Kaufman and to call the picture observed by us "anaclitic depression."

THE CONCEPT OF EARLY DEPRESSION IN THE LITERATURE. The psychoanalytic significance of the clinical symptomatology of melancholia was described by Abraham and Freud.[5] Both emphasized its similarity to cases of mourning, a psychic manifestation belonging to the field of normalcy. In all publications on the subject it was stressed that both melancholia and normal mourning originate from the same kind of trauma, i.e., a loss of the love object, the difference between normal mourning and pathological mourning being in the existence in the latter of fixation points on the oral-sadistic level. The primal parathymia observed by Abraham is placed in the years immediately preceding the oedipal conflict, and the examples given are typical of precursors of oedipal experiences.

These suggestions of Abraham of course do not exclude the existence of a depression in the first year of life. Accordingly, Fenichel states:[6]

The formulation can now be made that the disposition for the development of depressions consists in oral fixations which determine the reaction to narcissistic shocks. The experiences that cause the oral fixations may occur long before the decisive narcissistic shocks; or the narcissistic injury may create a depressive disposition because it occurs early enough to still be met by an orally oriented ego. It may also occur that certain narcissistic shocks, because they are connected with death (and the reaction to death is always oral introjection of the dead person), create the decisive oral fixation.

Regarding the factors that create oral fixations in the first place, the same holds true as for other fixations; the determinants are extraordinary satisfactions, extraordinary frustrations, or combinations of both, especially combinations of oral satisfaction with some reassuring guarantee of security; actually traumatic experiences in the nursing period can be found more often in subsequent manic-depressive patients than in schizophrenics (p. 405).

On the basis of our findings on 19 severe and 26 mild cases we believe that we are now in the position to offer clinical evidence for Fenichel's assumption that the equivalent of the primal parathymias described by Abraham can be observed during the first year of life.

In order to avoid the assumption that we are here speaking of what Melanie Klein calls "the depressive position" in infancy we now discuss her theoretical views.[7]

In psychoanalytic theory depression is an abnormal psychic manifestation, expressly considered the result of a specific environmental constellation. In the Kleinian system, depression is not only different in principle, but is also of primary significance as the cornerstone of the whole system. Melanie Klein considers depression the *fons et origo* of all human psychic development.[8] She and her school (Heimann, Isaacs, Rickman, Riviere,[9] Rosenfeld, Scott, Winnicott) postulate the presence of a so-called "depressive position" in infancy. This, in their opinions, is the fundamental mechanism of the infant's psyche, disposing of powerfully operating instruments of introjection and projection, upon which all further psychic development is based.

Our findings do not represent a confirmation of the view of Melanie Klein and her school. She states:[10]

The infantile depressive position arises when the infant perceives and introjects the mother as a whole person (between three and five months) ... the assumption seems justified that the seeds of depressive feelings, in so far as the experience of birth gives rise to a feeling of loss, are there from the beginning of life. I suggest that the "depressive position" in infancy is a universal phenomenon.

The coordination of functions and movements is bound with a defense mechanism which I take to be one of the fundamental processes in early development, namely the manic defense. This defense is closely linked with the "depressive position."

In other words: Melanie Klein posits a "depressive position" as an immutable stage in infantile psychic development, appearing between three and five months, irrespective of the child's individual history, experience, and environmental circumstances. She views the "depressive position" as part of the congenital equipment of every human being.

We are accustomed to consider our anatomical and physiological equipment as congenital. Of recent years, the tendency has been to restrict which psychic functions are to be considered inherited or congenital. Nonetheless, such endowments as: neural patterns based on anatomic and physiological premises, as well as on developmental sequences; perceptive modes as expressed in the principles of Gestalt; perhaps even certain basic reactions as described in the Watsonian triad of Love, Fear, and Rage,—are generally accepted as congenital and universal.

But the psychic element posited by Melanie Klein is of a very different nature from all of these. It is hard to conceive of the "depressive position" as a universal keystone of personality. We have become familiar with depression from the study of mental disease (of melancholia) in grownups. Psychoanalytic research, specifically that of Freud and of Abraham, demonstrated that it is a result of a regression to the oral-sadistic level of ego development. It would seem as if this finding had provoked a misinterpretation on the part of Melanie Klein. She appears to have concluded that since melancholia was a regression to the oral-sadistic level of the libido, the infant on progressing to this oral-sadistic level would have to develop melancholia. This of course is circular reasoning. Melancholia is the consequence of several factors, *one* of which is a fixation point at the oral-sadistic level of development. That fact in itself, however, is insufficient for the emergence of melancholia. Without the concurrence of certain experiential events dependent on environmental constellations, no melancholia will occur. The experiential events in question are of a severely frustrating nature and they presuppose the existence of some part of the ego organization which is to be frustrated. If these specific experiential events do not take place, or if they take place in a modified form, a completely different mental disease or perhaps even only a special character formation will emerge.

Melanie Klein, on the other hand, assumes that human beings are born with a finished and complete psychic structure. Here she falls into the same category as do other modifiers of psychoanalytic theory, like Adler, Jung, Rank,[11] and Reich. Mostly they had an axe to grind, whether that was for the purpose of eliminating the problems of infantile sexuality from psychoanalytic theory, or of satisfying the postulates of an ideological allegiance. Thus, with the help of the trauma of birth, Rank saddled heredity plus the experience of birth with the responsibility for the etiology of neurosis; and reduced the role of infantile sexuality, oedipal experience, and environmental influence to insignificance.

In contrast to Melanie Klein and her group, when we

speak of anaclitic depression in infants, we do not consider depression as *the* typical or as *a* typical mechanism of infantile psychic development. We do not consider depression as an integral element of the infantile psyche. To state that all human psychic development is determined by a "depressive position" in infancy makes as little sense as to state that erect human locomotion is determined by fracture or luxation in infancy—though some infants' gait at the outset may be vaguely reminiscent of a fractured or luxated limb. We speak of depression as a specific disease in infants arising under specific environmental conditions.

Diagnosis and Prognosis of the Syndrome

DIAGNOSIS. The problem of diagnosis of psychiatric disturbance in early infancy, during the preverbal stage, is difficult. In the first place, the question arises whether in this stage anything in the nature of psychosis can exist. Psychosis is by definition a disturbance in the relations between the different spheres of the personality. It would therefore look as if the formation of a superego or, at the very least, those abstractive functions of the unconscious parts of the ego that ensure conceptual thinking, would have to be present to enable us to speak of psychosis in the infant. For if anything is certain, then it is that the infant is not ruled by a superego, nor does it dispose of abstractive functions in any way demonstrable before the age of approximately eighteen months. Therefore that part of the psychotic destruction in the personality that involves the higher functions of the ego will not be manifested.

However, psychosis is characterized not only by delusion, disturbance of thought processes, abnormal thought production and mental confusion (memory defect, confabulation, impairment of apperception and attention, disorientation, ideational disorders, suspicion, etc.). It also involves modification of motility, grossly expressed by hypermotility, specific motor phenomena, or by hypomotility (catatonia, cataplexia, etc.); and it is more subtly manifested in the form of postural changes and pathognomonic expression. And finally, the most outstanding changes in the psychotic personality are those manifested in the affects. The changes in motility and the affective disorders are manifestations that do not require the presence of a fully organized ego capable of conceptual thinking, let alone the presence of a superego. Disturbance in these two fields presupposes an elementary organization of the ego, enabling it to perform the function of a coordinating center for elementary perception and apperception, for elementary volitional coordination of motility, as well as a capacity for such elementary differentiation of affect as is involved in the capacity to produce distinctly discernible positive or negative affective reactions on appropriate stimulation. This stage is reached when the child arrives at the second half of the first year of life.[12]

At this stage the child is capable, as we have stated above, of reacting to environmental experience by demonstrable affective disorders. We will show further on that gross disorders of motility are also manifested. The more subtle disorders can be detected in the dejected pathognomonic expression and posture of these infants. They show an obvious distaste for assuming an erect position or performing locomotion. It is in such behavioral changes that we have to seek the evidence of the pathological process.

Manifest evidence of this process is unmistakable to the

practised eye. The poverty of the symptomatology reflects the exiguousness of the modes of expression and the number of activities available to children of this age. As a consequence of the pathological process even this small number of expressions and actions is reduced—or expressions and activities in the normal course of development by the one-year-old do not materialize. Such a reduction in the performance, emotional and otherwise, of the infant are apt to impress the psychiatrist as an arrest in development rather than as a personality disorder. We believe—and we will bring proof of this in the further development of our case histories—that to consider the phenomena in question as an arrest in development only is to take a superficial view. The inadequacy of our means of communication with the infant is of course a severe handicap for diagnostic recognition of possible psychiatric disorders at this age. We are limited to the observation of behavior and its deviations; to the interpretation of visible manifestations of emotions; to the taking of a detailed anamnesis with the help of our own observation and that of the persons living with the child; and finally, to the quantifiable results of testing procedure. Thus the diagnostic signs and symptoms fall into the groups of static ones, genetic ones, and quantitative ones.

1)   The static signs and symptoms.

The static signs and symptoms are those observable phenomena that we are able to ascertain in the course of one or several observations of the infant in question. One of the outstanding signs is the physiognomic expression of such patients. The observer at once notices an apprehensive or sad or depressed expression on the child's face, which often impels him to ask whether the child is sick. It is characteristic, at this stage, that the child makes an active attempt to catch the observer's attention and to involve him in a game. However, this outgoing introduction usually is not followed by particularly active play on the part of the child. In the main it is acted out in the form of clinging to the observer and in sorrowful disappointment at the observer's withdrawal.

In the next stage the apprehensiveness deepens. The observer's approach provokes crying or screaming, and the observer's departure does not evoke as universal a disappointment as previously. Many of the cases observed by us fall into the period of what has been described as "eight months anxiety."[13]

The so-called "eight months anxiety" begins somewhere between the sixth and eighth month and is a product of the infant's increasing capacity for diacritic discrimination[14] between friend and stranger. As a result of this the approaching stranger is received either by what has been described as "coy" or "bashful" behavior, or by the child's turning away, hanging its head, crying, and even screaming in the presence of a stranger, and refusing to play with him or to accept toys. The difference between this behavior and the behavior in anaclitic depression is a quantitative one. While in anaclitic depression, notwithstanding every effort, it takes upwards of an hour to achieve contact with the child and to get it to play, in the eight months anxiety this contact can be achieved with the help of appropriate behavior in a span of time ranging from one to ten minutes. The appropriate behavior is very simple: it consists in sitting down next to the cot of the child with one's back turned to him and without paying any attention to him. After the above mentioned period of one to ten minutes the child will take the initiative, grab the observer's gown or hand—and with this the contact is established, and any experienced child psychologist can lead from this into playing with the child's active and happy participation. In the anaclitic depression nothing of the sort occurs. The child does not touch the observer, the approach has to be moderately active on the observer's part, and consists mostly in patient waiting, untiringly repeated attempts at cuddling or petting the child, and incessant offers of constantly varied toys. The latter must be offered with a capacity to understand the nature of the child's refusal. Some toys create anxiety in some children and have an opposite effect on others; for example, some children are attracted by bright colors but are immediately made panicky if a noise such as drumming is provoked in connection with this brightly colored toy. Others may be attracted by the rhythmic noise. Some are delighted by dolls, others go into a panic and can be reassured by no method at the sight of a doll. Some who are delighted by a spinning top will break into tears when it stops spinning and falls over, and every further attempt to spin it will evoke renewed protest.

When finally contact is made the pathognomonic expression does not brighten; after having accepted the observer the child plays without any expression of happiness. He does not play actively and is severely retarded in all his behavior manifestations. The only signs of his having achieved contact is, on the one hand, his acceptance of toys; and on the other, his expression of grief and his crying when left by the observer. That this qualitative distinction is not an arbitrary one can be seen from the fact that in a certain number of the cases in which the anaclitic depression was manifested late, we could observe the eight months anxiety as well as the anaclitic depression at periods distinct from each other. In one case, for instance, the eight months anxiety actually appeared at 0;7+14 and had already completely subsided and disappeared when the anaclitic depression was manifested at 0;11+2.

In the next stage the outward appearance of the child is that of complete withdrawal, dejection, and turning away from the environment. In the case of these children even the lay person with good empathy for children has no difficulty in making the diagnosis, and will tell the observer that the child is grieving for his mother.

2) The genetic signs.

The genetic signs can be disclosed with the help of a longitudinal investigation of the infant's development. A careful anamnesis reveals that before the above described attitude set in, the child was a pleasant, smiling, friendly baby. If the observer is lucky he may ascertain whether the child is already past the eight months anxiety, that it has come and gone. If the nursing staff reports a sudden development of changed behavior in the child without demonstrable organic disease and if this can be correlated to a separation from the child's mother or mother substitute, our suspicion as to the presence of anaclitic depression will be confirmed. It should not be overlooked that when we speak of the mother we are using a term which should really cover a wider field. "Love object" would be the more correct expression and we should say that these children suffer a loss of their love object.

3) Quantitative signs.

Quantitative signs can be detected by consecutive developmental tests which, if compared to each other, will at the beginning of the anaclitic depression show a gradual drop of the developmental quotient; this drop progresses with the progression of the disorder.

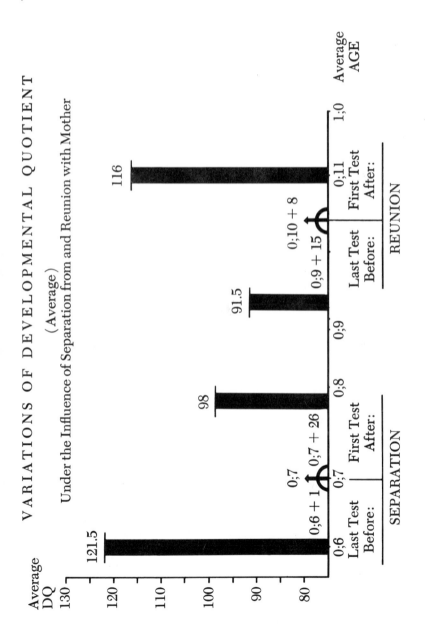

VARIATIONS OF DEVELOPMENTAL QUOTIENT
(Average)
Under the Influence of Separation from and Reunion with Mother

PROGNOSIS: WITH INTERVENTION. In the three case histories given by us in the beginning we ended by stating that a certain measure was taken in each case, whereupon the syndrome disappeared. The measure taken was in the nature of environmental manipulation. It consisted in returning the mother to the child. The change in the children's observable behavior was dramatic. They suddenly were friendly, gay, approachable. The withdrawal, the disinterest, the rejection of the outside world, the sadness, disappeared as if by magic. But over and beyond these changes most striking was the jump in the developmental quotient, within a period of twelve hours after the mother's return; in some cases, as much as 36.6 per cent higher than the previous measurement.

Thus one would assume that if adequate therapeutic measures are taken, the process is curable with extreme rapidity and the prognosis is good. The last statement requires some qualification. To our regret we have not been and are not in a position to follow the children in question beyond a maximum of eighteen months. It is therefore open to question whether the psychic trauma sustained by them as a consequence of being separated from their mothers will leave traces which will become visible only later in life. We are inclined to suspect something of the sort. For the sudden astonishing jump in the developmental quotient on the return of the love object is not maintained in all cases. We have observed cases in which, after a period of two weeks, the developmental quotient dropped again. It did not drop to the previous low levels reached during the depression. However, compared to these children's pre-depression performance, the level on which they were functioning after their recovery was not adequate.

The spectacular recovery achieved by the children we observed again places before us the question whether we are justified in calling the syndrome a depression and, if so, whether it should be considered as a phenomenon of more than transitory importance, whether it should not be equated to the transitory depression observable in adults—whether indeed it should not be equated to mourning rather than to depression. (See appendix, A. 1, paragraph 2.)

PROGNOSIS: WITHOUT INTERVENTION. The main reason why, apart from all physiognomic, behavioral and other traits, we feel justified in speaking of an anaclitic depression going far beyond mourning and even beyond pathological mourning is that we have observed a number of cases in which no intervention occurred and where it became only too evident that the process was in no way self-limiting. These cases were the ones observed in Foundling Home.* In that institution, where medical, hygienic, and nutritional standards were comparable to those obtaining in Nursery, the separation from the mother took place beginning after the third month, but prevalently in the sixth month. However, whereas in Nursery the separation was temporary and the love object was restored after approximately three months of absence, in Foundling Home the love object was not restored. The picture of depression was as clear-cut as in Nursery, with some additional developments: for the picture of children in advanced extreme cases varied from stuporous deteriorated catatonia to agitated idiocy.

If we compare the pictures of the two institutions we

* Described in earlier paper.[15] As there, to facilitate distinction between the two institutions, we call the one in which cases described up to now were cared for, *Nursery,* and the one we are about to describe, *Foundling Home.*

are confronted with a syndrome of a progressive nature which after having reached a critical point of development appears to become irreversible. It is this characteristic which causes us to call the picture depression and not mourning. And beyond this, in Foundling Home we encounter a phenomenon more grave than melancholia. Notwithstanding the satisfactory hygiene and asepsis, the rate of mortality of the infants reared there was inordinately high. In the course of two years 34 of the 91 children observed died of diseases varying from respiratory and intestinal infections to measles and otitis media. In some cases the cause of death was in the nature of cachexia. This phenomenon savors of psychosomatic involvement.

No intervention was effective in the case of the longer lasting separation in Foundling Home. This finding is one of the reasons why we spoke of three months as a critical period. The second reason is that in Nursery we observed towards the end of the three months the appearance of that kind of frozen, affect-impoverished expression which had strongly impressed us in Foundling Home. Furthermore, a curious reluctance to touch objects was manifested, combined with certain unusual postures of hands and fingers which seemed to us the precursors of the extremely bizarre hand and finger movements composing the total activity in those infants of Foundling Home whom we described as presenting a picture of stuporous catatonia.

After their recovery in the course of their further development, which to our regret could not be followed beyond one-and-a-half years, the children in Nursery did not show any spectacular changes. As indicated above it, it is therefore impossible at this point to state whether this early depression left any visible traces. One would be inclined to expect it. One would be inclined to expect some fixation.

The Therapy: Dynamic and Structural Considerations

THE RUDIMENTARY EGO. 1) As in melancholia[16] there occur in anaclitic depression more or less successful attempts to regain the lost objective world. The term "attempts at restitution" has been reserved by Freud for certain phenomena in schizophrenia. The attempts to regain the lost objective world in melancholia and also in anaclitic depression take the form of finding a substitute object.[17] We will therefore call this trend "attempts at substitution." These attempts form part of recuperative trends which become visible in anaclitic depression as they do in any other disease. We will encounter them in the course of our further discussion.

During the depressive stage of melancholia when the superego intolerably oppresses the ego, the outcome can only be a complete destruction of the individual, as in suicide. Against these demands of the supergo we have the reaction of the id drives. This reaction, however, is unsuccessful because the superego produces anxiety, forcing the id drives along the path dictated by the pleasure-pain principle; thus one part of the id drives is put into the service of the destructive superego demands. This part is represented by the desexualized id drive.

In case of a favorable outcome, however, the aggressive id drive is not completely desexualized. The sex-fused portion of the aggressive drive then may remain available to the ego. If such is the case it may be used in the interest of those self-curative tendencies which every living organization will manifest both in organic and psychic sickness. In its attempts to comply with the superego's demands the sex-fused id drive is used in the establishment of a compulsive system. Through the compulsive neurotic behavior and its rigid adherence to arbitrarily established rules, the superego can be at least temporarily satisfied that, with great sacrifices, its demands are being complied with. With this a remission (in the picture of an obsessional neurosis with compulsive ritual) begins, and thus interrupts the progress of melancholia.

2) Another outcome is possible if the ego does not succeed in putting the sex-fused id drives in the service of the appeasement of the superego, but the superego on the other hand does not succeed either in putting the defused drives into the service of its own destructive tendencies. In this case the id drives, aggressive and sexual, are shunted into an ego reinforcement. This then enables the ego to overpower, as it were, the superego, and to incorporate it into itself. As in the depressive phase the imago of the love object is introjected, whereupon the fury of the superego is unleashed against it, so in the manic phase the superego which in itself is the recipient of the archaic imagines of the original love objects, is now incorporated in the ego. The result is that the limits between the systems are abolished, and the manic picture develops.

Both outcomes of the manic-depressive process center around the ego and can be considered as representing attempts of the ego to escape annihilation, and it is in view of this that we consider them recuperative trends even when they are unsuccessful.

Such trends presuppose, however, the presence of the three systems, id, ego, and superego. In the infant the superego is absent, so that it is impossible to assume destructive hostility of the superego. However, the loss of the love object in itself is equivalent to a hostile deprivation for the infant. The organization with which the infant can react to this deprivation is its ego, inadequate as it is at this period. As Freud established, the ego at this early age is mainly a body ego. The organizations of which the ego disposes are 1) a very rudimentary ideational organization, barely adequate for diffuse hallucinatory processes, and 2) a rapidly developing locomotor system.

RECUPERATIVE TRENDS VERSUS INSTITUTIONAL CARE. At this same period the id drive in regard to the object is patterned on the anaclitic model. All locomotion will therefore be put in the service of an attempt to get gratification of the drive for anaclitic social relations.

The demand for social relations is subject to development in the course of the first year of life. Up to the sixth month these demands can be and are expressed only in a passive manner, since the infant has not achieved locomotion yet. Therefore the social demands of the infant are initiated not so much by the infant's activities as by the adult's activity.

From six to twelve months, however, its social demands are expressed actively, as shown in the results of the Hetzer-Wolf tests. At the age level of seven months, one of the test items consists of observing whether the infant already creates contact actively. At the level of nine months, the test consists in observing whether without intervention of the examiner the infant will grasp the hand or the coat of the averted adult.

One might also formulate this by saying that before the sixth month the passivity of the social demand is expressed in the fact that it is only manifested in the pathognomonic reaction of the infant to the adult. Before the sixth month the social contact manifestation is initiated by the adult and the child follows him; whereas after six months the infant takes the initiative and seeks for the adult.

In a certain percentage of our cases of anaclitic depression we have found that the infants did not show the anxious attitude immediately after being deprived of their love object. We were informed by the staff that these children were disturbed by the absence of their mothers. Nevertheless they seemed to turn with eagerness to the observer. We might interpret this behavior as an attempt at substitution of the lost object along the anaclitic mode.

However, if active attempts at substitution are to be initiated through social contact, locomotion is a necessary prerequisite for such an attempt. In institutionalized children both the opportunity to reestablish anaclitic object relations through social contact, and the opportunity for locomotion, are severely handicapped.

From the dynamic point of view locomotion and motility in general fulfills the important task of offering a necessary channel of release for the aggressive drive. When motor activity is inhibited in infancy, all normal outlets of the aggressive drive are blocked. In this case only one alternative remains for dealing with the aggressive drive: that is, to direct it against the self. The resulting dynamic picture is identical to the one we have previously described for melancholia. The only difference is that whereas in melancholia it was the superego which made use of the aggressive drive against the ego, in the case of inhibited motor activity in infancy the intervention of the superego is unnecessary.

Actually the difference between the dynamics in melancholia and those in anaclitic depression are not as great as might appear from a theoretical point of view. The hostile ego-oppressive authority in melancholia is the superego. In anaclitic depression the restriction of motility and the deprivation of the love object is imposed by the surrounding grown-up world. This world of grown-ups which forms the immediate environment of the infant is the identical one from which in the oedipal stage the imagines will be taken for the purpose of forming the superego. In other words, both in melancholia and in anaclitic depression the sadism which threatens the patient with extinction originates from the same source: except that in melancholia the source is an intrapsychic representation, while in anaclitic depression the source is the living original of the later intrapsychic representation.

An objection might be raised at this point: if anaclitic depression is provoked by inhibiting the locomotion of infants separated from their love object, why is it that a significant number of the infants observed by us in Nursery, the majority in fact, remained unharmed? And what is the reason for the severe nature of one group of infantile depression, for the milder course of the others?

The answer is that in both cases the outcome depends on the measure of success achieved in this institution in providing the infant with a substitute love object. The separation of the infants from their mothers takes place in Nursery between the sixth and the ninth month. Another of the inmates is then assigned to the care of the motherless child. The substitute mother thus cares for her own child and for a stranger. Though the enlightened management of Nursery exerts the greatest care, their selection is limited by the available number of inmates. Also it is hardly to be expected that a group of delinquent girls, as these were, will furnish very high grade mother substitutes.

We suggest that when the mother substitute is a good one, depression does not develop. Where the mother substitute turns out to be an aggressive, unloving personality, the parallel to adult melancholia is enacted in real life. Just as in melancholia the ego is oppressed by a sadistic super-ego, here the body ego of the infant is oppressed by a sadistic love object substitute.

Inhibited in its motor release, the pent-up aggressive drive is turned against the ego. The ego then is caught between a hostile love object substitute and its own aggressive drive. Bereft of locomotion, it cannot actively seek replacement for the lost love object among the other grown-ups in the institution.

An indirect confirmation of this view is contained in the following table, which refers to the original mother-child relatonship. In it we tabulate the number of children and the nature of their depression, on the one hand, the nature of the relations between the child and its mother, on the other. The mother-child relation was established by our observation of the way the mother behaved to her child. For the purpose of corroboration these observations then were compared with the information gathered for this purpose from the unusually able headmatron of Nursery. This somewhat complicated procedure made it impossible to procure reliable data on all the 95 children in question; but we did get them on 64, appearing in the table below.

Table 6.   Mother-Child Relation

	Good			Bad		
	In-tense	Moder-ate	Weak	In-tense	Moder-ate	Weak
Severe Depression	6	11	—	—	—	—
Mild Depression	4	—	3	7	—	4
No Depression	—	—	2	11	2	14

The figures speak for themselves. Evidently it is more difficult to replace a satisfactory love object than an unsatisfactory one. Accordingly depression is much more frequent and much more severe in the cases of good mother-child relationship. In bad mother-child relationship not a single severe depression occurs. It seems that any substitute is at least as good as the real mother in these cases.

In institutions motor activity is inhibited for organizational reasons: lack of adequate nursing staff requires that the children be mostly confined to their cots, and move freely on the floor only for very restricted periods, if at all. The ego therefore is impoverished by being deprived of the release of motor activity. The aggressive drive is pent up and directed against the ego.

This restriction, however, also precludes the children's actively seeking replacement for the lost object among the grown-ups present in the institution or through contact with other children. Thus institutional routine will jeopardize the chances of substitutive attempts of the ego both in the motor and in the emotional sector.

FACILITATION OF RECUPERATIVE TRENDS IN INSTITUTIONS. The theoretical considerations elaborated above on the parallelity of the roles played by the superego in melancholia on the one hand, and on the other by the originals of the later imagines in an anaclitic depression, hold promise of a much more successful and effective therapy in the latter. Changing the superego in melancholia or assuaging it is a laborious, time-consuming, and all-in-all not very hopeful task. Providing a mother substitute (if restoring the mother is precluded) for a child suffering from a not too advanced anaclitic depression, refraining from inhibiting its motility, should be matters for an efficient and adequate environmental manipulation. The correctness of the latter statement is borne out by our observations on the prompt results after restoration of the love object to the deprived infants. It is also borne out by the favorable results of liberating motility and providing an adequate mother substitute for those infants for whom the original love object could not be restored.

It is easy to visualize that these elements in the picture of infantile depression will be subject to a wide scale of variations, depending on the rapidly developing changes in personality that take place during the first year of infancy; and on the wide gamut of environmental facilitations offered by the different types of institutions.

As regards the first, the changes in personality, it is self-evident that no imaginable motor activity exists in the first six months of life which could conceivably be used for attempts at substitution of the lost object. During this period, routine care of the infant, at least during the first three months, covers a large part of its social requirements. This picture changes completely in the second half of the first year of life. Locomotion develops rapidly and the demand for love switches from previous passivity to activity.

Institutional confinement of infants to their cots after the sixth month thwarts their use of locomotion in attempts at substitution. The infant's active attempts to make contact with other infants or adults in the environment are blocked. The infant is at the mercy of the compliance of its environment, and of the ability of the institution to provide an adequate substitute object.

Hence we will find clinical pictures of increasing severity according to the capacity of the institution in question to afford children deprived of their love objects an outlet in the form of free locomotion and substitute love objects. This is the reason why the results of child care in the worst foster homes surpass (with a few exceptions) those of the best institutions.

In the case of the infants observed by us in Nursery, we found that in so far as the object was not restored, or an adequate substitute object not supplied, the depression progressed rapidly. Beginning with sadness and weeping, it continued into withdrawal, loss of appetite, loss of interest in the outside world, dejection, retardation, and finally, a condition which could only be described as stuporous.

THE ACTUAL THERAPEUTIC MEASURE. Our dynamic and structural model of the anaclitic depression suggests the obvious therapeutic measures. It is gratifying to find that for once in psychiatry they appear to be really effective where they can be applied. They fall into three classes:

1) prophlyaxis
2) restitution
3) substitution

1)   Prophylaxis: deprivation of infants, during the first year, of love objects for a prolonged period, should be strenuously avoided. Under no circumstances should they be deprived for over three months of love objects, during the second half of their first year.

2)   Restitution: if infants have been deprived of their love objects during their first year for a prolonged period, restitution of the love objects within a period of maximally three months will enable them to recover, at least partially, from the damage inflicted.

3)   Substitution: where neither prophylaxis nor restitution is possible, the substitution of the love object by another one is advisable. Particular attention should be given

to the facilitation of the infant's locomotor drives in the largest measure possible, and to the supporting of its tendencies to choose actively its own substitutes for the love object of which it has been deprived.

Summary

A.   A psychiatric syndrome of a depressive nature is observed in a series of infants and classified as anaclitic depression.

B.   Its etiology is related to a loss of the love object, combined with a total inhibition of attempts at restitution through the help of the body ego acting on anaclitic lines.

C.   Prophylaxis and treatment is suggested on the basis of these structural and dynamic findings.

D.   Some of the results of such treatment are reported.

E.   Theoretical assumptions concerning melancholia are discussed.

Appendix

A.   VARIOUS OBSERVATIONS WITH THEORETICAL IMPLICATIONS.

In the course of this study a number of observations were made which we have not cared to include in our general conclusions for several reasons. Some of these observations appear to us to lead to conclusions which are still of too speculative a nature for the purposes of the present study. Others again are too scattered and irregular to represent satisfactory findings for the purpose of establishing or confirming any theory. We therefore bring them here in order to call the attention of other investigators to these phenomena, in the hope that they may be utilized in later work.

1. The variaions of the DQ (developmental quotient) in the course of anaclitic depression.

In all our cases without exception a gradual decline of the DQ began when the infant was deprived of its love object. This decline paralleled the increasing severity of the developing symptoms. This is a welcome confirmation of our observations; an unexpectedly surprising and dramatic change in the DQ occurs when the love object is returned. We had the opportunity to test such cases immediately after the return of the love object, i.e., within twelve hours. DQs would jump as much as 36.6 per cent in this brief period. The developmental age of the children would take a jump from 0;11+0 to 1;4+0; or from 0;9+0 to 1;1+0. This in itself is surprising enough, but it is still more surprising that in the case of a child whose developmental age had jumped within three days from 0;11+0 to 1;3+28, it receded again, and for the following two months moved between 1;1+21 and 1;1+24.

It is an extremely striking finding that faculties already acquired should be lost in the course of the anaclitic depression, that when the love object returns they should be regained suddenly in a manner far surpassing the actual age of the child, but that after a short while the level of achievement should settle back again more closely to the performances to be expected according to the child's actual age. In view of our discussion of the fact that the ego at this period is mainly a body ego, that on the other hand the tests applied to establish the DQ require a good deal of body activity, one gets the impression of a sudden ego expansion having taken place on the return of the love object. This ego expansion is out of proportion to the age-adequate capacities of the child, and sinks back to a more normal proportion if no further disturbances intervene. The curious phenomenon of this sudden ego expansion which on the return of the love object replaces the depression makes us inclined to speculate whether there may be any anology between this manifestation and the replacement of a depression by a manic episode.

2. Some considerations in regard to assumptions of psychoanalytic theory and their verification.

The predominant role of oral eroticism in melancholia has always been stressed in psychoanalytic literature.[18] It is assumed that a regression to the oral biting phase takes place, with fantasies of introjection. Anal-sadistic trends appear enormously increased. Therefore we would expect to find striking oral biting and anal-sadistic phenomena in our depressed infants. Such was not the case, at least not in that measure which one would expect in view of the comparatively simple, elementary structure of early infantile psychic patterns.

a. Oral biting manifestations.

The one oral symptom common to all of the children was loss of appetite; on the other hand, we observed a greater tendency of the depressed children to stuff everything—hands, clothes, toys—into their mouths, and to keep them there. Prior to the depression these children were not noticeably prone to finger-sucking. During the depression finger-sucking increased conspicuously. We encounter biting phenomena in some of the depressed children, but not in all. In those cases in which we could observe them, they had not been present prior to the depression. It is an outstanding fact that the biting activities *never* were in evidence *during* the depression; they appeared after the depression had lifted. Interesting manifestations will be found in the following quotation from the protocol of one of our cases.

Aethelberta, white female:

From the beginning far advanced in her development, friendly, well liked. At 0;7+16 slightly depressive expression in the face noted, simultaneously with a decrease of the DQ. Inquiry elicits that she had been separated from her mother ten days before. In the following weeks she becomes weepy; by the time she is nine months old the nursing staff observes that the child is getting thinner and suffering from insomnia; she seems to be watching everything and allegedly cannot go to sleep for this reason. She finally is isolated for the purpose of overcoming her insomnia. Approaching her becomes difficult; she is mostly sitting in her bed, her dress in her mouth, or sucking her hand. In the following weeks she refuses to touch toys and lies dejected on her bed, face averted from the experimenter. Films taken by us during these weeks show a pathetic picture of sorrow, helplessness, and demand for assistance. The DQ drops further. The child, up to this point vigorously healthy, develops a stubbornly persisting cold. At 0;10+22 a mother substitute is delegated with instructions to be particularly loving to the child. The effect of this measure becomes immediately visible, though the child is by no means cured. She now accepts contact with other children in an aggressive form. At 0;10+29 she is biting, scratching, and pinching other children to the point of drawing blood. By 0;11+5 she tries for a prolonged period to bite the observer's nose, chin, neck, and hand. During these attacks she reaches out with her hands and vocalizes different incoherent sounds, among which the word "ma-ma" returns several times. At 0;11+19 the mother is returned. Simultaneously she has become friendly and positive, and her DQ has suddenly risen 29.28 per cent.

There are many traits in this picture which could be used to confirm psychoanalytic theory and we have quoted it for this reason. We do not at this point feel justified, however, in drawing conclusions because similar phenomena are manifested only by a minority of our cases.

b. Anal-sadistic manifestations.

Anal activities showed a somewhat different pattern. Like oral biting phenomena they were very striking in some cases and absent in others. However, in those cases where they were present they could be observed both during the depression and after the depression had lifted. The phenomena observed in these children were: playing with feces, with or without accompanying genital masturbation, and in some cases, coprophagia. Fecal games and oral biting manifestations appeared frequently, although not necessarily, in the same children. In the case of Aethelberta, for instance, as well as in that of another child, the games consisted in rolling fecal pellets, which seemed to be the only toy these children enjoyed. Aethelberta continued the fecal games after the depression had lifted, in the form of social games, trying to feed her play partner with the pellets. In another case in which biting and fecal games were simultaneously present, the pellets were used for covering the bed with the layer of feces and for throwing out through the bars of the cot, so that the surroundings of the bed were also completely covered with feces. Genital masturbation, which at this age is not particularly frequent in infants, was observed in nearly all of the children in whom fecal games were observed.

Process of Mourning

JOHN BOWLBY

In *Grief and Mourning in Infancy and Early Childhood*,[1] evidence was presented that the responses to be seen in infants and young children to loss of mother are, at the descriptive level, substantially the same as those to be observed when the older child or adult loses a loved figure; and it was argued that the underlying processes are probably similar. Both, it was contended, required the same description, namely mourning; in both age-groups the subjective experience appeared to be that of grief. Furthermore, in reviewing the psycho-analytic literature, it seemed that some of the implications of such losses had been overlooked. On the one hand many analysts seem not to have identified the processes in question as those of mourning or, if they have, to have believed that they differ radically from mourning in adults; on the other, some analysts have placed so much emphasis on grief and mourning arising from weaning and loss of the mother's breast that they have tended to become preoccupied with events of the first year to the neglect of later ones.

The main thesis I am advancing in these papers is twofold; first, that once the child has formed a tie to a mother-figure, which has ordinarily occurred by the middle of the first year, its rupture leads to separation anxiety and grief and sets in train processes of mourning; secondly, that in the

[1] See references in chapter notes at back of book.

early years of life these mourning processes not infrequently take a course unfavourable to future personality development and thereby predispose to psychiatric illness. Since I believe that an understanding of the nature of these unfavourable outcomes turns on a clear grasp being obtained of the nature of the mourning processes themselves, and of their variants and deviants, a discussion of their implications for psychopathology will be postponed until a later paper. Here the task is that of exploring some of the basic psychological processes engaged in mourning and their biological roots. Particular emphasis is laid on the function of weeping and of anger, which I believe are always or nearly always present, as means for the recovery of the lost loved object. Both, it is noted, are apt to be evoked at an especially intense level in early childhood.

The discussion closes at a point where it is entering the fields of psychopathology and psychiatry proper. It will be continued in further papers.

The hypothesis I shall be advancing is that unfavorable personality development is often to be attributed to one or more of the less satisfactory responses to loss having been provoked during the years of infancy and childhood in such degree, over such length of time, or with such frequency, that a disposition is established to respond to all subsequent losses in a similar way.

Although the way in which terms are used was defined in the previous paper, for convenience definitions are here briefly repeated. "Mourning" will be used to denote the psychological processes that are set in train by the loss of a loved object and that commonly lead to the relinquishing of the object. "Grief" will denote the sequence of subjective states that follow loss and accompany mourning. Although a common outcome of mourning is relinquishment of the object, this is not always so. By defining the term "mourning" to cover a fairly wide array of psychological processes, even including those that lead to a retention of the object, the different courses that mourning may take, healthy or pathological, are, I believe, more easily understood.

The term "depression" is used to describe an affect that, it is held, is as integral to psychic life as is anxiety. The clinical syndrome of which pathological depression is a main presenting symptom is termed "depressive illness."

The ground to be covered in this paper is already well-trodden. In tracing the paths that have been followed by others I shall begin by picking out certain main problem areas in the theory of mourning and indicating briefly what others have said about them and to what conclusions the evidence seems to point; I shall then attempt to trace historically the development of the main strands in the psycho-analytical theory of mourning.

Principal Issues

In the history of psycho-analytic thought the study of grief and mourning has usually been approached by way of the study of depressive illness and melancholia in adults. This has had advantages, but has not been without drawbacks. Here, because of the nature of the data we are seeking to understand, the task is different: we are studying grief and mourning in their own right, with particular reference to the courses they run in infancy and early childhood.

An examination of the psycho-analytic literature shows that few attempts have been made to conceptualize the processes of grief and mourning as such. Only Freud, Melanie Klein, Lindemann, and Edith Jacobson seem to have tackled the problem: and Lindemann appears to be alone in making the first-hand study of acute grief his main concern. Much of the clinical literature, indeed, is concerned exclusively with depressive illness, and some of it makes little or no reference to bereavement or other actual loss of object. Even when the roles of bereavement and mourning are clearly recognized, moreover, the bulk of the clinical literature is concerned more with pathological variants of mourning than with the normal process.

This one-sidedness is made good in some degree by contributions stemming from other traditions of psychological thought. Two of the most notable are those of Darwin[2] and Shand.[3] Because of his occupation with comparative studies, Darwin's interest in the expression of the emotions lay in the functions served and the muscles used. In keeping with conclusions reached on other grounds, his analysis traces much of the adult's expression in times of grief to the crying of the infant. Shand, drawing for his data on the works of English poets and French prose-writers, not only delineates most of the main features of grief but discusses in a systematic way its relation to fear and anger. As a sensitive and perspicacious study his book ranks high and deserves to be better known. Other authors whose work merits the attention of clinicians are Waller,[4] Eliot,[5] and Marris.[6]

Because the processes engaged in mourning are manifold and intricately related to each other, points of controversy are numerous. A selection has therefore to be made. In choosing some seven main themes I have been influenced partly by what have seemed to others and to me to be most relevant and partly by what can most usefully be discussed at this point in the exposition of my schema. They are the following:

(i) What is the nature of the psychological processes engaged in healthy mourning?

(ii) How is the painfulness of mourning to be accounted for?

(iii) How is mourning related to anxiety?

(iv) What sorts of motivation are present in mourning?

(v) What is the role of anger and hatred in mourning?

(vi) In what ways does pathological mourning differ from healthy mourning?

(vii) At what stage of development and by means of what processes does the individual arrive at a state which enables him thereafter to respond to loss in a healthy manner?

A theme that is omitted from this series of papers is that of identification; and to some a discussion of mourning that omits identification will seem like Hamlet without the Prince. There are several reasons for its omission. The main one is my belief that an attempt to discuss every aspect of mourning in a single series of papers is too ambitious, that it is therefore necessary to make a selection, and that what is selected must turn on the nature of the data under study. In selecting the process of identification with the lost object as his main focus of interest, Freud was governed by his concern to account for a special feature of melancholic patients, namely their tendency to direct reproaches, originally aimed at the lost object, against themselves. This, however, is not my point of entry. The primary data with which I am dealing do not derive from sick persons but from young children undergoing separation from their mothers; and these data do not seem to lend themselves readily to the study of identificatory processes and their deviations. On the other hand, they do call attention to other aspects of mourning which are of great interest. Indeed, I am inclined to the view that the role of identification amongst processes of mourning may become easier to discern after some of the problems to be tackled here have been clarified. The approach that I believe will prove most fruitful and that I hope one day to explore is the one outlined by Wynne.[7]

In order to orient the reader I shall in this section deal only briefly with the seven themes listed, indicating the views on each that have been expressed by leading workers in the field and the line I shall myself be taking. The reasons leading me to take that line will be amplified later.

All who have discussed *the nature of the processes engaged in healthy mourning* are agreed that amongst other things they effect a withdrawal of emotional concern from the lost object and commonly prepare for making a relattionship with a new one. How we conceive their achieving this change, however, will depend on how we conceptualize the dynamic of object relations. Because it is at this point that I find the concepts of Freud and other analysts inadequate, it is in regard to these processes that I find it most necessary to attempt new formulations.

Traditionally in psycho-analytic writings emphasis has been placed on identification with the lost object as the main process involved in mourning, such indentification being regarded as compensatory for the loss sustained. Furthermore, following Freud, the dynamics of mourning are commonly cast in a form of theory that (a) sees the process of identification as almost exclusively oral in character, and (b) sees libido as a quantity of energy which undergoes transformation, on the analogy of water under pressure. I am not satisfied by either of these formulations. First, evidence does not suggest that identification is the only or even the main process involved. Secondly, identification seems to be independent of orality, though it may be and often does become related to it. Thirdly, as I have made clear elsewhere,[8] the hydrodynamic model of instinct, which pictures instincts on the model of a liquid which varies in quantity and pressure, has serious shortcomings. The limitations of energy models of motivation are discussed by Hinde.[9] Instead I believe it to be fruitful to explore more systematically a theory of component instinctual responses similar to the one advanced by Freud in the *Three Essays* and more in keeping with modern biological theory.

In this paper therefore an attempt is made to formulate a theory of mourning based on this other model. It is a theory that sticks closely to the empirical data of Lindemann, Marris, and others. It differentiates three main phases of mourning. Taking as the point of departure the hypothesis that the individual's attachment to his loved object is to be understood as mediated by a number of instinctual response systems, the first phase is seen as one during which the systems are still focussed on the original object but, because of the object's absence, whenever activated cannot be terminated. As a result the bereaved individual experiences repeated disappointment, persistent separation anxiety, and, in so far as he suspects the worst, grief. This, however, is not all. So long as the response systems are focussed on the lost object there are strenuous and often angry efforts to recover it; and these efforts may continue despite their fruitlessness being painfully evident to others, and sometimes also to the bereaved himself. In this phase are sown, I believe, the seeds of much psychopathology. When the mourning process proceeds healthily, however, the response systems gradually cease to be focussed on the lost object and the efforts to recover it cease too. Disorganization of personality accompanied by pain and despair is the result. This is the second phase. The third phase completes the work of mourning and leads to a new and different state: during it a reorganization takes place, partly in connexion with the image of the lost object, partly in connexion with a new object or objects.

Such is the bare outline of the theory to be advanced. Before elaborating it, however, a word must be said about the six other themes, some of which have already been touched upon in the formulation above.

In previous attempts to account for the *painfulness* of mourning two main hypotheses have been advanced:

(*a*) because of the persistent and insatiable nature of the yearning for the lost object, pain is inevitable;

(*b*) pain following loss is the result of a sense of guilt and and a fear of retaliation.

It should be noted that these hypotheses are not mutually exclusive, and that there are therefore three possible schools of thought. In effect, however, there are only two. The first, to which Freud belongs, holds that the pain of yearning is of great importance in its own right; it may or may not be exacerbated and complicated by a sense of guilt or fear of retaliation. The second, represented especially by Melanie Klein, pays less attention to yearning as something painful *per se* and holds that, since guilt and paranoid fear are believed always to be present in bereavement and always to cause distress, taken by itself the painfulness of yearning is of little more than secondary importance. The first of these schools is the one evidence seems to favour.

Our third theme, *the relation of mourning to anxiety*, is

one already discussed.[10] In the papers mentioned, I have adopted and elaborated the view advanced by Freud in the final pages of *Inhibitions, Symptoms and Anxiety* that when the mother-figure is believed to be temporarily absent the response is one of anxiety, when she appears to be permanently absent it is one of pain and mourning. I have shown also how different this view is from that of Melanie Klein, which regards fear of annihilation and persecutory anxiety as being primary. Shand, I have found subsequently, in the decade before Freud's formulation had already advanced a view substantially similar to his. Fear, he suggests, presupposes hope. Only when we are striving and hoping for better things are we anxious lest we fail to obtain them.* Because, however, hope may be present in any degree, there is a continuum in feeling between anxiety and despair. During an experience of grief, feeling often travels back and forth along it, now nearer to anxiety, now to despair.

In exploring this line of thought Shand has also contributed to our understanding of our fourth theme, the complex *motivation present in situations evoking grief*, or, to use the word he favours, sorrow. The urge to regain the lost object, he points out, is powerful and often persists long after reason has deemed it useless. Expressions of this urge are weeping and the appeal to others for assistance, an appeal which inevitably carries with it an admission of weakness: "Thus the expressions and gestures of sorrow—the glance of the eyes indicating the direction of expectation, its watchings and waitings, as well as its pathetic cries—all are evidence that the essential end of its system is to obtain the strength and help

* In describing his feelings during escape from a prison camp Winston Churchill has recorded that "When hope had departed, fear had gone as well."

of others to remedy its own proved weakness." This appeal Shand regards, I believe rightly, as stemming from primitive roots and as having survival value: "The cry of sorrow . . . tends to preserve the life of the young by bringing those who watch over them to their assistance." It is a mode of conceptualizing the data that is strongly supported by the findings of Darwin[11] on the expressive movements occurring when grief is experienced. In my terminology it can be described as an expression in elaborated form of the instinctual response system of crying.

Although the accompanying emotions of hopelessness and helplessness have been recognized in several recent formulations (e.g. Bibring[12]), it is my impression that the urge to recall the lost object has been given too little attention in discussions of the motivating forces active during mourning. Yet it is plainly in keeping with experience and can be fruitfully linked both with Rado's picture of melancholia as "a great despairing cry for love"[13] and also with the view that an inability to mourn is an expression of an inability to tolerate being in a position of weakness and supplication.

In "Separation Anxiety"[14] I pointed out that loss of the mother in infancy poses very special stresses, since she is the person to whom the infant turns in all situations of anxiety. We can now add that she is also the person to whom he turns in all situations of sorrow and grief. Thus her loss can be seen as the cause not only of his anxiety and its going unmet but often also of his grief and his going unconsoled.

The fifth theme on our list and one of the most important concerns *the role of anger and hatred in mourning*. Although all are agreed that anger with the lost object (often unconscious and directed elsewhere) plays a major role in pathological mourning, there appears to be some doubt whether or not its presence is compatible with healthy mourning. Freud's position is not altogether consistent. On the one hand are many passages in which he makes it clear that in his view all relationships are characterized by ambivalence;* and a corollary of this would seem to be that ambivalence must enter into all forms of mourning also. On the other, however, is the view, expressed in *Mourning and Melancholia* and so far as I know never revised, that ambivalence is absent in normal mourning and, when present, transforms what would otherwise have been normal into pathological mourning: "Melancholia . . . is marked by a determinant which is absent in normal mourning or which, if it is present, transforms the latter into pathological mourning. The loss of a love-object is an excellent opportunity for the ambivalence in love-relationships to make itself effective." "Melancholia contains something more than normal mourning . . . the relation to the object is no simple one; it is complicated by the conflict due to ambivalence."[18]

I do not think the evidence regarding normal mourning supports this view. In the first place there can be no doubt that anger expressed in one direction or another is the rule. In the preceding paper reference was made to the observations of Lindemann[19] and Marris.[20] Eliot[21] also refers to it. Anthropological literature presents evidence either of the direct expression of anger, for example by the Australian aboriginals,[22] or of special social sanctions against expressing it.† Shand[23] does not hesitate to generalize: "The tendency of sorrow to arouse anger under certain conditions appears

* E.g. "Up to a point ambivalence of feeling of this sort appears to be normal." "This ambivalence is present to a greater or less amount in the innate disposition of everyone." "The unconscious of all human beings is full enough of such death wishes, even against those they love."[17]
† I am indebted to Dr. George Krupp for these two references.

to be part of the fundamental constitution of the mind." In the second place, there is reason to think that some part of this anger is commonly, if not always, directed towards the lost object.

The anger appears to have two main objectives: anger against those believed to have been responsible for the loss, and anger against those who seem to impede reunion. Although there may be many other individuals (including himself) who seem to the bereaved to be guilty in one or other of these respects, it is plain that the lost object is almost always sensed as being in some degree responsible also. This means that anger directed against the lost loved object is practically inevitable and universal.

There are probably many analysts who have long since adopted this view. Even so the mistaken distinction between healthy and pathological mourning drawn by Freud in his early formulations has lingered on in psycho-analytic theory. Examples are to be found in papers by Bibring[24] and Edith Jacobson[25] which are discussed later. The problem in understanding pathological mourning, it seems, is that of understanding not the simple presence of hostility directed against the lost object but its repression and/or displacement towards other objects, including the self. An understanding of its presence is made easier when we recognize that, of the several different and incompatible responses to loss of object, anger is one of the most frequent. I see it as a direct result of the frustration caused by loss and, in cases of separation other than those caused by bereavement, as having useful functions, namely those of overcoming such obstacles as there may be to reunion and of discouraging the object from straying away again. Looked at as a means that in other circumstances aids the recovery of the lost object and the maintenance of union with it, the anger characteristic of mourning can be seen to be biologically useful.

As already noted, this point of view is consistent with Freud's own formulations regarding the ubiquity of ambivalence. It is in keeping too with certain of the views he expressed in *Instincts and their Vicissitudes* (1915), e.g. his observation that "if a love relation with a given object is broken off, hate not infrequently emerges in its place."[26] Insofar however as Freud in this and other papers holds that "hate, as a relation to objects, is older than love" (*ibid.*) there are differences. The work of ethologists (e.g. Hinde, Thorpe, and Vince[27]) shows that in other species, if a positive relationship does not develop before fear or aggression become active, it is unlikely ever to do so. This leads me to think that in human beings also either a positive attachment to an object precedes hatred of it or else the two develop simultaneously. Indeed, a main function of anger directed towards the loved object seems to be to effect reunion with the object when separation threatens or occurs. Although when carried beyond a certain point it may defeat its own purpose, in moderate degree it promotes it. Whether it be wife, husband, or child, the individual who behaves like a doormat is more likely to be abandoned often or for ever than one who protests vigorously and on occasion expresses his rage.

The systematic discussion of our sixth theme, *the differences between healthy and pathological mourning*, will be postponed until a following paper. Although Freud in *Mourning and Melancholia* proposed at least three such differences, I do not find any of them satisfactory criteria.

The first difference suggested by Freud, that the presence of hatred for the lost object (expressed either directly or, indirectly, through self-reproach) betokens pathology has already been referred to, and discarded as out of keeping with the evidence. His second, that identification with the lost object is present only in pathological mourning, he abandoned a few years after he had proposed it (*The Ego and the Id*, 1923) because he himself found that it also is not in accordance with the evidence. His third is that one form of pathological mourning, namely melancholia, differs from healthy mourning in the disposition of the libido; in healthy mourning the libido that is withdrawn from the lost object is transferred to a new one, whereas in melancholia it is withdrawn into the ego and gives rise to secondary narcissism. Apart from this hypothesis being cast in a form of theorizing which I find unsatisfactory, it omits reference to the persistent though disguised striving to recover the lost object which is often at the root of the illness. In my next paper I shall try to show that some at least of the observed features of depressive illness and related conditions can be more satisfactorily explained in terms of the theory I am proposing.

Nor do I find Melanie Klein's approach satisfactory. Whilst I share her view that differences between healthy and pathological mourning are probably matters of degree rather than of kind, I doubt whether there is evidence to support her hypothesis that the anxieties to which loss of object habitually gives rise are to be equated with the early psychotic anxieties of her theoretical system. Nor for reasons already given do I find it necessary to attribute the anger both she and I recognize as always present in mourning either to the direct expression of the death instinct or to a reaction to the feelings of persecution which she believes arise from the very early projection of the death instinct.

My own approach to this issue is the same as that of

Lindemann who, in relating to their healthy counterparts the various morbid processes of mourning that he describes, regards them as exaggerations and caricatures of the normal processes. The more detailed the picture we obtain of healthy mourning, the more clearly are we able to identify the pathological variants of it as being the result of defensive processes having partially interfered with its progress. Many sufferers from pathological mourning, I believe, have become fixated in the first phase of the mourning process and, without knowing it, are striving still to recover the object that has been lost.

In his appraisal of acute grief Lindemann writes as though it were itself an illness. Melanie Klein takes the same view, claiming that "the mourner is in fact ill."[28] The justification for conceiving grief in this way has recently been considered by Engel,[29] who advances cogent arguments in its favour. "The experience of uncomplicated grief," he writes, "represents a manifest and gross departure from the dynamic state considered representative of health and well-being. . . . It involves suffering and an impairment of the capacity to function, which may last for days, weeks, or even months. We can identify a consistent etiologic factor, namely, real, threatened, or even fantasied object loss. It fulfills all the criteria of a discrete syndrome, with relatively predictable symptomatology and course." The concept of disease is therefore as appropriately applied to the results of a loss as it is to the results of a wound, a burn, or an infection.

I believe this to be a useful way of approaching the problem. Once the mourner is seen as being in a state of biological disequilibrium brought about by a sudden change in the environment, the processes at work and the conditions that influence their course can be made the subject of systematic study, in the same way that they have been studied for wounds, burns, and infections. What follows is an attempt to formulate a theory of mourning in these terms.

This raises our seventh and final problem: *At what stage of development and by means of what processes does the individual arrive at a state which enables him thereafter to respond to loss in a favourable manner?* Traditionally this question has been raised in the context of trying to understand the fixation point to which melancholics regress during their illness. Most psycho-analytic formulations postulate the phase as occurring in earliest infancy and carry with them the corollary that the capacity to respond to loss in a favourable manner should, if all goes well with development, be attained in this very early period. Following Melanie Klein, this critical phase of psychic development is now often known as the "depressive position."

An early dating of this phase of development, however, is open to much doubt. The evidence suggests that the capacity to react to loss in such a way that in course of time a resumption of object relationships can take place is one which develops very slowly during childhood and may perhaps never be as fully attained as we like to believe. The nature of the psychological processes at work and the conditions necessary for their favourable development require much more study than has yet been given them.

This completes our brief review of some of the main themes needing consideration in any discussion of mourning. What is impressive about mourning is not only the number and variety of response systems which are engaged but the way in which they tend to conflict with one another. Loss of loved object gives rise not only to an intensified desire for reunion but to hatred of the object, and, later, to detachment from it; it gives rise not only to a cry for help but to a rejection of those who respond to it. No wonder it is painful to experience and difficult to understand. As Shand rightly concludes: "The nature of sorrow is so complex, its effects in different characters so various, that it is rare, if not impossible, for any writer to show an insight into all of them."

Development of Psycho-Analytical Theories of Mourning

Only four psycho-analysts—Freud, Melanie Klein, Lindemann, and Edith Jacobson—seem to have given sustained attention to the psychology of mourning. The review is therefore in great part confined to their contributions.

As psychological processes in their own right grief and mourning were never at the centre of Freud's interest: only when he was concerned to elucidate certain other problems to which they seemed relevant did he turn to their examination. Thus *Totem and Taboo* (1913) is an enquiry into "some unsolved problems of social psychology"; *Mourning and Melancholia,* completed in 1915 and published two years later, is the study of an illness; *Inhibitions, Symptoms and Anxiety* (1926), which is more theoretical in outlook, is a re-examination of the problem not of grief but of anxiety. Freud's own views on grief and mourning as they occur in adults who are not mentally sick must be gleaned, therefore, in fields he cultivated for other purposes.

Freud's description of the task of mourning remains consistent throughout his work: "Mourning has a quite precise psychical task to perform: its function is to detach the survivor's memories and hopes from the dead"[30] Two years later he is writing: "Reality-testing has shown that the loved object no longer exists, and it proceeds to demand that all libido shall be withdrawn from its attachment to that object. This demand arouses understandable opposition . . . [which] can be so intense that a turning away from reality takes place . . . normally [however] respect for reality gains the day . . ." Finally, he suggests, there is "a withdrawal of the libido from this object and a displacement of it on to a new one."[31] The same formulation appears in *Inhibitions, Symptoms and Anxiety:* "Mourning is entrusted with the task of carrying out this retreat from the object in all those situations in which it was the recipient of a high degree of cathexis."[32]

In these accounts the pain of mourning is clearly regarded as an unavoidable accompaniment of the persistent and insatiable yearning for the lost object. In *Mourning and Melancholia,* after describing the conflict between the desire to maintain the old libidinal position and the demands of reality that it be abandoned, he proceeds: "Why this compromise by which the command of reality is carried out piecemeal should be so extraordinarily painful is not at all easy to explain in terms of economics. It is remarkable that [it] is taken as matter of course by us."[33] Later he conjectures an explanation: "Each single one of the memories and situations of expectancy which demonstrate the libido's attachment to the lost object is met by the verdict of reality that the object no longer exists; and the ego . . . is persuaded by the sum of the narcissistic satisfactions it derives from being alive to sever its attachment to the object that has been abolished" (p. 255).

In the final paragraphs of *Inhibitions, Symptoms, and Anxiety* he returns to the problem and arrives at the same conclusion. In likening the pain of mourning to that of bodily injury, he emphasizes the unappeasable character of bereaved longing and "the continuous nature of the cathectic process" which occurs after bodily injury and "the impossibility of inhibiting it." Each, he believes, produces "the same state of mental helplessness." That the retreat from the object which is necessary in mourning "should be painful," he concludes, "fits in with what we have just said, in view of the high and unsatisfiable cathexis of longing which is concentrated on the object by the bereaved person."[34]

That remorse and guilt frequently accompany mourning and lead to pathological depression and melancholia was known to Freud as early as 1897 (see Editor's Note by Strachey[35]), and is elaborated in *Totem and Taboo*[36] before providing a main strand in his theory of melancholia. His contrasts between mourning and melancholia make it clear, however, that he did not regard guilt as responsible for all the pain of mourning: "The disturbance of self-regard is absent in mourning."[37] In Freud's view, the pain of yearning is one thing, the misery of self-reproach another.

As regards the process of libidinal withdrawal from a lost object Freud in his later works came to the conclusion that this is commonly if not always accomplished by means of the ego identifying with the lost object: "When it happens that a person has to give up a sexual object, there quite often ensues a modification in his ego which can only be described as a reinstatement of the object within the ego . . .; the exact nature of this substitution is as yet unknown to us" (*The Ego and the Id* (1923), p. 36). "If one has lost a love object or has had to give it up, one often compensates oneself by identifying oneself with it" (*New Introductory Lectures* (1933) p. 86). This hypothesis had been adumbrated first in *Mourning and Melancholia* in order to account for the criti-

cisms which melancholic patients direct against themselves.
Freud had recognized that those criticisms often represent
criticisms initially directed towards the lost object and now
displaced on to the self. To account for this displacement he
had advanced the hypothesis that, instead of "a withdrawal
of the libido from this object and a displacement of it on to
a new one, . . . the free libido . . . was withdrawn into the
ego. There, however, it was not employed in any unspecified
way, but served to establish an *identification* of the ego with
the abandoned object."[38] Later this theory of identification
with the lost object was applied to cover normal as well as
pathological mourning.

One other feature of Freud's theory of melancholia is
of importance in understanding subsequent developments in
the theory of mourning: it is his emphasis on orality which,
Jones tells us, was due to the influence of Abraham.[39] Having postulated that in melancholia there is "a *regression* from
one type of object-choice to original narcissism" and having
previously linked primary narcissism with the oral phase, he
proceeds to refer to "this regression from object-cathexis to
the still narcissistic oral phase of the libido."[40] From this
source, through Abraham and Rado, stems much of Melanie
Klein's theorizing about the depressive position.

It is necessary at this point to distinguish between
Freud's clinical observations and the theory he advanced to
explain them. After a loved object has been lost, for whatever reason, criticism of the object and of the self he found
to be common; so is the tendency to identify with the lost
object. In melancholia, moreover, oral symptoms, such as
anorexia, are common. These observations, of course, are now
well confirmed. To explain them, however, Freud made use
of three hypotheses none of which I believe well-based—

namely the hydrodynamic theory of instinct, the hypothesis
that narcissism is primary and precedes object relations, and
the view that in melancholia there is regression to a narcissistic oral phase. Because of these differences of outlook,
therefore, the theory of mourning, healthy and pathological,
which I am advancing, differs at many points from Freud's.
Nevertheless there are also many points of identity. In particular the insatiable and persistent yearning for the lost
object, to which Freud repeatedly draws attention, is a feature of mourning that I believe to be of central importance
in understanding its psychopathology.

Abraham has little to say in regard to normal grief and
mourning. His early paper on melancholia,[41] although it advanced the view that the depressive psychosis is a pathological variant of grief, does not discuss the nature of grief itself. The main theme is that "the disease proceeded from an
attitude of hate which was paralysing the patient's capacity
to love,"[42] and that what is mourned is not the loss of object
but of the capacity to love. That this is his theory is made
explicit in his later paper on *The First Pregenital Stage*.[43]
Indeed in this second paper, although he again discusses depression and melancholia, attention is focused on orality,
and there is no mention of loss of object or of grief and
mourning. Only in his long study on *The Development of
the Libido*[44] is there a brief reference to our problem, and
here, in stressing identification, he does no more than follow
Freud: "The process of mourning thus brings with it the
consolation: 'My loved object is not gone, for now I carry it
within myself and can never lose it.' "[45]

Nor is there much discussion of mourning in the works
of Anna Freud except, as we have already noted, in her
clinical descriptions of young children undergoing separa-

tion from their mothers. As regards the pain of mourning her reference to the "natural pain of separation [which turns] into an intense longing which is hard to bear"[46] endorses Freud's view that ungratified yearning is itself painful.

It is a paradox that, whereas Anna Freud and Spitz have recorded valuable first-hand observations of grief and mourning in infants and young children but have contributed little to our understanding of theory, Melanie Klein has recorded no such observations but, having assumed the primacy of object relations, has recognized how crucial infantile experiences of grief and mourning are for personality development and has developed much valuable theory around it. Nevertheless, by concentrating attention almost exclusively on experiences of the early months, especially weaning, and by giving primacy to persecutory anxiety and regarding separation anxiety as secondary, much of her theorizing seems to me less useful than it would otherwise have been.

At a number of points the concept of mourning that Melanie Klein advances in her paper *Mourning and its Relation to Manic-Depressive States*[47] resembles that advanced here. Thus, she sees mourning as a phase of disorganization and of subsequent reorganization, and its painfulness as their consequence: "The pain experienced in the slow process of testing reality in the work of mourning thus seems to be partly due to the necessity, not only to renew the links to the external world and thus continuously to reexperience the loss, but at the same time and by means of this to rebuild with anguish the inner world, which is felt to be in danger of deteriorating and collapsing." The mourner, she believes, then has the task and must go through the pain of "re-establishing and re-integrating" his inner world. Further, our way of responding to the loss of a loved object in later life, she believes, is patterned on the way we responded to similar experiences which we may have had in infancy and early childhood; our mode of reorganizing our object relations subsequently will be in large part determined by the measure of success we achieved when doing so on these earlier occasions. This is a principle to which I attach great importance.

Controversy arises when Melanie Klein comes to specify the nature of the experiences of loss and grief in early life which are of consequence and the processes which constitute mourning. Like Freud, she approached the problem of mourning mainly through the study of depressive illness. Furthermore, she seems to have accepted without much criticism many of the theories regarding this condition which were current at the time she began her work. As a result not only is her theory of normal mourning cast in a mould of theory originally advanced to account for psychosis, but the theory in question is one which was elaborated at a time before the existence of the phase during which the child is attached to his mother had been clearly recognized. Most of the features which in my judgment are most controversial stem from her acceptance of views advanced during the twenties by Abraham and Rado. They include, first, great emphasis on orality, breast-feeding, and weaning, and, secondly, they postulate that in the infant's development paranoid anxieties precede depressive. The latter view leads directly to the conclusion that the pain of grief is inevitably shot through with persecutory anxiety and guilt.

Let us examine the roots of Melanie Klein's theory of mourning more closely. As is well known, Abraham had postulated that depressive psychosis represents a regression to a fixation point in the phase of oral sadism. This suggestion was elaborated by Rado[48] and it is his ideas which, in her paper *The Psychogenesis of Manic Depressive States*,[49] Melanie Klein singles out for approbation. The full passage, in which she twice quotes from Rado, reads thus: "Sandor Rado has pointed out that 'the deepest fixation point in the depressive disposition is to be found in the situation of threatened loss of love (Freud) more especially in the hunger situation of the suckling baby.' Referring to Freud's statement that in mania the ego is once more merged with the superego in unity, Rado comes to the conclusion that 'this process is the faithful intrapsychic repetition of the experience of that fusion with the mother that takes place during drinking at her breast.' I agree with these statements" adds Melanie Klein.[50] It is this line of thought which, fortifying ideas she already held, led her to give a central role to the experiences of breast-feeding and weaning and to the process of oral introjection as bases for identification.

The other line of thought which is also to be traced to the influence of Abraham and Rado is that paranoid anxiety is extremely primitive. Basing his argument on somewhat speculative premises, Abraham had postulated that paranoia stems from an earlier fixation point than does melancholia. Therefore, he argued, if the roots of melancholia are to be found somewhere in the oral phase, an even earlier part of the oral phase for the roots of paranoia must be searched for. Carrying this line of thought one step further, Melanie Klein advances the view, as we have already seen when discussing separation anxiety, that the infant comes into the world burdened with persecutory anxiety.

The outcome of this train of thought is that Melanie Klein sees the child's relation to his mother largely as a defence against paranoid anxiety, and loss of her as specially serious because it lets loose once more these persecutory anxieties. A warning, however, is necessary. The impression so often given by Melanie Klein that the pain of loss is *nothing but* the result of guilt and fear is probably unintended and misleading. In describing a male patient unable to experience sorrow, she reports that "he could not bear the fear of losing his *loved* mother" and how, during analysis, "he increasingly experienced the grief and longing for her which he had repressed and denied from his early days onwards" (p. 336). Earlier in the same paper she refers to the need for the ego "to develop methods of defence which are essentially directed against the 'pining' for the lost object" (p. 316). This view of defence is one I share.

The upshot is that, whilst grief and longing are recognized by Melanie Klein as in themselves painful, they are held never to occur alone; paranoid fear and guilt at having been responsible for the object's destruction are always present as well: "In my experience this fear of the total loss of the good object (internalized and external) is interwoven with feelings of guilt at having destroyed her (eaten her up), and then the child feels that her loss is a punishment for his dreadful deed: thus the most distressing and conflicting feelings become associated with frustration, and it is these which make the pain of what seems like a simple thwarting so poignant."[51]

In the preceding paper reasons were given for doubting the significance Melanie Klein attributes to the experience of weaning and to the very early months. In the next section of this one, where mourning responses in animals are discussed, reasons will be given for questioning the central role she attributes to guilt and remorse in the mourning process.

Here we will consider further the place she gives to persecutory anxiety.

In founding her whole theoretical structure on the assumption that paranoid anxiety is extremely primitive, Klein, it must be repeated, is doing no more than following a line of theorizing originating with Abraham and continued amongst others by Rado[52] and Glover,[53] all of whom have held the view that paranoia stems from an earlier fixation point than does melancholia. Their argument is, however, essentially theoretical and speculative, and Balint[54] has already given reasons for doubting the conclusions to which it leads.

First, he argues that, since clinical observation shows that both paranoid and depressive states have many narcissistic features and since there is much evidence (which Melanie Klein herself accepts) that narcissism is usually, probably always, a secondary and pathological state resulting from frustration in the love relationship, it is reasonable to conclude that both paranoid and depressive processes are themselves secondary and reactive to such experiences.[55] Later Balint seeks to assess the functional value of the phases of development termed respectively by Melanie Klein the depressive and the paranoid positions. These he evaluates very differently. As regards the depressive position he writes: "If we accept the view that a real adaptation—the acceptance of unpleasure—is only possible [providing] one can face depression without undue anxiety, then the depressive position must be considered as a . . . focus through which every line of development associated with adaptation must pass." The paranoid position, on the other hand, seems to him to have no such functional status. He therefore concludes that "the depressive position must be considered more fundamental, more primitive, than the paranoid" (p. 264).

In the upshot the sequence of healthy development that he postulates is, first, a phase of primary object-relationship in which there is "no fear . . . only naive confidence and unsuspicious self-abandonment" (p. 260) and, secondly, a phase after the depressive position has been reached during which the individual can face disappointment and depression without undue anxiety. Narcissism and paranoid attitudes he regards as pathological variants brought about by unfavourable experiences in the primary relationship: "Often we discover that the patient's early environment was anything but loving."

A sequence of this kind seems to me more likely. In my judgment far better evidence than has yet been advanced has to be presented before we can reasonably accept the hypothesis that paranoid anxieties are primary and that mourning and depression are inevitably shot through with feelings of persecution and guilt. My scepticism is strengthened by the fragments of knowledge we have regarding the mourning behavior of lower species. It is considerations such as these that lead me to be doubtful of much in Melanie Klein's concept of the depressive position.

Very many other analysts have written extensively on depressive illness, and in so doing some have discussed grief and mourning also.

In a recent paper on normal and pathological moods, Edith Jacobson[56] sets herself the task of studying the nature of moods and, in the course of it, draws a sharp distinction between sadness and depression as responses to the loss of something valued. She begins with two generalizations that I believe to be well founded: first that following loss there are two common reactions, a yearning to regain the lost object and a tendency towards aggression; secondly, that the balance of these two reactions varies greatly from individual to individual and that on this balance turns whether the response remains healthy or becomes pathological. The way she proceeds, however, and in particular her contention that aggression is absent from grief, I regard as open to criticism.

Much in her argument turns on her definitions of the terms "sadness," "depression," and "grief." "Sadness" she defines as a response to loss which is free of aggression. "Unlike depression," she writes, "sadness as such does not involve an aggressive conflict, either with external reality or endopsychically." "Sadness presupposes the presence of sufficient object-libidinous cathexes," and "a preoccupation with the happy experiences of the past . . . combined with painful desires to gain or regain them." Whenever aggression is present, she holds, the mood should no longer be termed sadness but "depression." Thus far it is only a matter of terms, but a difficulty soon arises. For in the context it seems clear that by "depression" Edith Jacobson has in mind a mood that is in some degree pathological*; and a corollary of this is that the presence of aggression following loss is regarded by her as in some degree pathological also. This seems mistaken.

In a discussion of grief and mourning, however, a more serious criticism of Edith Jacobson's position arises as a result of her defining "grief" as a special case of sadness.†

---

* In a footnote to her paper Edith Jacobson points to some disagreement with the views of Edward Bibring.[57] Much of the disagreement, however, seems less one of substance than one that arises from different uses of the term "depression." Whereas for Edith Jacobson the term seems to imply a pathological state, Bibring uses it in a way similar to that in which it is used here.

† "Since the term 'grief' singles out but a particular prolonged and profound state of sadness caused by the loss of a love object, I prefer not to restrict our study to the state of grief but to extend it to sadness in general."

For, having already defined sadness as free of both aggression and conflict, she inevitably reaches a definition of grief that makes it free of both these disagreeable characteristics also. Not only is this definition out of keeping with common observation and usage, but it makes for difficulty in understanding the relation of healthy grief and mourning to their pathological variants. The evidence seems to me clear that the common reaction to loss of a loved object comprehends both of the responses to loss that Edith Jacobson refers to, namely both the sorrowful yearning for happiness lost, often expressed in weeping, and also the aggression and conflict which she excludes from grief and identifies with depression. Indeed, it is this mixture of feeling which makes mourning so painful and also that makes it so liable to give rise to pathology.

Nevertheless, even though I do not find Edith Jacobson's terminology and concept of grief satisfactory, there is much in her point of view that I value. This includes her emphasis on the yearning to regain the lost object as integral to sadness and grief, and also her postulate that the happier the relationship with the lost object has been the easier it is for the bereaved to experience sadness and the less does aggression intrude to create conflict and difficulty. "An increase of aggression in the cathexes of the self and the world, that would lead to either angry or depressed mood," she writes, "is prevented by the previous memories of a happy past and of a previously rich self." Furthermore, in contrast to Melanie Klein, Edith Jacobson regards grief and sadness as moods independent of the guilt that so often complicates them: "Inasmuch as the sad person cherishes his past, he will feel deprived, but not bad and worthless or empty."

As in the case of many analysts, the main interest of

Bibring[58] is in depression and his reference to grief is short. Depression he sees as arising within the ego itself owing to its "shocking awareness of its helplessness in regard to its aspirations," that is, its inability to achieve its aspirations. Grief he regards as a special case of such helplessness; in this case the aspiration which cannot be achieved is the regaining of the lost object. In the "uncomplicated grief reaction," he maintains, there are only two components: the wish to regain the lost object and the experience of being helpless to do so. Though he takes a different route, Bibring's omission of aggression as an unavoidable ingredient of grief leads him to a conclusion similar to that of Edith Jacobson.

It is perhaps strange that, although as early as his *Studies on Hysteria* (1893-95) Freud had noted the relation of neurotic symptoms to bereavement and mourning,[59] fifty years were to elapse before a psycho-analyst undertook a systematic first-hand study of responses to bereavement as they commonly occur. The resulting paper by Lindemann[60] shows how immensely valuable for the progress of psychopathology such first-hand studies can be. As yet, however, I believe only part of its value to have been realized; not until there has been a thorough reconsideration of the theory of mourning and its relation to psychiatric illness in the light of his findings will the full harvest of his work be garnered.

By means of a series of psychiatric interviews on one hundred subjects, Lindemann made observations on the symptomatology and course of normal grief. In addition to his picture of the usual responses to be seen in this condition (on which I have drawn heavily both for this and the preceding paper), Lindemann described a number of deviations from the normal. These deviations he held to be due to shifts either in the timing of the whole syndrome or in the intensity of component parts of it. The syndrome of acute grief, he reports, "may appear immediately after a crisis; it may be delayed; it may be exaggerated or apparently absent. In place of the typical syndrome there may appear distorted pictures, each of which represents one special aspect of the grief syndrome." On the nature of the processes at work and of the conditions that determine which of these variants is manifested he touches, however, only briefly, and it is in these areas that his account seems to need most expansion.

Before making a fresh attempt to advance a theory of mourning, it is useful to review what is known of the responses to loss that are exhibited by animals.

The Occurrence of Mourning Behaviour in Animals

In the preceding paper it was demonstrated that overt responses to loss of loved object are similar in human infants and children to what they are in human adults. Here it will be shown that the responses of the higher animals conform to the same pattern. In theories of mourning this fact seems to have been overlooked, and on it, it is held, much turns.

Whereas in recent years much attention has been given by ethologists to the dynamics of mother-offspring relations and of sexual pair formation, unfortunately little or no systematic study has been devoted as yet to responses following rupture of these powerful bonds. As a result we are dependent on casual observation and anecdote. Nevertheless the high consensus in such records as are available suggests that the general picture that emerges is valid.

Though it would be possible to draw on a wider range

of animal species, I shall confine myself to two species of birds (jackdaws and geese), one of lower mammals (the domestic dog), and to two species of anthropoid apes (orang-utans and chimpanzees). The selection is governed partly by scientific requirements and partly by what is available. For scientific purposes it is useful to use both a low-power lens to review more than one order of animal and also a high-power one to look especially at the behaviour of man's nearest relatives. As regards availability, Lorenz happens to have recorded mourning responses in jackdaws, geese, and dogs, whilst the only accounts of primates I have found are concerned with orangs and chimpanzees.

The first impression we receive on reading these accounts is of the similarity of the responses to loss, both to each other and to those in man, that are exhibited by these different creatures. Behaviour designed to recover the lost object, followed by or coupled with withdrawal, apathy, and a rejection of potential new objects is the rule. Increased hostility is not reported for the two species of bird, but is a prominent feature in the behaviour of dogs and apes.

Lorenz has reported behaviour in both jackdaws and geese which he believes "certainly corresponds to grief." For instance, one winter all the members of his jackdaw colony escaped from their cage. Three days later one adult female returned. Her subsequent behaviour, however, suggested that in the absence of her mate she was lonely and sad. At first she repeatedly gave the "Kiaw" call, which has the function of uniting separated birds, and occasionally flew down to the meadows as though in search of her mate and other members of the flock. Later she was inactive and her calls subdued.[61]

In a personal communication Lorenz has described the

behaviour exhibited by a greylag goose which has lost its mate. At first there is a frantic searching and calling. Later this gives way to "depression," though the searching may be renewed in spring. In the phase of depression, there is a lack of energy, movements are slow, eyes seem smaller (because less protruding), feathers are loose and slightly fluffed,* head and neck are carried less erect, and there is a noticeably decreased readiness to fly. "These deserted solitary geese also show a decreased readiness for any social contact. They are generally ignored by other geese. Grief-stricken widows of this type are hardly ever courted by males, even if a quite considerable shortage of females prevails in the goose society. . . . The general picture of grief is just as clearly marked in a widowed goose as it is in a dog."

The distress of dogs who have lost a master to whom they are strongly attached is well known. Either they remain rooted to the spot where they last saw him or they search frantically for him. Subsequently they are bewildered and restless. Sometimes they became savage. This occurred with Stasi, a female mongrel of chow and Alsatian ancestry which Lorenz had bred. At seven months he began to train her, but a couple of months later he had to be away and left her at home. Her behaviour during this separation (of four months' duration) is not recorded, but on reunion she was in "a frenzy of joy." When after a few weeks, however, he began

---

* These observations of eyes and plumage in a bereaved goose bear a striking resemblance to observations made independently by Robertson of young children during short stays in hospital. He has records (unpublished) of how the eyes of young patients seem to go small and narrow and their hair lank and lifeless; and how, after return home, it takes a day or two for the hair to recover its former life and texture and the complexion to resume its bloom. A "lamp seemed to have lit up inside" is how he recorded his impression of a recovered child whom he had last seen in hospital.

to prepare for a second departure "the dog became noticeably depressed and refused to leave my side for an instant. With nervous haste, she sprang up and followed every time I left the room, even accompanying me to the bathroom." At parting she became desperate; and in the weeks following this second separation she became an unruly delinquent dog. She roamed restlessly about the district, was no longer house-trained, and refused to obey anybody. She also became increasingly ferocious.[62]

Two other features with which we are familiar in young human children who have experienced loss through separation are also to be observed in dogs. One is, during the initial phase of protest, a refusal to accept comfort or food from another person. In a recent newspaper report* it is recorded how a collie guide-dog-for-the-blind, when lost for 15 hours, ran frantically through London seeking his master, howled continuously on being caught and cared for by the police, and refused all food until his master came to recover him. A second is an inability to respond to the loved object, mother or master, on reunion. Lorenz has recorded that "the most sensitive and the most trusting dogs refuse to recognize their masters when they come to fetch them after a period of absence,"† and it is to him that I am indebted for reference to an account given of such behaviour by Thomas Mann.[64]

Bashan was a male mongrel which Mann had acquired at the age of 6 months and who for two years had formed a very strong attachment to him. Bashan developed a complaint and, since the cause was obscure, Mann placed him

* *Evening Standard,* 3 June, 1959.
† See Lorenz's contributions to the discussion of Robertson's film *A Two-year-old Goes to Hospital* in Tanner and Inhelder.[63]

for two weeks with a vet. When visited at the end of a week Bashan "lay there like a leopard, though a very weary disappointed leopard. I was shocked by the sullen indifference with which he greeted my entrance and advance." The attendant explained he had howled for the first twenty-four hours and then had "got used to things." On leaving again, Mann reports, "I made another attempt to cheer up Bashan's spirits by talking to him. But he was as little affected by my going away as by my coming." At the end of another week Mann decided to remove him. Bashan "lay upon his side, stretched out in a posture of absolute indifference. . . . He was staring backward . . . with eyes that were glassy and dull. . . . He paid no attention to me, and it seemed that he would never again be able to summon up enough energy to take an interest in anything. . . . We both called Bashan by name, alternately and both together—but he did not stir. He merely kept staring at the whitewashed wall opposite. He made no resistance when I thrust my arm into the cage and pulled him out by the collar. . . . There he stood with his tail between his legs, his ears retracted, a very picture of misery."

The misery and bad temper of the anthropoid apes when bereft of loved companions is now well recognized. Not only do they take every precaution possible to prevent being separated from a loved object, but when this occurs, at least when young, they respond much like a human child. First, Yerkes[65] reports, there is protest: "Taken forcibly from companion or group and left alone, the ape cries, screams, rages, struggles desperately to escape and return to its fellows. Such behaviour may last for hours. All the bodily functions may be more or less upset." Later there is depression and troublesome, unpredictable behaviour. Withdrawal, restlessness, a rejection of other individuals, and all the signs of depression are to be seen.

For instance the behaviour of Cleo, a female orang in the Berlin Zoo, after the loss of her husband is described by Zedtwitz.[66] Cleo behaved as though she was ill. She lay apathetically in her sleeping box or rolled up in a blanket, or else sat inert under the heating lamp. A month after she had lost her husband she gave birth to an infant; she was unmotherly towards the baby, however, and neglected it. Nevertheless, when, after being a widow for 18 months, she was introduced to a new husband she settled down with him fairly quickly.

At the Orange Park Primate Laboratories it has been observed that there is a marked response when a chimpanzee loses a companion, either chimpanzee or human, to whom it is attached. There is reduced activity and appetite, leading to loss of weight. Some animals are restless and may pick at their flesh and so cause bleeding. They also seem more prone to pick up infections, and occasionally even a death is believed to have resulted (personal communication from the late Dr. Henry Nissen).*

The urge to recover the lost object as the first response

---

* Pollock,[67] in a paper in which he has independently drawn attention to the mourning behaviour of animals, has quoted extensively from a paper by Brown (dated 1879) in which the responses of a male chimpanzee to the death of his mate are recorded. Points of special interest are his repeated efforts to arouse her, the yells of rage and accompanying anger, expressed at times by snatching at the short hairs of his head, the subsequent crying and moaning, and the tendency later to become more attached to his keeper and more angry when the keeper left him than he had been hitherto. Levy[68] has drawn attention to the report by Tinkelpaugh[69] of the responses of a male rhesus monkey, Cupid, first to the loss of his mate, and, later, to seeing her again. He bit himself repeatedly and severely, became restless and agitated, would not eat, and withdrew contact both from his second mate and his human attendants.

to loss is well-illustrated by an observation (made by a fellow of the Royal Society) which, when quoted by Romanes,[70] caught the eye of Freud.* After a female monkey had been shot and her body collected, a male "came to the door of the tent and, finding threats of no avail, began a lamentable moaning, and by the most expressive gestures seemed to beg for the dead body. It was given him; he took it sorrowfully in his arms and bore it away to his expecting companions."

It is unfortunate that reports in the literature are still so scrappy. Often one feature only, for example misery or bad temper, is mentioned, and we are left to guess whether the other features of mourning were present also or not. Loss of a particular loved individual is not differentiated from complete social isolation. Age is not treated systematically. Nevertheless the picture of mourning that emerges resembles that with which we are familiar in human beings, young and old, sufficiently that systematic study would plainly be rewarding. If the experimenter could bring himself deliberately to disrupt love relationships at suitable ages and perhaps repeatedly, it seems more than likely that neurotic conditions, psychosomatic ailments, and character deviations closely resembling those met with in human beings could be produced. As regards character disorders, Yerkes has warned us that the behavioural sequence following social isolation of chimpanzees during late infancy and early childhood "is profoundly significant for the understanding of chimpanzee nature. . . . Hitherto this violent reaction against social deprivation often has been attributed

* Freud's marked copy of Romanes's book is now in the library of the Psychiatric Institute of the College of Physicians and Surgeons of Columbia University.

to wilfulness, contrariness, bad temper, uncooperativeness, timidity, or fear, instead of to a compelling unsatisfied social need."[71] Students of human nature also have often made this mistake.

These records of mourning behaviour in sub-human species, fragmentary though they are, seem to make it fairly certain that each of the main behavioural features which we have listed as characteristics of mourning behaviour is in essential outline shared by man with lower animals. Members of lower species protest at the loss of a loved object and do all in their power to seek and recover it; hostility, externally directed, is frequent; withdrawal, rejection of a potential new object, apathy and restlessness are the rule. Furthermore, given time and opportunity, a reorganization of behaviour in connexion with a new object and recovery often follow. This does not mean that there are no features specific to human beings—obviously there are. But, methodologically, I believe we shall be wise in the next phase of psychoanalytical theorizing to identify first those features of human mourning that are shared with other species and only then to attempt a description of those that are specific. For the former it is sensible to seek explanations that invoke only those processes which can plausibly be credited to lower species: features seen only in man will probably require us to postulate more complex processes.

What features then, it may be asked, seem to be specific to man? Those which first suggested themselves to me were: the persistence over months and years of behaviour organized and oriented towards the lost object, the presence of hostility directed towards the self, and the tendency to identify with the lost object. It is doubtful, however, whether either the first or the second can be so regarded.

Lorenz's reports of mourning behaviour continuing over many months in birds and dogs cast doubt on the first.* The evidence of Yerkes[73] and Tinkelpaugh[74] regarding the aggression that young primates vent upon themselves casts doubt upon the second.† Only the tendency to identify with the lost object remains a possible. Not until much more systematic studies of mourning behaviour in sub-human primates are available than we have at present will it be possible to reach firm conclusions.

Three Phases of Mourning

We are now in a position to consider our problem afresh. In old and young, human and sub-human, loss of loved object leads to a behavioural sequence which, varied though it be, is in some degree predictable. In human beings, moreover, the behavioural sequence is accompanied by a sequence of subjective experiences which begins with anxiety and anger, proceeds through pain and despair, and, if fortune smiles, ends with hope. Not that either sequence runs a smooth unvarying course. On the contrary both behaviour and feeling oscillate violently, especially in the early phases: yearning, protest, and rage alternate with blank mute despair. Nevertheless there is plainly discernible a trend from protest through despair to some new equilibrium of feeling and behaviour. To the whole course of this

---

* Pollock[72] has quoted two cases of dogs which remained oriented towards the loved object they had lost for considerable periods of time. In one case the dog "returned to the railway station each day to await the master who would never return. He set out for the station in the morning and remained there until evening. Hachi made his daily trip to the station for ten years until he died."

† See also the recent review by Cain.[75]

subjective experience the term "grief," I believe, is applicable. Whilst our culture may encourage a patient resignation in the face of grievous loss, angry violent feelings nonetheless well up and must be recognized as an essential ingredient of grief. Grief, I believe, is a peculiar amalgam of anxiety, anger, and despair following the experience of what is feared to be irretrievable loss. It differs from separation anxiety in that anxiety is experienced when the loss is believed to be retrievable and hope remains.

Similarly, mourning is best regarded as the whole complex sequence of psychological processes and their overt manifestations, beginning with craving, angry efforts at recovery, and appeals for help, proceeding through apathy and disorganization of behaviour, and ending when some form of more or less stable reorganization is beginning to develop. Like all biological processes, however, mourning may take one of several different courses. Those which enable the individual ultimately to relate to new objects and to find satisfaction in them are commonly judged to be healthy, those which fail in this outcome pathological. The status in this respect of certain others is difficult to define.

Furthermore, there are some responses to loss which can hardly be included within the terms "grief" and "mourning," even if these terms are used, as they are here, to include a number of variants which are plainly pathological. Such for instance is the condition described by Helene Deutsch[76] as "absence of grief," and the tendency instead of grieving oneself to succour others who are grieving, described by Green.[77]

In trying to understand these different forms of mourning I am drawing on the hypothesis advanced in my paper regarding the nature of the child's tie to his mother. This hypothesis conceives the tie as mediated by a number of instinctual response systems, which are a part of the inherited behaviour repertoire of man. In the early months of life they come to be oriented towards a particular mother-figure, and it is she who habitually provides the stimuli that affect their operation. Although this theoretical model was proposed for the purpose of explaining the behaviour of infants and young children in a particular relationship, I believe it provides a useful model also for our other libidinal° relationships, for example sexual (genital) and parental ones. Such relationships are conceived as built on the same general pattern and incorporating many of the same instinctual response systems as that tying infant to mother, though it is evident that each contains also certain systems which are characteristic of itself. For example, nursing is specially characteristic of the maternal, and genital activity of the mature sexual relationship (though neither is confined to these relationships).

Within each such relationship, it is clear the loved object plays several roles, some of which at first sight may even appear contradictory. In the case of the mother much emphasis was placed in my earlier papers on her role in terminating certain instinctual response systems; for example, she often terminates crying by picking the infant up and escape from a frightening object by acting as a haven of safety. However, in addition to providing such terminating (or consummatory) stimuli for these systems, she provides activating stimuli for others. Thus the mere perception

° The adjective "libidinal" has for long been used in psycho-analysis to describe relationships which are expressed in physical contact between the partners and have deep emotional significance for them. It remains a valuable adjective for this purpose even when, as in this series of papers, classical libido theory is not utilized.

of his mother may lead the infant to smile and babble, and in her presence he is likely to smile and babble more than at other times.

Furthermore, it is now known that she not only activates smiling and babbling but also, by her ordinary behaviour, reinforces them. For example, Brackbill[77] has shown that the smiling response in infants of 3-4 months is susceptible to reinforcement when the infant is provided with social attention, and to extinction when this is withdrawn. Similarly, Rheingold, Gerwitz and Ross[78] were able to show that the spontaneous babbling of the infant of that age is open to influence in the same way. Social attention in the form of the presence of a friendly face, a cluck, and a pat led to increased babbling: their absence to its decrease. Some of the retarded development of infants in institutions is probably explicable in these terms. In such infants, it seems, behaviour patterns such as kicking, babbling, and smiling appear at much the same time as would be expected in the well-mothered baby, but, instead of increasing and becoming oriented towards a particular mother-figure, tend to die out (personal communication from Dr. Sally Provence). Such observations, if confirmed, are readily understood in terms of learning theory.

The model of a libidinal relationship that is presented is thus one wherein a selection of the instinctual response systems of each partner is enlisted and integrated, and the two sets adapted to one another in space and time. The presence and the reciprocal activities of the other partner provide the activating stimuli for some of the systems and the terminating stimuli for others; they also provide constant reinforcement for many or all of them. In this way the functioning of each partner is dependent on the presence and behaviour of the other. It is a circular system requiring the presence, actual or potential, of both. Mourning ensues when one or other is lost and the circular system is broken.

PHASE ONE: URGE TO RECOVER LOST OBJECT   Following separation or death the bereaved partner finds himself in disequilibrium, rather as a child on a see-saw is in disequilibrium if the child at the other end suddenly jumps off. At first he is bewildered and cannot truly believe what has happened. In consequence, as Lindemann and Marris have each shown so clearly, there is a strong tendency for him to continue to act as though the lost partner were still present. Coupled with incredulity, however, goes a strenuous effort, usually involuntary and sometimes unconscious, to recover him. This is exhibited not only in the hopes and phantasies which the newly bereaved entertains and the dreams he dreams but also in his actions. Irremediable though he may know the loss to be, his thought, feeling, and behaviour are none the less organized to achieve reunion. It is this, I believe, which accounts for both weeping and anger, two of the main features of the *first phase of mourning*.

When he misses his mother the infant's first response is to cry. This is a behaviour pattern that man shares with many lower species and which is adaptive: when the infant creature cries, his mother usually responds by returning to him. There seems no reason to doubt that it is this response system that is activated in the human adult who is bereaved. A situation of sudden loneliness evokes in him an ancient instinctual response. Though it might affront his sense of reality were he to be aware of its origin and function, when he weeps the bereaved adult is responding to loss as a child does to the temporary absence of his mother.

This explanation, which is so clearly in line with psychoanalytic concepts and has been touched upon amongst others by Fenichel,[79]* was first advanced by Darwin in his classical work on *The Expression of the Emotions*. In Chapters 6 and 7 he discusses the expressions exhibited in suffering, anxiety, grief, and despair, and advances the view that they all derive from the infant's screaming. After a detailed analysis of the muscle movements and their functions, he reaches the conclusion that the expression characteristic of adult grief is the resultant on the one hand of a tendency to scream and on the other of an unconscious inhibition of it. "In all cases of distress, whether great or small, our brains tend through long habit to send an order to certain muscles to contract, as if we were still infants on the point of screaming out; but this order . . . we are able partially to counteract" by means which are unconscious to us.

Weeping is only one component in the effort to recover the lost object. Anger is another. In the previous papers I have repeatedly emphasized the sharp increase of aggressive behaviour which occurs in young children separated from their mother-figure and earlier in this one have pointed out that it is the rule, too, in bereaved adults and also in bereaved animals. When the lost object is only temporarily missing this aggressive reaction is useful. When it is permanently missing the reaction ceases to be useful, though it may nonetheless occur and at high intensity.

Looked at in this way the hostility evident after a death or other irretrievable loss is easier to understand. Death of a loved object is a very rare event compared to the multitude of separations, mostly short and some long,

* What today is called grief is obviously a postponed and apportioned neutralization of a wild and self-destructive kind of affect which can still be observed in a child's panic upon the disappearance of his mother . . ." (p. 162).

that are the rule in life. Almost every separation has a happy ending, and often a small or large dash of aggression will assist this outcome. It may assist too in ensuring that it will not be repeated. There are therefore good biological reasons for every separation to be responded to in an automatic instinctive way with aggressive behaviour: irretrievable loss is statistically so unusual that it is not taken into account. In the course of our evolution, it appears, our instinctual equipment has come to be so fashioned that all losses have been assumed to be retrievable and are responded to accordingly.

It is in its function of ensuring that separation will not be repeated, perhaps, that we can see most clearly the adaptive function of aggression when it is directed against the loved object itself. On the reunion of a child with his mother after separation, anger directed against her is common, though it is not always openly expressed. When it is, its burden is a reproach against her for having left him. A dramatic example occurred in the case of Laura, the little girl of two and a half in James Robertson's film A Two-year-old Goes to Hospital.[80] For six months following her return home after eight days in hospital Laura kept her feelings to herself. Then through mischance, she saw a sequence from the film while it was being shown to her parents. When the lights were raised, agitated and flushed she exclaimed angrily: "Where *was* you all the time, Mummy? Where *was* you?" Then she burst into loud crying, turned away from her mother and went to her father for comfort.[81] It is not difficult to imagine the effect on parents. After such reproaches few would have the heart to subject their child to a repetition of the experience. Tyrannical it is sometimes said to be; adaptive it certainly is.

It is the service of this function, I believe, that explains why accusations and reproaches are habitually levelled by the bereaved at the lost object, the self, and third persons. Let us find the culprit, they seem to run, let us right the wrong, let us reinstate what has been lost, let us ensure it will never be repeated. Although reproaches against the dead are discouraged in our culture, they are not so everywhere. "For what have you left me?" moans the Polish peasant. "It is an accusation against the dead person," Anderson[82] remarks, "for having left and deserted the mourner." In a similar way there are accusations against the self and third parties. "I know it will do no good going over it all again and again," apologizes the mourner, "but . . ."; and in the unspoken "but" lies a secret hope that perhaps in some miraculous way to seek out the villain will lead to recovery of loss. Without exception all such blame, I suspect, is felt and expressed as part of the effort to undo the loss and to maintain intact the expected reunion. So long as it continues it is a sign that the loss is not accepted as permanent and that, whether realistic or not, hope still lingers on. As Marris comments in regard to the lady who gave her doctor a good hiding, it was "as if her rage while it lasted had given her courage."

Hostility to comforters is to be understood in the same way. Whereas the comforter who takes no side in the conflict between a striving for reunion and an acceptance of loss may be of great value to the bereaved, one who seems to favour acceptance of loss is as keenly resented as though he had been the agent of it. It is not comfort in loss that is wanted but assistance towards reunion.

Anger and ingratitude towards comforters, indeed, have been notorious since the time of Job. Overwhelmed by the

blow he has received, one of the first impulses of the bereaved is to appeal to others for their help—help to regain
the lost object. The would-be comforter who responds to
this appeal may, however, see the situation differently. To
him it may be clear that hope of reunion is a chimera and
that to encourage it would be unrealistic, even dishonest.
And so, instead of behaving as is wished, he seems to the
bereaved to do the opposite and is resented accordingly.
No wonder his role is a thankless one.

Thus, we see, repeated disappointment, weeping, anger,
accusation, and ingratitude are all features of the first phase
of mourning, and are to be understood as expressions of the
urge to recover the lost object.

Phases Two and Three: Disorganization and Reorganization as Adaptive Processes

Patterns of behaviour based either on the unthinking
assumption that the lost partner is still present or on a false
hope that a sufficiently strenuous effort will achieve reunion are plainly unstable. In the course of healthy mourning, therefore, they gradually drop away or, in terms of
learning theory, become extinguished. In Freud's words
"Each single one of the memories and situations of expectancy which demonstrate the libido's attachment to the
lost object is met by the verdict of reality that the object no
longer exists."[83] Subjectively this is experienced as a series
of repeated and painful disappointments.

As the sum of such disappointment mounts and hopes
of reunion fade, behaviour usually ceases to be focussed on
the lost object. Instead, despair sets in and behaviour, lack-

ing an object towards which to be organized, becomes disorganized. This is *the second phase of mourning*, and one
which Lindemann[84] has so graphically described: "There
is restlessness, inability to sit still, moving about in an aim-
less fashion, continually searching for something to do. . . .
Activities do not proceed in the automatic, self-sustaining
fashion which characterizes normal work. . . . There is . . . a
painful lack of capacity to initiate and maintain organized
patterns of behaviour."

This leads to a consideration of depression as an affect
which even the healthy individual experiences in certain
situations. In contrast to depressive illness, which is more
complex, depression is, I believe, in essence nothing else
than the subjective aspect of this state of disorganization.
The depressed individual of any age and species is the one
whose behaviour is no longer organized and self-sustaining.
Subjectively, because in certain key aspects of his total functioning interaction between himself and his world has
ceased, not only does he experience the world as poor and
empty but he feels himself to be the same. This, I believe,
accounts for much of the loss of self-esteem which is so
characteristic of depression.

In this respect the depressive phase of mourning is
probably no different from depression arising in other situations. In addition to our behaviour being organized towards
the maintenance of certain libidinal relationships, much of
it is concerned with the reaching of work or recreational
goals. So long as there is active interchange between ourselves and the external world, either in thought or action,
our subjective experience is not one of depression: hope,
fear, anger, satisfaction, frustration, or any combination of
these may be experienced. It is when interchange has ceased

that depression occurs. Often this is due to disappointment and the relinquishing of a goal; sometimes, and more surprisingly, to the goal having been successfully reached and so relegated to the past; on occasion it may be due to other and less obvious reasons. No matter what the cause, however, until such time as new patterns of interchange have become organized towards a new object or goal we experience restlessness or apathy, with concurrent anxiety and depression.*

If this general theory of depression is correct, the depressive phase of mourning must be regarded as a special case of the depression that arises as a result of the disorganization of behaviour patterns which is consequent on loss of significant object or goal in the external world. This simple but basic concept of depression is one I wish to emphasize. It is a concept which is as applicable to geese as it is to human beings, and one which, I believe, will enable us to see more clearly those components in the mourning response that are shared with other species and those that are limited to man. It is a view of depression which sees it, like separation anxiety, as an inescapable aspect of life and in that sense as normal. It is one, moreover, that can readily be extended to cover the clinical observation that depression arises not only when there is a loss of object owing to changes in the external world but also when loss is experienced owing to changes in the world of feeling, such as occurs for instance when love for the object is replaced by hatred of it. That in man it may be accompanied by more complex processes goes without saying. That, like

---

* It is to be noted that in the discipline of economics the term "depression" connotes a reduction in economic activity, accompanied by some degree of disorganization and, later, of reorganization.

every other biological process, it may take pathological forms provides the theme of the next paper in this series.

Looked at in this way the behavioural processes going with depression can be seen to have an adaptive function; whilst the painfulness of mourning and other forms of depression becomes more comprehensible. Since the patterns of behaviour which have grown up in interaction with the lost object or goal have ceased to be appropriate, were they to persist they would be maladaptive: only if they are broken down is it possible for new ones, adapted to new objects, to be built up. Although such disorganization is painful and carries with it the risk that satisfactory reorganization will never be achieved, it seems clear that it is an indispensable preliminary to new adaptation. Just as a child playing with Meccano must destroy his construction before he can use the pieces again (and a sad occasion it sometimes is), so must the individual each time he is bereaved or relinquishes a major goal accept the destruction of a part of his personality before he can organize it afresh towards a new object or goal. Although unwelcome, such phases are a necessary part of being alive.*

The view that a capacity to bear depression is a characteristic of the healthy personality has frequently been advanced by psycho-analysts. Freud described the task of mourning as being "to detach the survivor's memories and hopes from the dead"; and the notion that to recover from bereavement it is necessary to tolerate mourning and depression is now a commonplace amongst analysis. Melanie Klein has written extensively on the need, in the course of

* The painfulness of new ideas and our habitual resistance to them can also be seen in this context. The more far-reaching a new idea the more disorganization of existing theoretical systems has to be tolerated before a new and better synthesis of old and new can be achieved.

analysis, for the patient to be helped to experience and bear depression. Although her concept of the "depressive position" is different from mine, much of what she advocates is consistent with the theory advanced here; for instance, her notion that in mourning there is a disintegration of the inner world and a subsequent reintegration of it has already been noted. Balint also has expressed the view that depression is to be conceived as a phase of disorganization and has related it to the same biological principles that I am invoking: "Highly differentiated forms, both in biology and in psychology, are rigid and unadaptable; if a radically new adaptation becomes necessary, the highly differentiated organization must be reduced to its primitive, undifferentiated form from which a new beginning may then ensue." "A real adaptation—the acceptance of unpleasure— is only possible if one can face depression without undue anxiety."[85]*

Everyone who has undergone analysis and who has treated patients knows how reluctant human beings are to face disorganization and depression. Existing organization,

---

* That the depressive response may have an adaptive function is an hypothesis that has been suggested by Frank[86] in his discussion of the apathetic behaviour shown by soldiers in isolated outposts. There are, however, certain differences in his formulation from that advanced here. In the first place he seems to limit its occurrence to "conditions where either in actuality or in fantasy a relatively helpless individual is threatened with the loss of *suitable care, protection and sustenance*" (my italics). In my view this formulation underrates the importance of companionship as a need in its own right, a need vividly illustrated by another author, Christiane Ritter,[87] who describes her joy at finding some young eider ducks after many days alone in a Spitsbergen wilderness. In the second, probably because he is more concerned with the results of a situation in which function is gradually reduced rather than suddenly disrupted, he makes no reference to disorganization as a main underlying process. Perhaps for the same reason he seems also to underrate the role of aggression, which, for reasons already given, I regard as a frequent concomitant of depression and one which may be unavoidable in cases of sudden loss of love object.

in the form of "defences," is clung to; the prospect of disorganization, even though it be preparatory to reorganization on a new and better basis, is fought off.*

The process of becoming disorganized is not only intensely painful, it is also alarming. This Goldstein[90] made the core of his theory of anxiety, having reached it during his studies of brain-damaged patients. In his view anxiety is experienced when the individual is unable to cope with a situation and, as a result, is in danger of becoming disorganized. Although in his book there is no mention of bereavement as a cause of disorganization, his concept nevertheless is the same as the one I am advocating. It should, I believe, form a main ingredient in any comprehensive theory of anxiety. Freud's view that anxiety is provoked by excessive stimulation is not very different. Although it invokes as threatening an excessive *quantity* of stimulation, not a breakdown in the organization of behaviour patterns, his central concept is the ego's inability to respond to the stimulation in an effective, namely organized, way.

Let us return now to the processes of mourning. From what has been said it will be clear that a capacity first to tolerate the disorganization of mourning and subsequently to undertake a reorganization directed towards a new object can be looked on as valuable adaptive characters. There appear to be several ways in which failure to tolerate disorganization can manifest itself. The most evident is that which leads the individual to remain oriented towards the lost object and to continue living as though he were present, or at least retrievable. If the object is truly lost this

* The resemblance of analytic working through to the work of mourning has been noted by Freud[88] and a number of other analysts (see Lewin[89]).

may result in the individual living "in the past" and being unable to adapt to or take satisfaction in the present. Often, moreover, because uncorrected by reference to reality, the picture of the lost object becomes greatly distorted by wish-fulfilling phantasy and so even more difficult to relinquish. Coupled with an angry striving for reunion, and reproach against the object for desertion, it is a starting-point of depressive illness.

Another way in which disorganization is avoided, or at least partially avoided, is by an abrupt cleavage of the psychic apparatus of the kind Freud was studying at the end of his life.[91] All those instinctual response systems with their related phantasy which have been directed towards the lost object are split off from the main structure of psychic organization. Thenceforward they lead a more or less independent life, often almost wholly unknown to the conscious world of the individual concerned, but giving rise none the less to many neurotic symptoms and deviations of behaviour. It is a condition of this kind which seems often to be initiated in young children when they are bereaved or separated.

It seems easier to describe the processes at work in these two unsatisfactory forms of mourning than to describe those present in healthy mourning. It appears, however, that even in healthy mourning some elements of the two processes described occur; together they characterize *the third phase of mourning*. For instance, some persistence of behaviour oriented towards the lost object, who is often believed to continue his existence in another world, is the rule. In contrast to pathological mourning, however, in the healthy process such behaviour modifies as time passes. In particular there is discrimination between patterns that are clearly no longer appropriate and those that can reasonably be retained: in the former class are those, such as performing certain household duties, which only make sense if the lost person is physically present; in the latter maintaining values and pursuing goals which, having been developed in association with the lost person, remain linked with him and can without falsification of reality continue to be maintained and pursued in reference to the memory of him. It is in this way, indeed, that an effective and loving relationship with the lost person can be built afresh.

Similarly, even in healthy mourning some barrier is interposed in the psychic structure of the bereaved individual between the instinctual response systems which bind him to an object and the lost object itself. This is seen with tragic clarity for instance in women who believe themselves to be widows but whose husbands ultimately return. Lindemann[92] has described such cases occurring during World War II. The wives of service men whose husbands had been posted "missing, believed killed" were unable to respond to their husbands when eventually they returned. A similar, though less complete, form of unresponsiveness was common when long-held prisoners-of-war returned to their families. Often in the early days of reunion neither side was able to respond in the way they had each expected of the other and imagined in themselves: mere physical presence failed to bridge the emotional gulf which time and absence had created. The resulting "disappointment about the lack of feelings" is a theme to which Therese Benedek[93] has drawn attention. "An officer, father of two children, described this lack of feeling vividly," she reports. " 'Before I left,' he said, 'I took them for granted. They were a part of my life. Now I have to look for my feelings. I have to search for them and therefore they become so important; everything has to be expressed, to reassure me that I love them.' His complaint," she comments, "expressed articulately what many veterans feel."

The literature describing the psychology of prisoners-of-war is of great interest in this connexion, for it is plain that prisoners pass through a sequence of experience and behaviour similar to though not identical with that of the bereaved. A vivid description is provided by Cochrane,[94] himself a prisoner for some years. He emphasizes two main features—aggression and apathy. In his experience the hatred was directed principally against the prisoner's own officers, until then experienced as good objects. "In conversation no officer who left Crete free [i.e. uncaptured] escaped the most biting criticism. . . . It was also typical that the attacks were launched in the foulest possible language." Apathy took the form of a sullen isolation and personal neglect. Men who a few days earlier had been good soldiers allowed themselves to become dishevelled and dirty, were wholly unresponsive to their compatriots and often "surprisingly uninterested in food." Cochrane reports his own "colossal inertia." As time wore on, however, a reorganization of behaviour and personality developed. This had its dangers, since it was a reorganization adapted to the peculiar environment of a prison camp and, as such, unsuitable elsewhere. This was shown all too clearly on repatriation. "Those who were best adapted to imprisonment," records Cochrane, "found the greatest difficulty in readapting in England." Newman[95] and Curle[96] have described some of these difficulties.

The sequence of responses shown by individuals to experiences of social isolation also exhibits many similarities to the processes of mourning. Lilly,[97] in reviewing some of the records of behaviour during social isolation, emphasizes first that "isolation *per se* acts on most persons as a powerful stress." In the case of sailors who have deliberately sailed alone or who have found themselves alone after shipwreck, he points out, the first days are the dangerous ones: Bombard speaks of "the terror of the first week." At this time there may be panic and even impulses towards murder or suicide. Later, in those who survive the disorganization of this first period, a new form of adaptation develops in which phantasy, sometimes amounting to delusion or hallucination, commonly plays a large part. For instance an intense need for companionship may be met by conversing with a doll, by delusion of a companion being present, or perhaps in an experience of being "at one with the universe." This phase persists and can be regarded as one of reorganization adapted more or less appropriately to the new environment. "Most survivors report, after several weeks' exposure to isolation, a new inner security and a new integration of themselves on a deep basic level," reports Lilly. Nevertheless, as in the case of prisoners-of-war, their new integration is not without its disadvantages; for there grows a love for the situation and a reluctance to leave it that leads to great difficulty in resuming social relations at its end. This brings home to us forcibly how stable any form of psychic organization, however peculiar, tends to become and how reluctant the individual is to move into a new environment, even a normal one, if it demands disorganization of what exists and a fresh organization appropriate to the new circumstances.

In writing this section illustrations have often been taken from the world of the adult. All that has been said, however, applies equally to infants and young children of over six months. When for any reason they lose their loved object the three phases of mourning described are experienced. At all ages, we now see, the first phase of mourning is one of Protest, the second one of Despair, and the third one of Detachment. What Robertson and I had described as typical for young children has a generality greater than we knew. Nevertheless it would be wrong to suppose there are no differences. In determining the course of mourning age is probably a main variable. In the young, it seems, mourning is specially apt to take a pathological course.

Conclusion

In this paper I have been concerned to understand the basic psychological process occurring in mourning. Points I have stressed particularly are the intimate relationships of grief and separation anxiety, the urge to recover the lost object that is dominant throughout the first phase of mourning, the weeping and the aggressive acts that are a part of it, and the roles of disorganization and subsequent reorganization that are the main processes occurring in the second and third phases. Throughout it has been my aim to discern the potentially adaptive function of the processes concerned, a potential that is realized when the object can be recovered but which cannot be realized in the statistically rare cases when recovery is impossible. In drawing attention to mourning responses in lower species I have sought to emphasize the primitive biological processes that are at work in human beings, whilst at the same time recognizing that there are probably also features of mourning specific to man.

Reasons have been given for thinking that the painfulness of mourning is to be accounted for by the long persistence of yearning for the lost object and the constant repetition of bitter disappointment on not finding it. Phantasies of having destroyed the lost object and their accompanying guilt may exacerbate the pain, but cannot be regarded as its main determinant.

In the final section, I have suggested that the persistent seeking of reunion with a permanently lost object is the main motivation present in pathological mourning, although it appears in forms which, because of repression and splitting, have become disguised and distorted.

Dynamics and Therapy of Depressive States

SANDOR LORAND

The fundamentals of the psychogenesis of depressive states were first described by Freud; with the elaborations upon them by the detailed studies of Abraham and Rado, among others, they have made possible our present valid insight into the condition of melancholia. To carry *ad absurdum* the theoretical speculations, as is done with so many analytical problems, is not the aim of this paper, which will, instead, stress certain points about the dynamics of depression. Probably because of the insufficiency of adequate clinical material these points have in the past been somewhat overlooked. In addition this paper will attempt to indicate certain important features of the technical approach, which is an extremely difficult one.

Abraham was the first to point out that in manic-depressive states the patient regresses to a fixation point at the oral stage of his libidinal development, and that this fixation point is closely connected with the stage to which the obsessional neurotic regresses, namely, the anal

321

stage. It follows from this formulation, that both points of fixation—oral and anal—are prominent and of the greatest importance in such states. And the more nearly contemporaneous the oral is with the anal, the better the chances for readjustment and analytical treatment; the more remote, the more difficult the treatment and the more dubious the outcome.

We may take it for granted that patients who come for the treatment of depression usually have had several similar phases before; but it is of cardinal importance to stress the fact that the earliest depression-like state must have occurred in infancy, a fact which will always be proved in a prolonged and thoroughgoing analytical treatment. Depression in an adult presupposes a painful and severe early childhood with strong feelings of conflict and ambivalence, which, parallel with the infantile neurosis, form the fertile soil in which the later adult depression grows. Moreover, it will become clear during the analysis that the adult situation that precipitated the current depression is emotionally identical with the patient's childhood environment.

A prolonged, uninterrupted analysis of from more than two to four years' duration helped establish in at least five cases under my immediate observation the fact that these patients had endured shocking experiences, causing severe infantile neuroses, which we may look upon as the earliest depression.

The wealth of material gained in such long drawn out analyses afforded an opportunity to follow up the theoretical constructions of the rôle played by the early fixations, and helped to clarify the rather complicated psychic mechanisms concerning the fixations and aggressions resulting from these first emotional disturbances. Such detail about depressive states teaches us more about Ego functions, brings us closer to the deep-rooted insecurity which is so prominent a feature in depression, shows us more clearly what fixation implies, and makes the regression more comprehensible.

It demonstrates the importance of the Ego function in both the well and the ill, and I believe it will be of aid in determining the criteria for the selection of cases amenable to analysis. I mean, that the degree of plasticity—or of rigidity—of the Ego may be of decisive importance in selecting the type of patient suitable for psychoanalytic treatment of depression. Too much plasticity, too great elasticity, in the Ego of these patients means a great degree of instability; such patients are likely to show extreme regressive tendencies. Their adjustment after analysis is less satisfactory because their Egos were so feeble and plastic. Whereas if a degree of rigidity is present in the patient's character, denoting a certain strength in the Ego, restitution by psychoanalytic treatment is more complete. It is this Ego function, therefore, which must be responsible for our observing different patterns in the different cases of depression, since the same factors responsible for all depressive states are found to bring about quite diverse quantitative emotional disturbances in the various patients.

All the cases under my observation showed the characteristics of all depressions: tremendous sadism, distrust of the world, constant complaints of mental insufficiency, retardation in social functions, hypochondriacal body complaints, panicky situations and reactions, mild delusions of persecution, and suicidal tendencies. But the degree of self-abasement and self-reproach, the inhibitions and sadness, varied in the various cases. This will be clear in two cases I shall present. In one the lack of impulsiveness was noteworthy, the inhibitions, rigid melancholy, self-abasement, and psychomotor retardation dominating the picture. Whereas in the other case, although at times dazed by the hardships of routine, the motility, contact with reality, and interest in the world around were present in a greater degree. This patient was in general able, although with difficulty and at times to only a limited degree, to maintain his general relationships and interests.

The conflict in the depressive patient is centered not only around the mother but around all the members of the family who are responsible for the loss of the loved object in early childhood. The patient's memory retains from the very earliest years the frustrations by the mother; it is this frustrating, threatening, punishing attitude of hers which stands out most conspicuously in the patient's recollections, overshadowing the mother's love. It is probable that a constitutional factor, defined by Abraham as a constitutional heightening of oral erotism, is also to be taken into consideration, as creating a keener sensitivity in the child, and causing him to react more violently to attachments and frustrations. And when, in the early environment the siblings and the father interfere with his sole possession of the mother's love, an unlimited jealousy is aroused in the child against all the members of the family, which then becomes responsible for the tremendous envy which is so notable a characteristic of all depressions.

Aggression directed against the whole world concerns primarily, as we know, the first environment, in which the "whole world" was represented, then, by the siblings and the father as well as by the mother.

In the following case histories I intend to illustrate

clinically how the psychological mechanisms familiar to us as a result of the above-mentioned investigations make intelligible the processes of the development of depressions, as well as making the depressions amenable to therapy.

The outstanding complaint of the patient whom I shall describe first was deep unhappiness, a feeling of being alone and forlorn. From early puberty on he remembered feeling depressed most of the time. At times, for a few months, he might feel himself "better balanced," but then, especially in his later life, something that required his making a decision would arise, and he again would begin, in his own phrase, "to slip back into a depression." He recalled how from the age of fourteen onwards he used to walk the streets in the evening, sometimes excited, looking for someone to love him. At the time he came to analysis and during part of the analysis he continued these lonely walks, seeking someone to love. When he tired of the streets he went to moving picture shows, wandering in and out from one to another; or he frequented hotel lobbies and theatres. After that he began to drink, taking only enough to raise his spirits, never getting drunk. During the analytical period he might sometimes spend a whole hour crying and repeating incessantly: "alone, alone, alone!" On such occasions he shed no tears but beat his head and face with his fists. The picture resembled the tantrums of a child.

The youngest of a large family, he was in his twenties when he came for treatment complaining of: depression, suicidal thoughts, lack of interest in his business (which he conducted against his will), a feeling of embarrassment and inferiority to others, even to his subordinates, so that he could not speak in a loud, assertive voice; distrust of people, and fears of a bad odor from his mouth or body.

It will give some conception of the important material gained in the more than three years of his analysis to describe some of the happenings of his life, as they emerged in the course of analysis, accompanied by strong emotional charges which were an important factor in furthering the analysis. Among his earliest memories, possibly the earliest of all, was the recollection of being wheeled in his baby cart under the elevated train structure and left there alone. Another memory that recurred vividly during the analysis was of an operation around the age of five. He was anaesthesized and his mother left him with the doctor. He recalled how he had kicked and screamed, raging at her for leaving him.

Around this time, he thought, he might have seen his parents having intercourse. "I remember as a very little child that they always closed their door at night, but in the early morning I used to slip into their bed."

At about the age of seven he had what he called "hallucinations." He would lie in bed and provoke them, because they were pleasant. He would see the room getting closer and closer to him, finally closing in on him. During the analysis, after seeing O'Neill's play, "Mourning Becomes Electra," he again experienced the feeling, and imagined that the room that came closer and closer meant his mother's breast, his mother approaching to feed him with her large breast. When he was not yet ten his foot once slipped between an elevated train and the station platform, but his mother pulled it out.

During his analysis he formed the curious habit of sleeping in hotels at odd intervals. He would rent a room, take up some newspapers, and spend the night there. Early in the morning he would leave, slip into his own home, and get into bed for an hour or so that his parents should not know he had not spent the night at home. His reason for this behavior was equally curious. He said that his mother always asked him whether he would be home for dinner. From the question he inferred that she did not want him, so he stayed away.

At times he would sit in an arm chair at home after dinner and fall asleep there, not awaking until the early hours of the morning, when he would go to his room and to his bed. He had a delusion connected with eating: his mother, who was always urging him to eat, prepared his breakfast and wanted to wait on him at dinner. She cooked delicious food, but he thought he detected a peculiar taste in it. He became obsessed with the idea that she wanted to poison him, make him sick so that she could take care of him, and that was why she put something into the food which gave it the queer taste. Yet at the same time he imagined that she wanted to make him strong and potent. At one period of the analysis he also had the idea whenever he rode in a cab, that he was being followed in another cab by gangsters who wanted to kill or to kidnap him.

He also worried about a number of oral symptoms which shaded over into the anal. Sometimes he spoke with a spray of saliva, which made him shy of meeting people, for fear of what they might think of him. He fancied that he had an unpleasant mouth odor. This particularly distressing idea was discovered, on analysis, to have multiple determinants. It meant on the one hand and primarily, aggression: overcoming people by the bad odor; and along with this, blowing people away, "killing with a breath." On the other hand it had also the significance of attracting people to him, as if with perfume, and of impregnation, in the biblical sense of the creation of man by blowing the breath of life into him. It was also connected with his knowledge of the fact that physicians sometimes resuscitated blue babies by blowing breath into them. In this connection he would be the blue baby, to be revived by life-giving breath, which was equated with nourishment and his mother's breast. Blowing was also the equivalent of flatus, and this invested the bad breath with anal attributes, namely, attracting the mother's attention again as in infancy, when soiling himself meant getting her prompt attention.

Two dreams of his, of which one was the first in analysis, may illustrate the importance and the identification of both anal and oral odors. The first was a dream of which he said: "*I am sitting in the toilet having a movement. My mother calls me, finally coming and pulling me out. . . .*" His mother actually was in the habit of knocking at the door when he was in the bathroom and calling him to dinner, a habit which always infuriated him. The other dream was of "*being in the toilet, having a good bowel movement which smelled and girls standing outside enjoyed it.*" He was deeply interested in odors and could identify by the smell which member of the family had preceded him in the toilet.

He complained a great deal of his mother's selfishness and

stinginess; at the same time speaking of the analysis and the analyst with love, for his "taking me into the care of analysis." He himself was very selfish, and although he had spells of extravagance, he was also very stingy, never giving anything to the members of his family, nor contributing any share of the living expenses at home although he had a good income.

In his upbringing not only his mother, but also his grandmother, whom he remembered with love, took an active part. Therefore, he really had two mothers, and both of them, as analytical material revealed, deceived and deserted him. His grandmother died during his childhood and his mother had early made him independent; but his attachment to them persisted, permanently disrupting his healthy adjustment, as a result of the unconscious rôle of his mother in his life. His sexual maladjustment showed this most clearly, pervaded as it was with peculiarities, inclinations toward perversions, unconscious homosexual tendencies, etc. Although consciously he was able to have coitus and to enter into temporary relationships with prostitutes, he never really enjoyed these. He enjoyed only being convinced of his potency, and the sadistic pleasure implicit in intercourse. At times he needed alcohol to give him courage to approach women and on these occasions his perverse tendencies appeared, especially in the form of cunnilingus and fellatio.

His fundamental distrust of women was the strongest inhibiting influence in his enjoyment of any relationship with them; and the catastration anxiety led straight back to the mother as castrator. This fact was made abundantly clear during analysis in his fantasies and dream life. Many of his dreams were incest dreams.

The *second case* was that of a young dentist who came to analysis because of recurring depressions, which always came on in the spring and lasted two or three months, compelling him to stop work. On these occasions he went away for a rest, while his friends helped his family.

This patient's inhibitions were more pronounced than those of the first case; his self-accusations and delusions more frank, his sadness more rigid and his suicidal tendencies more constant. His repressive state took an acute turn after his marriage and especially after the birth of a child. He felt more and more handicapped, and his anxiety centered around the torturing fear of becoming poor, destitute, and unable to support his family.

He came for treatment as the immediate result of a slight affair with a woman, after which he had a panicky fear of being found out by his wife, his family, or by his patients. And he became increasingly worried that this time if he had a break-down his friends would all desert him. Other incidents out of the past began to worry him, all connected with women, so that he tried to seek relief from his panic by coming to analysis.

From the start of the treatment he complained a great deal about his difficult childhood. He had been reared from infancy in a religious atmosphere, sent to denominational schools, compelled to go to church regularly, against his own inclinations, and always threatened, always warned of the consequences of sin. During his treatment his mother insisted that he attend divine services with her, but the result of her efforts at sympathy and kindness was an increase in his sense of guilt, because he himself resented all this religious schooling. He grew worse to expiate his guilt because at that time he was consciously raging against her. Being ill and talking about himself and how unworthy he was of her love he made his mother reassure him that she did care for him; which was, in fact, one of the chief aims of his illness.

It was her love he had always desired from earliest infancy, when he experienced all the frustrations at her hands. At the same time, it was her love that he could not enjoy, on account of the many guilts that accompanied his desires. As analytical material revealed, his super-ego was endowed mainly with the qualities of the mother.

In his childhood, since he had younger brothers and sisters, he had had opportunity to observe his mother's frequent pregnancies, which made a distinct impression on him, embarrassing him greatly before the other children. He recalled numerous childhood shocks during the course of his analysis. One of the

earliest memories was of the death of a younger child, and of
seeing the baby in its small coffin. He remembered also, how
when he himself had been ill the older members of the family
had paced the floor with him the whole night through.

Before he was ten his mother found him masturbating and
beat him severely. Her usual way of punishing was to slap his
hands, which left an indelible impression. It is interesting to
note that he became remarkably skillful with his hands and
during the analysis had the idea of cutting them off in order
to cease practicing dentistry. At the same time, in childhood
he was actually threatened with having his penis cut off. During
an adult illness he had fears that his glans would disappear
in intercourse, an idea directly connected with the threats of
childhood.

This patient was very unstable emotionally, even as a child,
and easily flew into rages. He often pretended to be ill in order
to stay away from school, which he hated. The same excuse
of illness served him even when he was an adult coming to
analysis; he would make use of it to stay at home in bed.

In his first year at school he was badly frightened when
some of the children were beaten with a stick, and he ran
behind a teacher's skirts. At the same time he used to masturbate
by moving his legs and the teacher told him to stop. He said,
"When I wanted to go to public school mother said she had
rather see me in a coffin than in a public school."

Before he was ten, too, he was seduced by a servant, who
used to play with him, making him lie on top of her. In his
early teens he had a slight concussion of the brain from playing football and had to give up the game. He had always
wanted to be a doctor but compromised by becoming a dentist,
the reason for this being, as was revealed in analysis, and as
he was fairly well aware, that he feared the responsibilities of
being a physician and was afraid of his strong sexual drive and
curiosity about examining women.

He was afraid of all kinds of disease, especially of pneu-
monia, of which he had had a touch in his childhood. He was
obsessed with fears about his health and had a particularly

strong dread of dying. At times he could imagine himself lying in his grave, disintegrating. He was full of feelings of revenge whenever he was insulted or punished, and these feelings were especially fierce against his mother, who had so often humiliated him. For instance, at fifteen he went to a prostitute and was aware that he did so out of revenge against his mother, because he had noticed that very day that she was pregnant again and he felt like choking her—in his own words, "Like killing her with her big belly. She was always whining and going to church and always having a big belly."

Thus the idea of pregnancy in his youth was connected with a resentment against women, which he carried over into all his later dealings with women and into his marriage. For him, intercourse meant making the woman sick, ruining her; and touching meant doing something wrong for which he was always punished, yet for which he always wanted to revenge himself. Thus he was involved in perpetual conflict. On the one hand, doing something wrong to women which would anger his parents if they learned of it; and on the other, obtaining gratification from the action, which was sexualized.

It was remarkable how doing something to a woman with his hands was applied from his unconscious to his work. The dental work in which he was skillful and eminent was completely sexualized. He used to say that his eyes were in his fingers.

He was tormented by the idea that he was infecting his patients when he pulled or handled their teeth, and the infection was always of a venereal nature. Needless to say, this idea covered the double wish to impregnate the patients and to attack them sexually and kill them. So painful was this idea that he might infect his patients, especially the women, and that he might have impregnated them by his touch, that he was often on the verge of giving up his practice altogether.

The religious conflicts which had been so prominent at the beginning of his depression receded more and more into the background, and gave hardly any material in analysis. This was a natural consequence, as the religious conflicts proved to be a secondary elaboration of his deeper and primary conflicts concerning the attitudes of his parents. His identification with his mother became increasingly noticeable. He was afraid of taking a bath, and at the same time he was afraid of his body odor, which he described as the odor of menstruation.

The overwhelming childhood fear of his father also came to the fore in analysis. His periods of trembling in analysis were a revival of actual tremors in childhood, when he had feared his father. At one time he divided the analytical hour into two periods, during the first of which he complained, raved about his unhappiness, and trembled; and during the second phase he cursed and displayed great aggressiveness against the analysis, his parents, and the whole world. There were periods in analysis of alternating depressions and rage, which were repetitions of childhood moods. These had constantly been changing, just as the parents' attitude toward him and the other children was a constantly changing one.

His distrust had much to do with this constantly shifting parental attitude. He was always afraid of his parents and their moods. They were both moody and the children always had to be on their guard, watching out for the next change. "Always changing from good to bad, and then punishing," the patient described them.

At times he showed great devotion to his mother and even more to his wife. But behind this devotion was revealed strong aggression, for which the devotion was merely a compensation. The aggression was connected with his envy of his wife's good health and the possibility that she might be going about with his friends while he was sick. He was extremely jealous and angry when he saw her talking to anyone, even to his best friend. On such occasions he felt like choking her and if he happened to be working at the time his fear of infecting the patients was stronger than ever. He was afraid to take out an inlay lest it slip down the patient's throat. In the same way, when he had a decayed tooth he was afraid to have it pulled, and in telling me about it made a slip. He said, "Because I might get pregnant," intending to say, "infected." He never gave an anaesthetic himself, fearing that the patient might not wake up.

It must be obvious from the material already presented that

he had difficulties in his sexual life. He got very little pleasure
from intercourse, and was always afraid of impregnating or infecting his wife. Both fears covered strong feelings of aggression,
as was revealed in such dreams as this: *"I am eager to have
lots of intercourse for revenge, to lie on top of women and choke
them."* These dreams were associated with his feelings toward his
mother.

He obtained relief from his sexual tension by frequent masturbation, intercourse *inter femora* when his wife was in pyjamas,
and intercourse with condoms, which caused him to feel guilty
because his church considers the practice sinful. He had been
taught that intercourse was permissible only for the purpose of
propagation and that it should not be indulged in otherwise.

As was natural, the castration fear was always on the surface,
with fears of the father and mother as castrators. There were
strong homosexual tendencies, plainly revealed in his desire to be
taken care of, since his original fear at the onset of his illness was
that his friends and family would refuse to support him any longer
because of the affair with the woman.

The constant unhappiness of depressive patients, their
fundamental distrust of everyone and everything, which is
a result of the original distrust caused by the sufferings of
early environmental influences, combine to make the therapy extremely difficult. The first purpose of the therapy,
naturally, will be to change the distrust and to diminish
the aggression and guilt in such a manner that the patient
will become less terrified and panicky.

The analytical process itself is an incessant battle in
which the patient must go through all the periods of
adaptation that he skipped in his childhood. He must learn
to react with less anxiety to the frustrations arising in the
course of analysis.

Depressed patients are those in whom the so-called
"negative therapeutic reaction" is most prominent. This
fact alone presupposes certain modifications of and devia-

tions from what we are accustomed to in the regular analysis of neuroses.

These patients constantly desire—and as constantly fear their desires. Their fear is always of the repetition of the traumatic frustration of the earliest separation. This is why the anxiety is overwhelming, and why, as soon as one fear is dispelled, a new panic-situation springs up to replace it, with the same aim of defense and protection.

For as long as fear is present the patient is not in danger of being dismissed from the analysis, where the help he seeks is really not that of treatment and cure but that of attention and care.

The defensive means he employs, the fear and the panic, reveal the vast extent of the insecurity. And the self-depreciation serves the same purpose of showing how worthless and insecure the patient is, so as to assure him pity and help even at the sacrifice of all his chances for happiness.

The first approach will be an attempt to bridge the negative attitude in a persistent endeavor to bring about a positive reaction. In other words, a positive transference, which should promptly be strengthened, as was pointed out by Abraham. To bring about and strengthen this positive reaction will take all the ingenuity the analyst possesses, and it must be accomplished anew nearly every day; again because of the fundamental distrustfulness of these patients.

Abraham also advised that this positive transference should not be analyzed. Both his injunctions are important, although the latter, not to analyze the transference, may be valid only in short, superficial analyses, where a deep penetrating, prolonged analysis is not feasible. If one wishes to achieve a permanent adjustment and cure of the patient, the transference will have to be analyzed, although at a later phase of the analysis, when the patient can better endure frustrations, and can make demands without feeling guilt or fearing dismissal.

One must be sparing and cautious with the frustrations which we are accustomed to impose early in the analysis of neuroses. It is more helpful to reassure the patient, to see his point of view and to agree with his or her assumptions. There are times when interpretations will not be of much avail but may on the contrary merely add to the confusion.

In one case I had to agree with a patient that under the existing circumstances she was quite right in wishing to commit suicide. From both the logical and emotional points of view her arguments were sound, and I really could not contradict her. (All her arguments concerned her childhood environment, particularly her parents.) When she had ended her tirade, I pointed out that being right, and having felt as she did for so many years, and yet continuing to live, must indicate that there was some desire or at least willingness to be alive, if for no other reason than to exist as a perpetual reminder to her parents of their mistakes in her upbringing. Later, when the suicidal impulses had diminished in intensity, she reacted violently and furiously against me, accusing me of making it impossible for her to die; of keeping her alive.

Now in this case, for example, it was clear that what the patient really wanted was to see whether and to what extent I was concerned about the danger of her suicide, because she felt that I could not be really concerned, just as her parents and the physicians she had consulted were not concerned, and that I did not believe her and would only belittle all her threats. In such a situation it would have been a mistake to be passive and only listen, or to display an attitude of annoyance or weariness at the patient, or to interpret her suicidal tendencies. This patient was occasionally quite childish in her behavior. I once had to force money upon her so that she could spend the night at a hotel, instead of in Grand Central Station.

With this patient and another I sometimes had to discuss their ways of dressing, telling them that they were shabby, that they looked like derelicts, thereby emphasizing their unhappiness and wishing that people would take an interest in them. The patients reacted to such discussion as to a scolding. But from the material in connection with these habits, it was clear that they were intended to irritate the analyst. At the same time, if their attitudes had not been met with frank annoyance, they would have felt confirmed in what they always suspected: that the analyst was not trustworthy, not truthful, and did not say what he thought nor show what he felt. One patient, for example, put it like this: "Show me emotion, that I may know I make a difference to you." For to him the analyst's attitude seemed to be one of indifference, and he wanted to find out whether that was the actual reaction to his productions. Obviously, with such patients questions must be answered frankly if at all. Many of their actions were not analyzed until a much later date, and I think should not have been analyzed until there was good reason to believe that the patients could understand and accept. For instance, a patient would ask to have a check cashed because he had no money with him, or ask for a match or a cigaret.

The analysis of such actions (and the period of more open frustration) should be postponed until one feels sure that the possibility of relapse into deep depression is over. It is not difficult to determine when this stage has been reached. The patient's general attitude is improved, the suicidal tendencies hardly appear, and the delusions are gone. In their place more neurotic symptoms come to the fore, among them numerous obsessions, and from this point on the handling of the situation will be easier, because in this period the object relationships are stronger and the attitude towards the analyst and the world, friendlier.

The usual rules for analyses do not suffice in depressions. The tremendous aggression, guilt and anxiety, all concern the parents, as does the patient's desire to be taken care of. To sit back quietly and repeat the superego pattern with which the patient is already all to well acquainted from his early childhood, because all his difficulties concern that superego, would be to reproduce his emotional entanglements, not to solve them. We must bear in mind that in order to reorganize the inter-psychic powers responsible for his depression and to affect its structure, we cannot afford to appear to the patient to be sadistic. We must become more tolerant, more elastic, more understanding, so that the patient feels that he is understood, and is getting sympathy even though the analyst's attention does not completely satisfy the craving for love in the desired manner.

During the course of treatment the analyst will meet frequent discouragement, and for each step forward the patient will seem to slip back two. The analyst must always keep alert, have inexhaustible patience, and be prepared for a tedious, time-consuming process. On occasion the patient's condition will seem alarming, so dramatic may be the analytical process. And even after one has made certain that the patient is on the road to improvement, the analysis will still go on for a long time, to guide the patient to a better adjustment, or at least to the beginning of one.

Transference Problems in the Psychoanalytic Treatment of Severely Depressive Patients

EDITH JACOBSON

I have been invited to stimulate our discussion today by a brief communication on my analytic experiences with severe cases of depression. I was very reluctant to accept this suggestion because I feel that what I have to say and can say in the available time is not substantial enough to deserve being presented.

May I first briefly define the type of cases which I want to discuss. Of course, almost all neurotics tend to develop temporary depressive reactions. But the patients to whom I shall refer were persons whose whole life problems hinged on their predisposition for severe depressive conditions, and who sought treatment because of such states.

Among the depressive cases which I accepted for psychoanalysis proper have been only a few true manic-depressives; most of them were cases with psychotic features, but not to the point of permitting, even under long observation, a clear-cut differential diagnosis of psychotic versus neurotic depression. Clinically, they presented largely differing syndromes. They were chronic depressives, patients with irregular mood vacillations, depressives with severe anxiety states, patients with hypochondriacal and paranoid forms of depression, or with severe reactive depressive states, schizoid types of depression, and so on, and so forth.

In other words, most of these patients were borderline cases, ranging from borderline to both manic-depressive and schizophrenic psychosis.

In all these cases the infantile history had a rather characteristic pathogenic pattern and played a decisive role in the illness, although the influence of hereditary factors was rather evident. This tends to confirm that the depressive constitution is much farther spread out than the clinical disorder as such. But the weight of the heredity and the severe pathology in such patients justify the question—even if they are accessible to analysis—how far we can accomplish what is the real goal of psychoanalytic treatment: not a symptomatic but a causal cure; in other words, a change of their predisposition for severe depressive states or breakdowns.

Certain clinical experiences are apt to relieve such doubts: A woman now forty-seven years old had suffered from the age of sixteen to twenty-eight from typical depressive phases for which she had been regularly hospitalized, though without ever getting psychotherapeutic treatment. When she was twenty-eight her father died. Half a year later she began her first love affair, and after two years without relapse into illness got married. Despite tragic experiences, such as the suicides of her mother and her only girl friend, she has never again had a real breakdown. But she still shows conspicuous mood vacillations and suffers from mild depressive states. Such cases are not so rare. If life can achieve so much, analysis should be able to do even more.

With this optimistic attitude let me turn to the discussion of problems arising in the analytic treatment of such patients.

The indistinct but convenient term "borderline" epitomizes certain common features in such patients regarding their personality structure and their devices of conflict solution. They present ego distortions and superego defects, disturbances in their object relations, and a pathology of affects beyond what we find in common neurotics. For this reason they usually need many years of analysis with slow, patient, consistent work in the area of ego and superego, with great attention to their particular methods of defense and to their affective responses in which these defenses find special expression. This work is so difficult because such patients call into play auxiliary defense and restitution mechanisms which impair their reality testing to a greater or lesser extent, engaging at the same time the outside world, and in particular the significant objects for the purpose of their pathologic conflict solutions. For these reasons they may require modifications of our usual technique, which neurotic patients do not need. To be more specific: depressives try to recover their own lost ability to love and to function through magic love from their love object. As a melancholic patient once put it: "Love is oxygen to me." For this purpose, they use varying defensive devices. When failing to get such help from without, they may retreat from their love object or even from the object world and continue the struggle within themselves.

In the course of analysis, the analyst becomes inevitably the central love object and the center of the depressive conflict. With advancing analysis, the patient may thus develop even more serious depressive states and, in general, for long periods of time, go into states of ego and id regression deeper than ever before. In other words, we may be confronted with a special variety of what we call negative therapeutic reactions.

Of course, this state of affairs causes great technical difficulties, especially with regard to the handling of the transference. How are we to cope with them? How far and in which way is the analyst supposed to deviate from the usual practice and respond to the pathological, defensive needs of the patient for active emotional or even practical help from without? Is it dangerous to let his sadomasochistic fantasies, his profoundly ambivalent impulses come to the fore?

I may introduce the discussion of these problems with some more general remarks. Of course, manic-depressive patients do not seek treatment when hypomanic or manic, because in such states they lack insight. But even though the analytic process advances best during so-called healthy intervals once the patients are in analysis, they usually do not come for treatment during such periods. One patient, whose third depressive phase had suddenly subsided after he had managed to break his leg, decided to do something drastic for himself. But he soon changed his mind; he now felt "too well," after all. Evidently the restitution processes in such patients do work too well, i.e., involve denial mechanisms constituting strong resistances to treatment.

In my experience the attitudes described prevail quite generally in depressive patients. They regularly begin treatment in a depressed state. Of course, the prerequisite for any sort of psychotherapy with depressives is a sufficient transference basis, which in my experience with such patients can be evaluated already during the very first interview. Questions regarding the patient's feeling about the mutual rapport are indicated and commonly elicit a frank, simple response; it is mostly yes or no. In other words, depressives tend to establish either an immediate, intense rapport, or none. This makes it very hard and risky, for instance, to refer them to another therapist.

In the case of typical, periodic depression, the treatment starts off best in the beginning or end stage of the phase; i.e., stages where the withdrawal is not yet or no longer at its peak. The therapeutic approach to depressive patients depends, of course, on the individual case and the special type of depression. But in some respects the course of analysis shows common, characteristic features in all such cases. This I would like to sketch out by briefly describing a rather typical development of transference manifestations and corresponding symptomatic reactions during the analysis of a depressive patient. Thereby I shall neglect all the details relating to the forthcoming material. What I want to show are characteristic treatment phases: the initial, spurious transference success; the ensuing period of hidden, negative transference with corresponding negative therapeutic reactions, i.e., waxing and more severe states of depression; the stage of dangerous, introjective defenses and narcissistic retreat; and the end phase of gradual, constructive conflict solution. The case tends to confirm my impression that analytic work is most successful with patients who, when not depressed, show a mixture of mildly hypomanic and compulsive attitudes.

Mr. L., a brilliant scientist in his forties, has suffered since childhood from irregular states of depression, severe anxieties and functional intestinal symptoms. When depressed he struggles against the threat of passivity and retardation by starting hectic sexual and professional activities. He is thus often simultaneously depressed, severely anxious, excited, and obsessionally overactive rather than retarded. His personality reflects his conflicting strivings. He is a warm, appealing, lovable human being, eager to please but proud of being a fighter and of owing his remarkable career to nobody but himself.

The patient lost his depressive mother in early childhood by an accident. After her death, the father developed a chronic depressive state, gave up home and work, and placed his children with foster parents where they were brought up in an indifferent emotional atmosphere. The patient's conflicts revolve around his disappointing marital relationship and his unsettled status on the faculty of his university. He has had previous treatment, with little improvement. The patient selected me among other analysts whom he had met socially, because I seemed to be not only competent but "so warm, so motherly and unaggressive." He feels in immediate rapport with me. Thus he starts off his treatment with a suspiciously strong enthusiasm for the analyst and for his future analytic work. His transference fantasies reflect his idealization of the analyst and closeness to her, who has become the most valued part of himself. In the starlight of this initial positive transference the patient's condition improves rapidly. He is feeling better, that is more hopeful, than in years. His work seems easier, he feels closer to his wife who now appears to be much more acceptable. Despite continued mood vacillations and anxieties, the patient goes on feeling subjectively markedly improved for at least a year. The analysis develops seemingly well, with dramatic revivals of certain traumatic childhood events, in a general atmosphere of optimism and of admiring, affectionate gratitude to the analyst who is giving so much.

So far, the course of events and the transference success would not much differ from what we may see in any case of hysteria, were it not for the highly illusory, magic quality of his transference feelings; for his exaggerated idealization and obstinate denial of possible or visible shortcomings of the analyst. Important is the refusal of the patient to see that despite his subjective feelings of improvement, no drastic objective results have as yet been achieved. He just feels ever so much more hopeful; he knows his analysis is but a promise; it will take a very long time; but he believes in ultimate success, though in the distant future. This attitude, the neglect of the present situation, is very characteristic. Instead of realizing and accepting the past in their present life, depressives live on hope for or fear of the future.

After about a year, the situation begins to change. We enter a stage of insidiously growing disappointment. The beginning menopause of the patient's wife precipitates severe depressive reactions, during which for the first time fantasies and doubts emerge regarding the advanced age of the analyst, her fading charms, her dwindling sexual and mental functions, her ability to give. Such signals of irresistible disillusionment enter consciousness only sporadically, to be followed by immediate attempts to retransform the analyst into a good, ideal, loving image. At that time feelings of hopelessness and doubts about his own advanced age, about the biological impairment of his sexual and intellectual abilities, and the like, increase. His emotional state and the transference manifestations indicate that the ambivalence conflict begins to assume dangerous proportions and to be focused on the analyst. But the wife is still used as scapegoat for the patient's hostility. He now feels sexually and emotionally repelled by her and withdraws from her with a mixture of anger at her demands for love and sex, and intense guilt feelings. He is frankly resentful that he can no longer find comfort in sexual escapades, as in previous years. His social relations are also deteriorating. He suspects correctly that his intense absorption in the analysis may account for his loss of interest in other persons and matters. However, while constantly blaming his wife for his worse condition, he becomes even more closely tied up with the analyst than before.

There follows a long, typical period during which the patient lives only in the aura of the analyst and withdraws from other personal relations to a dangerous extent. The transference is characterized by very dependent, masochistic attitudes toward the analyst, but also by growing demands for a self-sacrificing devotion from the latter in return. Feelings of rejection by the analyst provoke brief outbursts of defiance, the slogan being: "I don't need you." His transference fantasies assume an increasingly ambivalent, sadomasochistic coloring, with corresponding fantasy and childhood material coming to the fore. In rapidy changing moods, the patient accuses the analyst alternately of being too seductive, or of being herself frustrated and sexually needy, or of being cold and rejecting. To any professional failure or success, as to any "harmful" or "helpful" interpretation, he now reacts with depression and anxiety. In some cases this period is especially critical because of the patients' exhausting, sadomasochistic provocations. They may unconsciously blackmail the analyst by playing on his guilt feelings, hoping in this way to get the longed-for response; failing to do so, they may try to elicit from the analyst a show of power, strictness, punitive anger, serving the alternate purpose of getting support for or relief from the relentless superego pressure.

To return to our case: A spring vacation of the analyst opens up a new and even worse phase. The patient feels abandoned by the analyst as by his mother, whom he lost in the spring at the age of seven, and is thrown into a severe depression. Suspecting correctly that I left him to present a paper at a convention, he decides defiantly, as in his childhood, to make himself independent. He himself begins to write a scientific book, supposed to outdo the one that I was allegedly writing. From now on this book becomes a devouring, obsessional interest; on the one hand, the one great ideal goal in his life; on the other hand, a monster which tortures him day and night with depression and anxieties. What he expects and ought to write is the best work ever done on the subject; whatever he has written appears to be a completely worthless production. The book period represents a definite, narcissistic withdrawal from me and the world in general. He has indeed tried to replace the analyst by a book, a book of which he has robbed her. His severe intestinal symptoms, with pain radiating into leg and genital, and the correlated analytic material at this time indicate the underlying incorporation and ejection fantasies. He equates what he calls the frightening, painful lump in his stomach with the analyst, with his mother and with the book whose subject relates directly to his mother's violent death. At the same time, the lump represents a "baby-penis" of which his penis is but an outside extension. He wants to throw up and deposit (ejaculate) the lump on the analyst's lap, but is scared of dying in this act. Whenever he feels freer of pain and anxiety, he is afraid to lose the lump and be empty. He is equally frightened of ever terminating the analysis or of finishing the book. The final success will be the end of him. At this point the analyst's deliberate, supportive counterattitude helps him over the most critical stage. I show a very active interest in his book, as far as my vague familiarity with the subject permits; in other words, I share the book with him and win him back by allowing a temporary situation of participation.

A phase of drastic transference interpretation, along with the analysis of deep homosexual and preoedipal fantasy material, opens up. The tide turns at last when the primalscene material and his sadomasochistic identifications with both parents can be worked through in the transference. At this point I may stop the case report. The book has been a great success among his colleagues, which for the first time he could accept. He now feels a recognized member of his professional group and is identified with it. I believe that his marital and sexual problems are in a state of final resolution, and hope to terminate the analysis this year. He has been in analysis for almost seven years. Regarding the final success, much credit must be given to this patient for his unusual insight and his ceaseless co-operation.

I hope the case illuminates the technical problems and in particular the transference difficulties to which I referred in the beginning. The point is: how can we manage to let the intensely ambivalent transference of such patients de-

velop sufficiently for analysis, and yet prevent that the patient ends his treatment in resistance; i.e., either after
emerging from a depression with a spurious transference
success, or with a negative therapeutic result, that is with a
severe depression and retreat from the analyst? Can we
avoid or do we promote such results by gratifying the patients' need, first for stimulation of their vanishing libidinous
resources, then again for an either punitive or forgiving
superego figure?

I do not think I am able to give satisfactory answers
to these questions. Generally speaking, I may express the
belief that we are at present better equipped for the analysis
of such patients by our increased insight into the ego, its
infantile developmental stages and its complex methods of
defense. Regarding modifications in our technical approach,
we can nowadays at least rely on our analytic understanding rather than our intuition.

Analysts such as Abraham,[1] who many years ago dared
to treat severely depressive and manic-depressive patients,
have commonly considered their oral overdemands, though
not understanding them in terms of defensive needs. The
prevailing attitude has been to give severely depressed patients daily sessions. My experiences with regard to the structure of the depressive conflict have taught me differently. I
believe that much more depends on the emotional quality
in the analyst's responses than on the quantity of sessions.
In fact, many depressives tolerate four or even three sessions
weekly much better than six or seven. To set a distance of
space and time between themselves and the analyst tends
to reduce their ambivalence rather than increase it. Daily
sessions may be experienced once as seductive promises too
great to be fulfilled, or then again as intolerable oralsadistic

obligations which promote the masochistic submission. If patients during a depressive period are very much retarded, we may have to prolong and, in times of suicidal danger, to increase the sessions. But I remember a very retarded, paranoid depressive patient who would frequently need ten minutes to leave the couch, but later on blame me resentfully for having stimulated her demands by the sixty-minute sessions.

As long as patients are severely retarded and blocked in their feeling and thinking, they cannot either associate freely or digest any interpretation. Even if they are able to establish and maintain contact, they may be so absorbed by anxieties, guilty fears, compulsive brooding, that they may need the therapist mainly as a patient listener to whom they are allowed to address their repetitious record of complaints. All the profit such patients may get from the treatment may be for weeks or months not more than support from a durable transference, which may carry them through the depression. Abraham stressed that, in manic-depressives, analysis proper is commonly restricted to the free intervals. But in some cases the analytic process may proceed during the depressive periods even when there is marked retardation, provided that the analyst has sufficient patience and empathy to adjust to the slowed-up emotional and thought processes of such patients. This adjustment to their pathological rhythm is especially difficult in patients with strong and rapid mood vacillations. One such patient would accuse me correctly of either being too quick and impulsive or of being too slow and torpid in my responses and interpretations. In this respect I have learned much from trial and error. There must be a continuous, subtle, empathic tie between the analyst and his depressive patients; we must be very careful not to let empty silences grow or not to talk too long, too rapidly, and too emphatically; that is, never to give too much or too little.

In any case, what those patients need is not so much frequency and length of sessions as a sufficient amount of spontaneity and flexible adjustment to their mood level, of warm understanding and especially of unwavering respect; attitudes which must not be confused with overkindness, sympathy, reassurance, etc. In periods of threatening narcissistic withdrawal, we may have to show a very active interest and participation in their daily activities and especially their sublimations. I have observed that analysts who are rather detached by nature seem to have difficulties in the treatment of depressives. Beyond this warm, flexible emotional atmosphere, without which these patients cannot work, supportive counterattitudes and interventions may occasionally be necessary; but they are only a lesser evil for which we have to pay. With these patients we are always between the devil and the deep, blue sea; this cannot be avoided. Despite the greatest caution, the analyst's attitude and his interpretations will be experienced during certain analytic stages in turn as a seductive promise, a severe rejection and lack of understanding or a sadistic punishment, all of which may increase the insatiable demands, the frustration, the ambivalence and ultimately the depression. The most precarious point is the patient's temporary need for the analyst's show of power. My experiments in this respect have not always been fortunate, but, at critical moments, the analyst must be prepared to respond with either a spontaneous gesture of kindness or even a brief expression of anger which may carry the patient over especially dangerous depressive stages. Since these patients are frequently very provocative and exasperating, such a deliberate show of emotional responses naturally presupposes the most careful self-scrutiny and self-control in the analyst. However, what I wish to stress is less the necessity or the danger of such supportive counterattitudes, but the way in which they can and must be utilized for the analysis. It seems advisable to begin early during the period of positive transference to connect interpretation of the illusory nature of the transference expectations with warnings for the future. Whenever critical transference situations arise that require special emotional counterattitudes, we must keep them carefully in mind, refer back to them later on, and explain the motivations for our behavior in terms of the patient's defensive needs and methods. In paranoid cases I have learned to avoid such interpretations carefully during periods when they accuse the analyst of wrong emotional attitudes. At such times any explanations are misused to blame the analyst even more for what appears defensive behavior on his part.

Finally, some words about the question whether it is indicated to carry the analysis of such patients to the point where their preoedipal fantasies and impulses are produced and interpreted. It appears that in some depressive patients this is simply not possible. In such cases we must limit ourselves to interpretations in the area of their ego-superego and transference conflicts, i.e., in terms of their introjective and projective mechanisms rather than in terms of the deep, underlying incorporation and ejection fantasies. But my experiences suggest that the most thorough and lasting therapeutic results could be achieved in cases where this deep fantasy material could be fully revived, understood and digested. In this connection I may refer to Gero's[2] excellent paper which shows how the analysis of these pregenital fixations will then bring the castration fears into focus and promote the progress to the genital level. (My case report showed that decisive dynamic changes seem to occur when such patients become aware of their unconscious equation of their genital with the incorporated "bad object.") When the patients are carefully prepared for this material by a slow and careful analysis of their ego-superego and transference conflicts, they can tolerate it and work it through successfully. When such deep preoedipal fantasies come to the surface, the patients may go through transitory, very disturbed or even slightly confused emotional states, often with violent psychosomatic (respiratory, circulatory, intestinal) reactions of a kind never experienced before. But apart from the recurrence of depressive periods during the treatment, in true manic-depressives, I have never had the experience of a patient going into a psychotic state provoked by the breaking through of deep id material. What seems to me important in all borderline and prepsychotic cases is to discourage and discard premature, isolated, fragmented productions of such deep material which may be brought up very early, without adequate affects, in a peculiar, easy manner, remindful of but quite different from the detached, rationalized id interpretations which obsessional-compulsive neurotics are inclined to give. In the type of cases to which I refer here, such productions have the true, uncanny coloring of the id. But they are and must be interpreted as defensive, regressive escapes, until years later they turn up again and can be understood in the infantile frame of reference and related to what is going on or what has been interpreted for years in the area of the ego and its defenses. Mostly the therapeutic success with depressives can be gauged by their ability to remodel an unfortunate life situation which prior to analysis was bound to precipitate depressive states.

Some Suggestions for Treating the Depressed Patient

SIDNEY LEVINE

Most depressed patients who consult psychoanalysts do not have the more severe forms of depression that are diagnosed as "depressive illness" but suffer essentially from neurotic disorders. Furthermore, since most neurotic patients feel depressed to some degree, in practice one is confronted more often with a depressive component of neurosis than with a typical depressed state. Treatment for many depressed patients therefore uses the general techniques of psychotherapy and psychoanalysis; yet when a patient is even slightly depressed therapy must be influenced by our understanding of repression as a disturbance of the ego. Bibring[1] defined "basic depression [as] a state of the ego whose main characteristics are a decrease of self-esteem, a more or less intense state of helplessness, a more or less intensive and extensive inhibition of functions, and a more or less intensely felt particular emotion." This definition applies not only to depressive illness, but also to the whole range of lesser degrees of depression found in neurosis.

353

The numerous contributions of psychoanalysts to depression have been ably summarized by Mendelson in his comprehensive review of the literature.[2] Most of these contributions deal with theory and only a few refer to treatment. This paper contains suggestions for treating depressive symptoms and neglects consideration of other aspects of these patients' neuroses. This does not mean that the author believes that therapy of every neurotic patient with depression should be directed chiefly at the depressive symptoms; that is not so. Nor is treatment of depression a simple matter, though a condensed paper such as this may make it seem so. The suggestions presented may have to be repeated, modified, and combined with other therapeutic efforts in a variety of ways over a period of months or years. The analysis of depressive currents, either in psychotherapy or in psychoanalysis, is not less difficult and prolonged than that of other aspects of neurosis.

General Considerations

Many patients with definite signs of depression are not conscious of feeling depressed. They may complain of fatigue, insomnia, or other symptoms, and may require much analysis of their defenses against depressive affect before becoming aware of it. A twenty-year-old male college student, who entered therapy because of academic failure, initially complained of severe fatigue but denied feeling depressed. It was found that this denial was his defense against the memory of a sister's suicide and against feelings of weakness and lack of masculinity, which were equated in his mind with being depressed. It was only after the reason for the denial was clarified that he became aware of his depressive feelings.

In some patients, depressive feeings may not be denied but remain unrecognized or poorly defined until the therapist points them out. By using the term "depression" or "depressive feelings" at appropriate times, the therapist can give the patient a label to apply to his psychic state which is so often experienced with bewilderment and fear.

Some depressed patients may express the same self-critical complaints over and over again—the "broken record" response. Such a patient may be helped to see that by this he is avoiding exploration of his problems, and that by directing all his complaints against himself he is blotting out the external world. The therapist, by exerting gentle continuous pressure and introducing topics which he thinks the patient can discuss, may often help him talk of a wider range of subjects. Also, by asking specific questions the therapist may help the patient overcome his inability to talk about particular subjects and furnish those details conspicuously absent. If the therapist is too passive, the patient's silence may increase, or he may become drowsy, and after each interview may experience a sense of failure with increased depression. Unfortunately, the reluctance of some therapists to use active techniques such as asking questions may hamper their treatment of inhibited patients. Such reluctance may occur in those who believe a good analyst or analytically oriented therapist is not active in his therapy. It may also occur in those who are somewhat inhibited themselves and therefore limited in the degree of activity they can comfortably employ. Some of these are not fully conscious of the degree of their blocks and rationalize their involuntary silences as decisions to wait for the patient to talk.

Patients who bring little psychic content to therapy frequently report their dreams. In some instances the dreams have to be written down on awakening to avoid forgetting them by the time the therapeutic hour arrives. When this special effort is made, the patient often has a sense of relief, because he then feels better prepared for his therapeutic session and does not expect the intense emotional suffering he has experienced in the past when facing his therapist in stony silence.

It is characteristic for depressed patients to have pre-conscious or unconscious fears of insanity. Some of these fears result from depressive symptoms such as lack of energy and diminished ability to perform certain tasks. If the patient has difficulty concentrating or feels confused, he may interpret these symptoms as early manifestations of severe mental disorganization. Furthermore, there may be some return of the repressed, which often leads to obsessive fears. Brought to consciousness, these fears tend to lose some of their intensity. One may also help the patient to understand that depression is typically accompanied by some depletion of psychic energy which may lead to a variety of symptoms such as fatigue, sensitivity to outside stimuli, fearfulness, and withdrawal.

A not uncommon symptom is unrealistic fear of the consequences of losing control of aggressive and regressive impulses. It is often helpful to point out that the patient's fears of losing control imply lack of confidence in his "automatic control." He may be able to see that control is to a high degree involuntary. The therapist might use as an illustration the automatic controls that come into play when a person drives for long distances in his car. The driver may be absorbed in fantasy, yet his basic patterns of behavior persist. When the patient has less fear of losing control he may be ready to analyze the genetic basis for this fear, proceeding, for example, to explore childhood experiences of bladder and bowel incontinence or sexual and aggressive acts. Thus he can understand why he has no confidence in his automatic controls; often it is because he saw that his parents lacked this confidence and believed vigilance necessary to check impulses.

Many patients do not know the immediate precipitating causes of their depressions. A teacher became depressed immediately on hearing of the promotion of one of his colleagues but did not realize the effect this news produced in him. Helping such a patient examine the circumstances of onset of his depression may make him willing to explore further, give him hope, and make therapy more meaningful. The patient who believes that his depression arises entirely from hidden internal sources may feel victimized by forces over which he sees no hope of getting control. When he understands that events of his life have contributed he may become more optimistic.

A middle-aged man with recurrent depressions entered psychotherapy in a depressed state one year after terminating a successful course of treatment. It soon became clear that, although he had acquired considerable insight during his treatment, he was not aware of a major precipitating cause of his depressions. When the circumstances surrounding the onset of several depressions were carefully reviewed, a common incident stood out: each depression had developed shortly after he had become associated with a highly aggressive man. His current depression came a few months after he started a new job under such a man whom he had initially idealized, but who, as time went on, became increasingly overbearing. The patient, who felt weak and unassertive, unconsciously attempted to borrow the strength of aggressive men, but sooner or later became the object of their aggression. When he finally understood his pattern, he decided to work for an unaggressive man whom he could respect for ability alone. After this change there was improvement.

When a person becomes depressed his use of projection may increase, especially projection of self-critical feelings. Early in treatment the patient can often become aware of his tendency to project, even though he may still not be able to control it. This understanding enables him to suspend retaliatory action and to view his projections with some scepticism. A young doctor who entered therapy with a moderately severe depression was considering quitting his job because he thought his associates were dissatisfied with his work. He mentioned that after he had presented a case at a recent staff meeting those present were highly critical. When asked how they showed it, he could say only that one doctor made a disparaging remark and that the others hurried off after the conference. Pressed for details, he stated that one doctor had commented "nice going" in a sarcastic manner; he had considered this remark sarcastic because of the doctor's tone. Now he began to wonder if he might have misinterpreted the doctor's attitude; after the staff meeting, he recalled, he had at first thought the doctor sincere, but something told him this was not so and he brushed the idea aside.

He also began to doubt whether the other doctors, who were always in a hurry, had really left the conference more abruptly than usual. He soon came to see that he projected his self-criticism in many other situations and perceived his associates to be unfriendly whether they were or not. He tended to suppose that the rejections of others made him feel depressed, when in fact his state of depression made him feel constantly rejected. He became aware that it was only after onset of his depression that he felt generally rejected by his associates; furthermore, this feeling fluctuated in intensity with the level of his depression. This understanding led him to resolve not to quit his job but to remain and work out the reasons for his depressed state.

Another depressed patient, a middle-aged woman, withdrew from her bridge club because she felt the other members rejected her, supposing that they avoided her. The truth was that their "avoidance" began only after she became depressed and seemed to her friends to want to be left alone. She had misinterpreted as rejections the attempts of others to be considerate of her feelings. Knowing this helped her return to the club where she was welcomed. Psychic impotence and frigidity often become an obsessive preoccupation and are seen as causes of the depression rather than symptoms of it.

Much attention must be given to the complications and vicious circles that develop when a patient becomes depressed. For example, failures in performance may lead to depression; the resulting depression by its inhibitions of thought and action leads to further failures in performance, which accentuate the depression. Such failures may have disappointed others—employers, for instance—in the patient. It is important for the therapist to acknowledge the possibility of such changes of attitude in others, regardless of how much the patient seems to be distorting them, so that they may be realistically evaluated.

His family often urges the depressed patient to "pull

yourself together." Their critical responses may increase his
depression and lead him to complain that they do not understand his difficulties. Such a patient can often be helped to
see that it may be as unrealistic for him to expect his family
suddenly to understand his emotional difficulties as it is for
them to expect him suddenly to get over his depression.

Depressed patients are usually unaware of their intense
anger, much of which is redirected internally through the
superego, leading to guilt and loss of self-esteem. Efforts
directly to counteract the guilt and loss of self-esteem are
generally unsuccessful and frequently elicit a distrustful
feeling that the doctor is merely trying to be supportive.
One usually has greater success if he points out that the patient castigates himself primarily because much of his anger
has nowhere to go but toward himself, since certain inner
forces do not permit its discharge toward external objects
or even its abreaction. The patient may then realize that his
excessive guilt will continue until he finds and eliminates
the source of the anger or finds some temporary outlet for
it. This helps the patient avoid seeking reassurance or ease
for his guilt from the therapist and leads him instead to
search for the sources of his hostility.

Attempts to counteract directly the archaic superego of
"borderline" or melancholic patients are also bound to be
unsuccessful. An archaic superego is characterized by regressive narcissistic aspirations and pathological guilt, both
of which occur only when there is considerable regression.
Regressive narcissistic aspirations reflect primary narcissistic libido directed into the superego, and pathological guilt
results from primary aggression directed into the superego
and then turned against the self. Until the underlying regressive process is reversed and new outlets for libido are

found, the archaic superego tends to persist. This type of superego should not be confused with the strict superego that arises from internalization of excessive demands of parents and parent-substitutes in early life. A strict superego is nonregressive and may be directly counteracted by insight, by suggestion, or by encouraging identification of patient with therapist, which permits replacement of the excessive demands of parents by the more moderate demands of the therapist.

Some depressed patients turn so much of their hostility inward that the therapist may not know how much hostility is being aroused by his therapeutic efforts unless he watches the patient closely, especially for indirect indications of hostility. If a patient becomes self-critical or bemoans his fate immediately after an interpretation, the therapist can infer that the interpretation has met resistance and that the hostility thus aroused is being detoured into the superego and then directed against the self. A comparable detour of hostility through the superego may occur following frustration of unconscious transference wishes; this anger, instead of being directed at the therapist, may be expressed through guilt, self-castigation, or feelings of inadequacy. By observing these reactions the therapist can evaluate how much interpretation and how much frustration of transference wishes the patient can tolerate without becoming more depressed.

When a patient becomes conscious of hostile feelings, he may begin to discharge some of them outside the therapy. A middle-aged man who had entered psychoanalysis for treatment of long-standing depression became conscious of his hostility toward his thirteen-year-old son, and after abreacting some of this felt less depressed. But before his hostility could be analyzed he decide to express it directly to his son. He began to criticize the boy and his son became more rebellious. The patient then increased his attack, believing he must do so to prevent his son from becoming delinquent and to protect himself from severe depression. Urged by the analyst to restrain his criticism until he understood his hostility, he at first said that the therapist did not understand how intense were the son's provocations. Gradually he began to see that he had formerly dealt with his anger by repression and withdrawal but now by tantrums. It then became clear to him that awareness of hostility should lead to exploration of its sources. The patient checked his outbursts without experiencing the recurrence of depression he had feared, and as he gained new insight his relation with his son improved.

In many depressed patients therapy must be directed largely toward relieving excessive repression of libido, which prevents adequate sexual satisfaction and causes depression. A nineteen-year-old college girl complained of depression and weeping for about a year. She was preoccupied with thoughts of her mother's death six years before and supposed that this was a delayed grief reaction. Psychotherapy revealed that she was inhibited sexually and could tolerate little bodily contact with men. She was convinced that she could never marry or have sexual intercourse. The sexual inhibitions were the chief cause of her depression and her preoccupation with her mother's death showed a powerful regressive wish to return to "the good old days" of childhood. Therapy was directed chiefly to increasing her tolerance for sexual fantasies, feelings, and impulses.

Analysis of the transference is of great importance in depression. Libido is sometimes withdrawn from important objects and concentrated on the therapist; transference frustration becomes intense and the depression becomes accentuated. If the concentration of libido on the therapist is pointed out, the patient can usually see that by disengaging himself from outside relationships he has created a state of frustration that cannot be satisfied by the relation with the therapist. A twenty-five-year-old married woman who attributed her depression to being completely blocked in writing her Ph.D thesis developed an intense positive transference and expressed a variety of sexual fantasies toward the therapist, such as lying close to him or masturbating him. During this phase of treatment she became more discouraged about her thesis and was convinced that she would never complete it. As therapy continued she regressed to a masochistic transference in which she had fantasies of the therapist beating her and forcing her to write. These fantasies were related to childhood fantasies of being beaten by her father. After analysis of this content, her writing block was temporarily relieved, but in a few days it returned and she again felt hopeless. When it was pointed out that she was withdrawing from her husband and her friends she was surprised but recognized that she had been doing so for many months and did not understand why. She was told that concentration of her sexual interest in the therapist indicated withdrawal of sexual interest from major objects; that she wished to get everything from the therapist and could therefore expect only frustration. Next day she did not seem depressed and was neater; she was also more optimistic about completing her thesis on which she was again at work.

Analysis of a patient's tendency to withdraw may cause him to change and quickly become overengaged with others.

A depressed young physicist, who had withdrawn to his laboratory for several months, suddenly became consultant for a number of other projects. His resulting competition with several highly aggressive scientists made him feel inadequate and depressed anew and he fell behind in his own experiments. When he understood the counterphobic nature of his activity and how it caused his depression to return, he confined himself to more appropriate jobs.

In treating depression, one obviously tries to support the patient's hopefulness; a hopeful therapist transmits this feeling to his patient. Also, the manner of presenting interpretations can determine the degree of support they offer. After an operation for herniated disc a middle-aged woman in my care developed a postoperative infection which prolonged her hospitalization and depressed her, chiefly because of intense fear of death. She complained that her wound took long to heal and that it seemed she had been in the hospital for several months (actually for only four weeks). I told her I could understand her dissatisfaction and suffering but that ten years later her hospitalization would seem a brief interlude, diminished by time. After this brief conversation the patient was less depressed. By indirectly transmitting the idea that she would be alive ten years hence, I was able to make her more hopeful and, since this idea was slipped in as an incidental comment, it was not perceived as a direct effort to reassure and therefore did not meet the natural resistance to such efforts. Eissler[3] produced a similar effect in a dying woman by giving her a subscription to the monthly programs of her favorite broadcasting station. Aside from its symbolic significance, this gift conveyed the message that the doctor expected her to live long enough to enjoy the subscription. It therefore counteracted her fear of imminent death.

A therapist usually cannot "manipulate" a patient out of feeling hopeless,[4] but he can often help the patient see that the hopelessness is not realistic but rather an inevitable manifestation of depression itself and deserving analysis. Hopelessness is usually associated with fears and a moderate amount of pressure may be necessary to help the patient spell out what he fears is going to happen. For example, when a patient expresses a fear of losing his business, one can encourage him to elaborate on what he thinks would happen after its loss. He may give voice to childhood notions about poverty and starvation. He may thus be helped to face the expected humiliation of being exposed as a failure and also to say whose ridicule he fears most; this may show the importance of object relationships he previously minimized.

Hopelessness is often expressed as "I can't do this or that." The patient's conviction that he never will be able to face his fears is analyzed. The graduate student who "cannot" write a thesis may be saying not only that he fears exposing his thoughts in writing but also that he believes his fears will continue to be overpowering. This conviction is often related to early experiences of intense anxiety or humiliation.

Some patients retain false hopes in defense against underlying feelings of hopelessness; they are reluctant to abandon highly cathected goals and fear intense humiliation if they admit defeat. The business of a sixty-two-year-old man began to fail and he was unsuccessful in attempts to refinance it, sell it, or merge it. His attorney convinced him that the business was hopeless and should be liquidated, but the patient could not bear to do this and lived in hope of finding an investor to save it. His underlying hopelessness was warded off by false hope. Unfortunately his therapist, because of countertransference, at first supposed the hopelessness merely a product of the man's depression, identified himself with the patient in his wish to save the business, and thought refinancing it a realistic plan. When the therapist understood his countertransference, he analyzed the situation, noting that the patient feared not only loss but also humiliation from business associates if he admitted defeat. The patient accepted liquidation as wise and began to work through his grief over loss of the business.

A similar problem was present in a first-year medical student who became depressed after failing his mid-year examinations and sought psychotherapy with the hope that it would help him succeed. In college serious academic difficulties had necessitated repeated tutoring, summer school courses, and a fifth year of study. Psychoanalysis at that time had yielded insight but little improvement in his work. He passed all premedical courses but had great difficulty gaining acceptance to medical school; he had had, he said, to "sell myself" to the director of admissions. All the evidence indicated that he was ill-suited for medical school. However he was extremely reluctant to consider withdrawing and talked of taking summer courses and repeating his first year of study. It was necessary for the therapist to explore the patient's fear of leaving school which led to analysis of his relation to parents and siblings and his fear of their ridicule. A change now appeared: the patient saw that he was compulsively repeating a pattern and that, if he continued, his work would continue to be poor if he survived at all. He decided to withdraw and at once became less depressed; after his mourning over loss of a highly cathected goal, he turned to a vocation for which he showed talent.

It is common for a depressed patient to believe that the therapist has underestimated both his suffering and the severity of his illness. The therapist can help by showing that he knows how depressed the patient feels and is willing to face the difficult problems of treatment. It is generally better for the therapist not to minimize the severity of the depression but to seem hopeful concerning its outcome.

Fluctuations in the level of depression are likely to be confusing not only to patient but also to therapist. A temporary relapse may convince the patient that he is getting worse, but the therapist should expect these relapses and must interpret them to the patient as not necessarily indicating lack of progress. The patient's course may be generally a rising curve though fluctuations produce many hills and valleys. To sketch such a hypothetical graph may encourage the patient.

In some instances interviewing two members of a family together may be effective in treating depression in one of them, especially when the one who is well has unconscious ego-syntonic patterns of response that put continuous stress on the other member and is reluctant to undertake therapy. After a few unproductive interviews with a severely depressed thirty-year-old woman. I called her husband into the office with her. He spoke fluently and had complete mastery of the situation. When after some time it appeared that his wife wanted to say something, I turned to her and she made a brief comment but she was quickly and subtly squelched by her husband; he monopolized the interview. His tyranny forced her to submit to repeated narcissistic wounds. She feared him intensely and internalized her hostility toward him; the more depressed she became the more dependent on him she grew, and the more fearful of antagonizing him. The three of us continued to meet and I told them what I saw. It was not long before the wife began to assert herself and her husband reacted with overt hostility; shown this, he checked his aggression and began to examine it. When they understood their interaction and its effects she was cured of her depression and has stayed well for the five years since.

Thus "identification with the aggressor" can contribute to depression, provided the aggression is directed toward the self, a process that is fairly common and can at times resemble *folie à deux*. A twenty-eight-year-old married woman, severely depressed, at times had hysterical reactions during which she pounded the walls of her room and screamed at herself in despair. She praised her husband for his tolerance and patience and in general idealized him. He prided himself upon never losing his temper and always being polite to his wife. She is emotionally disturbed, he said, and thus he is more fortunate than she; he would show himself a man of endurance who had married for better or for worse and would live up to his marital vows. He considered her emotional state to be similar to a physical illness and denied that he contributed to it in any way. Therefore he was a devoted, long-suffering husband. It soon became apparent, however, that he was a highly intolerant man who managed to hide his hostility and maintain a polite and disarming façade toward both his wife and his colleagues. She had responded by becoming intolerant of herself—one might even say that she had permitted herself to be "brainwashed" by him—and also critical of herself, rather than fighting back against his subtle aggression. Becoming aware of the underlying hostility of her husband she saw how he contributed to her own; she pointed out to him some of his responses and eventually helped him to become aware that he did in fact have intense angry feelings and

was scornful and disrespectful toward her. Thereafter he
sought therapy for his own emotional difficulties.

Masochism, which is usually found in states of depression, puzzles us because experiences we should expect to
interfere with satisfaction actually produce it; but we can
understand this if we appreciate how often experiences that
appear to create disturbances in libido economy really improve it. A simple example is a depressed patient, suffering
from impotence, who found that only when he subtly provoked his wife to attack him could he freely show anger
toward her and then become reconciled with her, with the
result that his impotence temporarily disappeared. He
masochistically sought narcissistic injury—a circuitous route
toward improved libido economy.

It is important not to confuse nonmasochistic behavior
that happens to result in unpleasant consequences with behavior in which the "aim" is masochistic. For example, a
patient's failure in an examination is not necessarily due to
a "wish to fail" for it may be the result of inhibitions in
studying that accompany a depressed state.

Analysis of masochistic patterns is important in treatment of depression; since it has been discussed by many
authors[5] only a few technical suggestions are mentioned
here. When the masochistic patient bemoans his fate and repeatedly castigates himself, I have at times found it helpful
to tell him that he is behaving like a person who throws himself into a ditch, smears himself with mud, and then complains about how dirty he is. Such a comment can facilitate
analysis of underlying self-destructive tendencies. If the patient indulges in "brinksmanship," I may compare him to a
man who leans over the bank of a river to see how far he can

lean before falling in but must fall in to find out. Such preliminary clarifications are to be followed by more careful
analysis of the sexual and aggressive components of the
masochism.

Some therapists have argued that one should freely
express anger at such patients to satisfy some of their masochistic needs, a recommendation, unfortunately, likely to
come from those who find it difficult to control their anger
and seek to justify behavior they cannot control. Others out
of shame try to hide their anger from the patient and even
from themselves. But we ought to accept the fact that we
sometimes get angry, for some patients are adept at evoking
our anger and are strongly motivated to do so. To tell the
patient that he has succeeded in evoking the therapist's
anger often helps to clear the way for analysis of his provocations; to understand that he has achieved a neurotic victory is an important insight.

The negative therapeutic reaction, not uncommon in the
depressed, may reflect not only a desire to defeat the analyst
as well as oneself, but also a re-enforcement of this desire
due to the mounting hostility likely to result from sensitivity
to the analyst's interpretations as severe narcissistic injuries.
Careful dosing of interpretations and tactful clarification of
sensitive reactions to them may help to counteract the negative therapeutic reaction. This reaction may also arise from
intense transference frustration due to concentration of libido on the therapist. When this is clarified, redistribution of
libido to other objects may occur and relieve the negative
therapeutic reaction. In still other instances, negative therapeutic reaction may result from the therapist's reluctance to
use active techniques when the patient is severely blocked;
the patient tries unsuccessfully to overcome his block and
hence feels failure after each interview.

Many patients seek relief from depression by acting out sexual impulses. A thirty-five-year-old man entered analysis because he wished to understand why he was repeatedly unfaithful to his wife. He said his marriage was a happy one but, nevertheless, he sought extramarital affairs which, although temporarily satisfying, left him feeling guilty and anxious. It soon became apparent that his infidelity counteracted feelings of depression. As he examined his depression he gradually became aware of the problems in his marriage; but he was afraid to acknowledge them to himself because of fears, for example, that he might be tempted to get divorced like his cousin who was now lonesome and unsuccessful. He also feared that if his marriage broke up his father would disown him. The patient eventually saw that he was very angry at his wife and was repeatedly running away from her in actuality or in fantasy, even though he was much in love with her. All his life he had run away—when he was young, for example, into military service to get away from his mother with whom he fought. After long analysis this patient became able to deal with the tension in his marriage without developing a depression and running away.

A thirty-year-old married man entered psychotherapy because of depression of a year's duration, accompanied by impotence. After a while he confessed that when most depressed he sought homosexual affairs, which disgusted him and convinced him that he was basically "a homosexual." The patient's employer had replaced his father who died when he was eight and at first they had worked closely together, but as business expanded and new assistants were employed the patient felt brushed aside, although actually he had simply withdrawn in a sulky manner and become depressed. Moreover during the previous year the boss had been going through a trying period and was also depressed.

The patient saw nothing of this; he found it hard to believe that this man whom he had so idealized could have emotional problems of his own. But as the patient saw that his employer's irritability was not directed only at him he began to seek out and respond to his employer and the improved relation ended his depression, his impotence, and his homosexual activity.

Analysis of Reactions to Psychological Stress

Four categories of psychological stress may contribute to depression: loss, attack, restraint, and threats.[6] These categories have theoretical as well as clinical utility. A thirty-year-old man undergoing analysis became depressed when a contract upon which his business depended was cancelled. Convinced that his business would fail, he spoke mostly of his own guilt; he was responsible for losing the contract since he had failed to meet the requirements of the "parent" company. It became clear that he was directing all his aggression against himself in a manner typical of the depressed. It was difficult to mobilize his anger at the executive who had cancelled the contract, but when he finally expressed it, he revealed that the man was generally considered ruthless and gave several examples of his unfairness to the patient who had made many concessions to him. The patient had always withdrawn from conflict with men. As a child he had feared his father and repeatedly tried to appease him and he ran from fights with other boys. He was doing the same thing now, blinding himself to the other man's aggression and dishonesty. As the patient saw that he had been cheated and had not deserved to lose the contract he began to fight back rather than surrender as he had always done previously. This roused anxiety until he could understand his fears of the other man and of his father. He took successful legal action and reorganized his business and his depression improved.

Continuous pain may have depressing effects and may be experienced as an attack, even a frightening one. It is common for patients with continuous pain to imagine that they have serious illness, even though repeatedly reassured, and it is also common for these notions to disappear when the pain is relieved. The attending physician may not realize how important it is to give the patient an adequate amount of pain-relieving medication. Some physicians become especially reluctant to give narcotics when a patient is depressed, supposing depressed persons more susceptible to addiction.

Realistic fear often causes depression. For example, a young man in service overseas became depressed because his orders for returning home were delayed, causing him to fear he was to be sent to Laos. As soon as the crisis there subsided, his depression disappeared.

Once depression develops from any cause, minor physical symptoms seem to mean serious physical illness, rousing unconscious fear of death. Making the fear conscious helps but only relief of the depression can remove the fear. Showing that the patient's fears are groundless may relieve the depression, as in the case of a scientist who feared—needlessly, since only he could provide evidence to substantiate them—that his ideas had been stolen for another man's book.

Awareness of the effects of "restraint," both external and internal, can also be useful in treating depression. When a patient with a coronary attack is kept in bed for several weeks, he may become depressed as much from restraint as from reaction to his illness. Modification of the medical regime to permit greater mobility usually can be effected. In such a case one must also take into account not only the immobility imposed but also the patient's reaction to the physician's recommendations. The restrictions placed upon a patient by his own fears are often most important.

A woman referred—seemingly with full agreement and acceptance—to a gynecologist by her doctor revealed in psychotherapy that she resented the doctor's having, as she felt, constrained her to accept the consultation. Her sense of restraint was due to her fear of self-assertion; understanding this she told her doctor that she wished to be free to decide herself whether to submit to any gynecological procedures recommended. After this she felt freer to reserve judgment. The same patient supposed, wrongly, that her therapist did not approve of her dating a man unless there was a clear possibility of marriage. Analysis showed that she imputed to her therapist some of her father's attitudes about dating which she had made hers at an early age. Her self-restraint was now mitigated and she became freer in her dating.

Narcissism and Depression

Those susceptible to depression are at times called highly narcissistic. Freud[7] noted that their object choices are made "on a narcissistic basis" and that when they are disappointed by the loved object they readily regress to "original narcissism." Yet much evidence indicates that these individuals are vulnerable not only to loss but also to other types of psychological stress. Many such persons can remain free of depression only if they are largely free from stress. Therefore they tend to seek relationships that promise to protect them from loss, attack, restraint, and threats. They also employ a variety of narcissistic defenses such as the illusion of excessive love. Menaker[8] described a patient who maintained his libido economy by the illusion that he was greatly admired by the analyst and became depressed when the analyst pointed out his marked passivity.

Since patients susceptible to depression may need excessive love, their ability to obtain it may be critical. The readiness to initiate relationships—to give love to others— is important if one is to receive love, but narcissistic individuals tend to be blocked in this ability. Some of them search for love not only from specific objects but also from people in general. One patient who spoke often to audiences was not satisfied unless he could have their full and favorable attention. Patients susceptible to depression may over-react to lack of warmth in others. Unless their advances find a response their libido economy becomes disturbed; once such a person has shown positive feelings he becomes enraged if they are not returned. Hence he may size up the situation carefully before revealing his feelings in order to make sure that the other person is ready to reciprocate.

The ego ideal of the narcissistic individual shows his intense desire for freedom from stress: through attainment of high aspirations he hopes to obtain excessive quantities of love from external and internal objects as well as sure protection from attack, restraint, and external and internal threats. Such a person may therefore make great demands not only upon others but also upon himself and be highly perfectionistic.

Analysis of the narcissistic core of the depressed patients personality is essential, with constant effort to delineate over-reactions to innumerable experiences of stress.
There must be repeated clarifications of what Murray calls
attitudes of "narcissistic entitlement,"[9] attitudes that follow
the basic formula "I have a right to what I want" and are
likely to produce both indignation when one's self-defined
"rights" are not recognized by others and a sense of righteousness in making repeated demands for such recognition.

We must pay attention to the patient's sensitivity. When
a patient becomes aware of reacting sensitively, he has made
a significant step forward and another comes when he realizes that his sensitivity fluctuates with the level of his
depression. A young woman patient, moderately depressed,
became upset when a friend made a not unkind remark
about the patient's excessive sweating; the patient was
helped by her therapist to see that she was ashamed of her
sweating and resented having it pointed out to her, and that
it was only when she was depressed that she was so very
sensitive. Many patients deny their sensitivity and rationalize their responses by exaggerating the intensity of the
stimulus, a distortion of reality. A simple illustration can
make this clear to the patient; for example, that an oversensitive person may explain his over-reaction to dental pain
by claiming that his dentist is very rough, even eventually
charging that all dentists are sadistic.

A highly sensitive patient may have to learn to avoid
certain stresses to protect himself against recurrences of
depression. Sometimes the patient gravitates toward the
very stresses to which he is most sensitive. A sensitive young
graduate student repeatedly dated hypercritical girls who
depressed him. Understanding his ambivalent attachment

to his mother helped him avoid his oedipal problem by finding pleasure in more tolerant girls.

Highly narcissistic patients may have to be helped to obtain increased narcissistic satisfaction to get relief from depression. Some patients, by achieving more, attain a sense of increased competence and greater admiration of others. Some can obtain increased narcissistic satisfaction from love objects if their relation with them can be improved. Hence insight into how the patient complicates his major relationships is essential. A young narcissistic woman who entered analysis in a state of moderate anxiety and depression complained that her husband repeatedly withdrew from her. It was necessary to clarify the subtle excessive demands she made upon him and her spitefulness toward him when he did not meet her demands; she thus became aware of the reason for her husband's withdrawal.

Tact is necessary to protect the patient from narcissistic injuries during treatment. The patient's self-esteem is already broken down, and any clarification or interpretation may lead to a narcissistic injury. The therapist may convey that he knows the blocked patient is trying to talk and is not being uncooperative. We can support the patient's narcissism by recognizing his efforts to live up to his principles in therapy and elsewhere. In discussing a patient's hostility, it can be made clear that one is fully aware of his repeated efforts to be kind and considerate. The therapist's tact depends in part on careful observation of the patient's sensitivity to specific types of therapeutic intervention, a sensitivity the patient often attempts to hide.

It is not uncommon for patients to use for defense the understanding acquired in therapy concerning events in their early lives. When a patient revives memories of early traumatic experiences, he may use this knowledge to justify his present difficulties by blaming his parents and others for some of his current failures,—for his trouble in learning, for example, whereas further analysis shows the parental pressure he complains of came after the trouble started from a different cause. Such a patient may justify his anger at his parents by comparing them to his idealized analyst. This sort of narcissistic prop for the patient's self-esteem may tempt us to analyze it prematurely, accentuating the patient's depression. Such defenses may even have to be temporarily re-enforced to support a shaky narcissism until the patient's depression improves sufficiently to enable him to tolerate analysis of them.

The strong oral character traits and the excessive envy that accompanies them in many depressed patients must be analyzed. This envy is often expressed thus: "Others get whatever they want; why not I?" This patient does not perceive clearly the inevitable frustrations of other people and the innumerable compromises they must make, and his failure to perceive is probably defensive. If others get what they want, the patient also hopes to gratify all his wishes. Such illusions perpetuate envy and, as a result, the patient who acts on this principle may lose his friends. Such patients also envy the therapist, who seems to be omnipotent and able to gratify every wish.

Depressed patients often demand special consideration from the therapist, sometimes in a subtle way, as did a middle-aged woman who repeatedly brought her psychotherapist inexpensive gifts. When she brought a small sculptured donkey it was learned that she thought of donkeys as being as clumsy as herself and the gift was a way of leaving a symbol of herself in the therapist's office. Her gifts turned out to be motivated not, as she rationalized, by the golden rule but by her special modification of it: so do unto others as to force them to treat you as you want. The underlying wish was for special attention. When she did not get it she became angry and shouted "ingrate!" because she did not get what she claimed was merely an appropriate response. When she finally understood her forcing maneuvers she also understood why her gifts were not as well received as she had hoped.

In treating depressed patients it is important to analyze those patterns of behavior that lead them to feel humiliated. At a recent symposium on narcissism, Waelder[10] told of a young man who could not say "no" to his girl for fear of losing her love. He would reluctantly agree to her demands but this made him feel humiliated and impotent. His consequent anger and depression led him to pick arguments with her and she, in turn, would also become angry. Analysis of his inability to say "no" and its consequences led to his becoming less compliant and no longer depressed. A man I treated was equally unable to refuse his mother's demand that he and his wife travel one hundred miles every weekend to visit her. These visits made him irritable and his appeasements of his mother made him feel ashamed before his wife. Only when his fears of his mother were brought to consciousness and analyzed was he able to change his behavior and protect himself from the humiliation that led to his depressed state.

Humiliation causes shame and to analyze the origins of shame is a long process. These origins are two in number. Sexual thoughts, feelings, and impulses mobilize shame and are inhibited or repressed in consequence. More superficially, a secondary shame is roused by the basic shame and its accompanying inhibitions; or to put it simply, "one feels ashamed of reacting with shame." This secondary shame leads one to hide inhibitions and "carry on" in spite of them. Both levels of shame require analysis if economy of the libido is to be improved and relieved.

Some persons are easily made ashamed by encountering overfriendliness. The therapist may therefore have to remain somewhat aloof initially to avoid arousing uncomfortable shame while he and the patient get to know each other; otherwise the patient may break off treatment. Later the patient can tolerate greater warmth from the therapist and communicate without experiencing intense shame, though it may take some time for the patient to reveal his fantasies or to relate embarrassing events. Many patients fail to reveal basic problems because of intense shame but may speak so that the therapist can guess the secret and thus help expose the problem. (Freud[11] tells of doing this in a case of depression. When the "Rat-man" could not bear to describe the punishment that so disturbed him, Freud said, ". . . I would do all I could . . . to guess the full meaning of any hints he gave me. Was he perhaps thinking of impalement? 'No, not that . . . ,'" the patient replied, but with this help gradually and haltingly went on to tell what he had in mind.) A single woman of thirty-five with a moderately severe depression talked a great deal about her fear that she would never be able to marry because men invariably dropped her after a brief relationship. It was only when the therapist introduced the topic of homosexuality that the patient confessed her homosexual affairs and her intense shame concerning them. It is worth noting that this patient had previously been in treatment with another therapist for over a year without revealing these facts.

When the patient through treatment ceases to avoid tasks, formerly feared, that satisfy his narcissistic aspirations, his depression may be replaced by fear. If he continues to face some of these tasks in spite of his fear, he may gradually become less afraid.[12] A young physician undergoing analysis for anxiety and depression avoided all professional activities other than his practice. When he saw that this avoidance was due to fear of speaking up in professional groups, he began to attend hospital meetings regularly, making himself heard increasingly as time went on. As he thus became more satisfied with himself he experienced considerable relief from depression.

Sometimes, after becoming aware of certain fears, a patient goes too far and undertakes tasks that severely frighten him; if this causes mild feelings of depersonalization, new fears appear. A thirty-five-year-old man who undertook for the first time to speak without notes before a large audience sensed mild depersonalization and when his talk was over feared he was going insane. When he understood that the depersonalization arose from intense fear of a large audience, the secondary fear of insanity disappeared. Such a patient can thus learn how much fear he can tolerate without depersonalization—and, thereafter, usually stays within his range of tolerance.

The patient's withdrawal from everyday activities may, by depriving him of major satisfactions, accentuate his depression. A forty-year-old man rarely accepted invitations to social functions unless urged to do so. He avoided many tasks around the house such as bringing in his young children's bicycles or playing with them. He explained that his work demanded most of his energy. Becoming aware—to his surprise—through analysis how many activities he was avoiding, he resolved to seek out other people instead of hiding behind a book. His new participation pleased him, he saw that it caused only slight tension, and it rendered unnecessary the fantasies of successful business ventures and torrid sexual affairs that had compensated him for his feelings of weakness and impotence.

In many patients, analysis of fears that prevent their taking advantage of their opportunities is essential to relieve depression. A twenty-two-year-old woman with recurrent severe depressions had been used by her very disturbed divorced mother for narcissistic purposes. The mother repeatedly attacked the girl, her only child, shattering her self-esteem and convincing her that she was responsible for all the mother's suffering. Her jealous, emotional, and even violent mother taught her to expect that if she showed interest in anyone else the mother would desert her or murder her. Although she had made one attempt to live away from home, she had to return after a few months. In therapy her fear of her mother's threats and their implications had to be made conscious and worked through before she could seek new objects and new aims. She became able to live away from home, to satisfy some of her own narcissistic aspirations, and to recover from her depression.

Depression may diminish when a patient gains new sources of satisfaction in physical activity such as golf or dancing, which led to a career and largely prevented depression in an adolescent patient of mine. It is especially helpful to direct the depressed patient into satisfying activity; in fact one should be wary of doing anything to discourage activity in the depressed patient even if some of it is clearly symptomatic. As long as the patient is not destructive to himself or to others, his activity may give him purpose and narcissistic satisfaction. To be verbally blocked deprives one of interchange of positive feeling with others but withdrawal from activity causes an even greater loss.

To reverse the depressed patient's tendency to withdraw may take much therapy, as the following case shows. A thirty-five-year-old man, depressed to varying degree for many years, entered psychoanalysis because of what he wrongly considered lack of success at his work. The fluctuations in his depression proved to correspond with the state of his marriage. He was often angry at his wife for what he supposed to be coldness. He would often stay up reading much later than she and then, furious at finding her asleep, would feel rejected and would masturbate. After this he would be depressed for several days, distant and spiteful to his wife, pushing her away if she tried to be affectionate. After he had punished her thus for several days, his depression would begin to lift and they would have sexual intercourse. Although he reached orgasm, he experienced only partial satisfaction, blaming his wife's "frigidity." If she delayed even briefly when he made advances to her he accused her of unwillingness to have intercourse. She feared his irritability, but when she fought back he became temporarily more considerate and less depressed and found more satisfaction in the relationship.

After many months of analysis the patient saw that it was when he was most hostile to his wife that she seemed to him most rejecting and that it was mainly when his impotence was most pronounced that he supposed her frigid. He realized that by his hostile behavior he had intimidated her and had even subtly threatened her with divorce—a thought he could not admit to having entertained until analysis made him more conscious of it. He recognized that to feel affectionate embarrassed him and made him hostile. As he now saw the problem, he said, he had the choice of resolving his embarrassment and liberating his affectionate feelings or going through life as a chronically depressed man. At first he found it difficult to overcome his embarrassment and show affection, but although he still became angry at his wife, especially if she was reluctant to have sexual relations, he gradually ceased to sulk and withdraw. He found that his previous notion that he could get relief from depression only through sexual intercourse was incorrect, and he tolerated postponements of intercourse without anger. His wife became less depressed as he improved and he realized that she was far from frigid, although she was less responsive sexually when she was depressed, just as he was.

The patient attributed some of his improvement to finding out how stubborn he was and to learning how to "give in" rather than remain trapped in a neurotic battle against his wife. He also stated that, since he could not always obtain quick relief from his tension, he had to learn to be patient. His anger had to be resolved to some degree before he could become affectionate. He became able to trust his wife and know that she loved him. Whereas he had gained much of his sense of strength from stubbornness and rebellion, he now obtained it from "giving in" and taking responsibility for resolving some of the tensions in the marriage.

Negative Reactions to the Depressed Patient

Depressed patients can be frustrating especially if they resist treatment or show negative therapetuic reaction. Some are highly provocative, in particular those who repeatedly complain that they are making little progress in therapy and imply that the therapist is not doing enough to help. In addition, just as enthusiasm is contagious, so is depression. The physician treating a depressed patient may become mildly depressed himself, partly through identification (as in treating a patient dying from malignancy). The therapist may therefore develop his own resistances, resent the depressed patient, and wish to avoid him. The therapist's resentment may lead him to imagine that the patient is exaggerating his suffering, "putting on a show" to gain sympathy. The negative reaction of the therapist may also take the form of general lack of interest, theoretical and clinical.

Since major precautions against suicide cannot be taken for all depressed patients, one is often in the uncomfortable position of knowing that if the depression should increase the patient may attempt suicide—a threat to the therapist's reputation since suicide may expose him to criticism either as a poor therapist or as one who takes too many risks. Many therapists therefore avoid treating patients with tendencies to suicide. The justifications used for transferring such patients to others are many and ingenious; in fact, when an analyst refers a depressed patient to another, it is not uncommon for him to minimize the risk of suicide to avoid having the patient rejected.

When a depressed patient comes to a therapist for his first interview, he may present himself as incompetent, inadequate, and even hopeless. He may do so partly to protect himself from the narcissistic injury of rejection, like students who do little studying before examinations so that if they fail they can feel sure that had they really tried they could have done well. The therapist may be misled by a patient's manner of presenting himself, since he may appear more disturbed than he actually is. Furthermore, the therapist may intuitively feel the patient's strong narcissistic need and may fear the expression of transference hostility which may arise if narcissistic supplies are not forthcoming. Such reactions can lead therapists to avoid psychotherapy or psychoanalysis of many depressed patients who would benefit from it.

EPILOGUE

Epilogue: The Meaning of Despair

What has been presented here is the evolution of a psychoanalytic theory of depression. Through the diverse approaches of many authors a unified concept emerges. However, to claim the definitive answer, or even to claim objectivity would be arrogant and naive, as any book which selects a dozen articles out of hundreds written on the subject must be subjective. The very act of selection, unless it is random and purposeless, must define a point of view.

The first three articles would be included in any psychoanalytic study of depression. They represent an ordering of the clinical data, a defining of basic concepts, and a point of departure for all. The early researchers were superb clinical observers, and since psychiatry remains preeminently a clinical branch of medicine, this explains why students still find that reading these authors is rewarding.

Patterns of behavior seen in neuroses today remain essentially unchanged from those of fifty years ago. What has altered has been the understanding of the causes of the neurosis. In some conditions this has led to an ironic reversal in that which was considered cause and effect. The relationship of anxiety and repressed libido is perhaps the most

interesting example, because the reversal was made within
the cycle of Freud's own writing.

Freud originally viewed anxiety as a purely derivative
phenomenon. It was a result and expression of repressed
libido. In *Inhibitions, Symptoms, and Anxiety* he completely
reversed the relationship between the two. Here he viewed
anxiety as a primary response mechanism of the organism
to danger, and saw repression of libido as its resultant. That
is, whereas formerly anxiety was caused by repression of
libido, now anxiety causes repression of libido. This brilliant
reevaluation published in 1926 confounded many of Freud's
followers, who were quite content with his earlier explanations. Some of them still have difficulty accepting its implications, which perhaps explains why it took ten years for
an English translation to be prepared.

It has been my feeling that a similar reevaluation of
cause and effect is needed to understand depression, and the
subsequent articles demonstrate the evolution of that reversal. Originally, Freud saw self-attack and diminished self-
esteem as the *result* of depression (which in turn was due
to the loss of a loved object). In this sense it was again
purely derivative, an accidental result of the hostility toward
the loved object. We begin to see an enlargement of the
role of self-esteem and its movement from the periphery to
a more central position in the writings of Rado and Fenichel.
Nonetheless, it is still seen as effect rather than cause. Bibring
took the final position of reversing the roles and stating
that diminished self-esteem is the *cause* of depression. He
should have gone one step further.

It is intriguing to notice that, throughout his paper,
Bibring refers to the crises in self-*esteem* when, more specifically, he is describing self-*confidence*. In this he is con-

sistent with Fenichel. A careful reading of Fenichel indicates that he is talking about confidence in the operating capacity of the ego—coping, if you will. He does not mean self-esteem in terms of self-love, but rather the trust one has in one's own ego, in its ability to meet and solve problems essential to survival.

It is in paranoia that one sees a true crisis in self-esteem, with the consequent emphasis on shame and self-disgust. It is not the lovability but the dependability of self that is questioned in depressed patients. They feel helpless and hopeless, not humiliated. Recall the quotation from Bibring:

Depression can be defined as the emotional expression (indication) of the state of helplessness and powerlessness of the ego, irrespective of what may have caused the breakdown of the mechanism which established his self-esteem.

Obviously, the sense of helplessness will result in a lowered self-esteem, but it is caused by a shattered self-confidence. This inexactness is not characteristic of Bibring (nor of Fenichel, for that matter) and seemed puzzling to me until a colleague suggested (rightly, I think) that self-esteem is a residual of thinking in terms of libido theory. Having spent a lifetime explaining neuroses in terms of the disposition of sexual drive and energy, Bibring and Fenichel unwittingly are thinking in terms of cathexis. Self-esteem and self-love are traditionally explained in terms of investment of ego with sexual energy, whereas confidence is a step removed from that frame of reference.

There is a type of depressed patient in whom self-esteem does seem to be the paramount issue. This is the infantile and narcissistic individual who has never developed a sense of trust in the executive capacity of his ego. For him survival is always seen in terms of infantile dependency. Convinced of his weakness, he survives because of the protection of the strong and loving figures in his life. But loving figures require one to be loveworthy or lovable, and when a patient with this dynamic pattern loses his sense of self-worth, he feels he loses his loving protector and, with it, his security. This is precisely the patient who will have a depression precipitated by the loss of a loved object. Childhood depression is characteristically of this type.

What is important to realize is that depression can be precipitated by the loss or removal of *anything* that the individual overvalues in terms of his security. To the extent that one's sense of well-being, safety, or security is dependent on love, money, social position, power, drugs, or obsessional defenses—to that extent one will be threatened by its loss. When the reliance is preponderant, the individual despairs of survival and gives up. It is that despair which has been called depression.

Hopeless and helpless, he gives up the struggle. It is this abandonment which makes depression different from other psychological conditions. Bibring says the ego is paralyzed because it feels incapable of meeting life's dangers and Rado, too, talked of adaptational paralysis in depression.

This paralysis is what is so unique in depression. We are conditioned to look for the "meaning of symptoms"; a meaning in terms of problem-solving. Symptoms are the attempts of the individual to compromise his way out of a conflict situation. They are the reparative maneuvers and manipulations of the threatened ego. In depression, however, the distinguishing feature is the paucity of such maneuvers. The "symptoms" are the non-symptoms of passivity, inactivity, resignation, and despair. Here the reparative mechanisms are at a minimum. The depressive is not like the phobic who has found an illusion of safety through the mechanisms of displacement and avoidance. He has no illusions.

The disease represents the dissipation of the reparative movements, and as the nightmare indicates the breakdown of the dream mechanism, depression is the breakdown of the reparative function of symptom formation.

I have talked of paucity of reparative maneuvers rather than absence, because in psychiatry nothing is one hundred percent. It is true that the depressive has given up all hope of either fight or flight, but despite Bibring, and Rado before him, these are not the only survival mechanisms. They are not even the most fundamental. *Dependency* is the basic survival mechanism of the human organism. In the critical early period of life, the human animal is capable of neither fight nor flight—only clutch and cling. In the human being, with his disproportionately long period of helplessness, the very survival of the species is based on the built-in dependency maneuvers of the infant and the biologically determined sympathetic responses they elicit in the adult.

When the adult gives up hope in his ability to cope and sees himself incapable of either fleeing or fighting, he is "reduced" to a state of depression. This very reduction, with its parallel to the helplessness of infancy becomes, ironically, one last unconscious cry for help, a plea for a solution to the problem of survival via dependency. The very stripping of one's defenses becomes a form of defensive maneuver.

It is part of the wonder of man that even the state of hopelessness can be used to generate hope.

References

Chapter 2

1. Presented at the Third International Psycho-Analytical Conference, Weimar.
2. MAEDER, A. "Psychoanalyse bei einer melancholischen Depression," *Centralblatt für Nervenheilkunde und Psychiatrie,* 1910. A. A. Brill, "Ein Fall von periodischer Depression psychogenen Ursprungs," *Centralblatt für Nervenheilkunde und Psychiatrie,* 1911, *Bd. i.* Ernest Jones, "Psycho-Analytic Notes on a Case of Hypomania," *Bulletin of the Ontario Hospital for the Insane,* 1910.
3. MAEDER, A. *Op. cit.*
4. *Der Witz und seine Beziehung zum Unbewussten* (Vienna, 1905; fourth edition, 1925).
5. Liepmann, *Über Ideenflucht* (Halle, 1904).
6. See reference 1.

Chapter 3

1. The German "Trauer," like the English "mourning," can mean both the affect of grief and its outward manifestation. Throughout the present paper, the word has been rendered "mourning."
2. ABRAHAM (1911), to whom we owe the most important of the few analytic studies on this subject, also took this comparison as his starting point. Freud himself had already made the comparison in 1910 and even earlier. In some remarks in a discussion on suicide at the Vienna Psycho-Analytical Society in 1910 (Standard Ed., 11, 232), he stressed the importance of drawing a comparison between melancholia and normal states of mourning, but declared that the psychological problem involved was still insoluble.
3. Pain and the organism's method of dealing with it are discussed in Chapter IV of *Beyond the Pleasure Principle* (1920), *Standard Ed.* 18, 30. The subject is already raised in Part I, Section 6, of the "Project" (1895, *tr.* 1950).
4. Cf. "A Metapsychological Supplement to the Theory of Dreams," *Complete Works of Freud, Standard Ed.,* Vol. XIV, p. 230.

5. This idea seems to be expressed already in *Studies on Hysteria* (1895d): a process similar to this one will be found described near the beginning of Freud's "Discussion" of the case history of Fraulein Elisabeth von R. (*Standard Ed.*, **2**, 162.)

6. A discussion of the economics of this process will be found below on page 65.

7. "Use every man after his desert, and who shall scape whipping?" (Act II, Scene 2).

8. See "The Metapsychology of Dreams," *Complete Works, Standard Ed.*, Vol. IV, p. 233.

9. In the first (1917) edition only, this word does not occur.

10. In 1914.

11. See "Instincts and Their Vicissitudes," *Complete Works, Standard Ed.*, Vol. XIV, p. 138. Cf. also Editor's Note, pp. 241–2.

12. Abraham apparently first drew Freud's attention to this in a private letter written between February and April, 1915. See Jones's biography (1955), p. 368.

13. The whole subject of identification was discussed later by Freud in Chapter VII of his *Group Psychology* (1921), *Standard Ed.*, 105 ff. There is an earlier account of hysterical identification in *The Interpretation of Dreams* (1900), *Standard Ed.*, **4**, 149–51.

14. Much of what follows is elaborated in Chapter V of Freud's *The Ego and the Id* (1923).

15. For the distinction between the two, see paper on "Instincts and Their Vicissitudes," (*Complete Works, Standard Ed.*, Vol. XIV, pp. 138–9.)

16. Cf. "Instincts and Their Vicissitudes" (p. 136).

17. Later discussions of suicide will be found in Chapter V of *The Ego and the Id* (1923) and in the last pages of "The Economic Problem of Masochism" (1924).

18. This analogy of the open wound appears already (illustrated by two diagrams) in the rather abstruse Section VI of Freud's early note on melancholia (Freud, *The Origins of Psychoanalysis*, 1950, Draft G, probably written in January, 1895). See Editor's Note, *Standard Ed.*, p. 229.

19. The "psycho-analytic impression" and the "general economic experience."

20. The economic standpoint has hitherto received little attention in psycho-analytic writings. I would mention as an exception a paper by Victor Tausk (1913) on motives for repression devalued by recompenses. (Freud's note.)

21. "Dingvorstellung." See p. 201n, *Complete Works, Standard Ed.*, Vol. XIV.

22. Pain and the organism's method of dealing with it are discussed in Chapter IV of *Beyond the Pleasure Principle* (1920), *Stand-*

ard Ed. The subject is already raised in Part I, Section 6, of the "Project" (1895, *Tr.* 1950).

23. (Footnote added 1925:) Cf. a continuation of this discussion of mania in *Group Psychology and the Analysis of the Ego* (1921). (*Standard Ed.,* 18, 130–33.)

Chapter 4

1. ABRAHAM, K. "Notes on the Psycho-Analytical Investigation and Treatment of Manic-Depressive Insanity and Allied Conditions" (1911), *Selected Papers.* London: Hogarth Press, 1927.
2. FREUD, S. "Mourning and Melancholia" (1916), *Collected Papers,* Vol. IV. London: Hogarth Press and the Institute of Psychoanalysis, 1924.
3. ———— *The Ego and the Id* (1923). London: Hogarth Press and the Institute of Psychoanalysis, 1927.
4. ABRAHAM, K. "A Short Study of the Development of the Libido, Viewed in the Light of Mental Disorders" (1924), *Selected Papers on Psycho-Analysis.* London: Hogarth Press, 1927.
5. FREUD, S. "Mourning and Melancholia."
6. *Ibid.*
7. RADO, S. "An Anxious Mother," *International Journal of Psychoanalysis,* Vol. IX, 1928.
8. *Ibid.*
9. FREUD, S. *Introductory Lectures on Psycho-Analysis.* (1916/17). London: Allen and Unwin, 1922.
10. FREUD, S. *Hemmung, Symptom und Angst* (1926).
11. *Ibid.*
12. RADO, S. "The Psychical Effects of Intoxicants" (1926), *International Journal of Psycho-Analysis,* Vol. IX, 1928.
13. BERNFELD, S. *Psychologie des Säuglings.* Vienna, 1925.
14. FREUD, S. *Group Psychology and the Analysis of the Ego* (1921). London: Hogarth Press, 1922.
15. ABRAHAM, K. "A Short Study of the Development of the Libido."
16. *Ibid.*

Chapter 5

1. RADO, S. "Mind, Unconscious Mind, and Brain," *Psychosomatic Medicine,* Vol. XI:165, 1949.
2. ———— "An Anxious Mother: A Contribution to the Analysis of the Ego," *International Journal of Psycho-Analysis,* Vol. IX:219, 1928. S. Rado. "The Problem of Melancholia," *International Journal of Psycho-Analysis,* Vol. IX:420, 1928.
3. ———— *Patterns of Motivation in Depression.* 12th International

Psychoanalytic Congress, Wiesbaden, 1932. S. Rado. "The Psychoanalysis of Pharmacothymia (drug addiction)," *Psychoanalytic Quarterly*, Vol. II:1, 1933.

4. ────── Lectures at Columbia University.

5. FREUD, S. "Mourning and Melancholia," *Collected Papers*, Vol. IV: 152. London: Hogarth Press and the Institute of Psychoanalysis, 1924.

6. ABRAHAM, K. "Manic-Depressive States and the Pregenital Levels of the Libido," *Selected Papers*, p. 418. London: Hogarth Press, 1927.

7. RADO, S. "An Anxious Mother: A Contribution to the Analysis of the Ego," and "The Problem of Melancholia."

8. ────── *Patterns of Motivation in Depression.*

9. ────── "Emergency Behavior: With an Introduction to the Dynamics of Conscience," in *Anxiety*, Hoch and Zubin, eds. New York: Grune and Stratton, 1950.

10. ────── "An Adaptational View of Sexual Behavior," in *Psychosexual Development in Health and Disease*, Hoch and Zubin, eds. New York: Grune and Stratton, 1949.

11. ────── "Emergency Behavior: With an Introduction to the Dynamics of Conscience."

12. FREUD, S. *The Problem of Anxiety.* New York: W. W. Norton, 1936.

13. RADO, S. Lectures at Columbia University.

14. ABRAHAM, K. "Manic-Depressive States and the Pregenital Levels of the Libido."

15. RADO, S. "Emergency Behavior: With an Introduction to the Dynamics of Conscience," S. Rado. *Four Types: The Depressive, the Extractive, the Paranoid, and the Schizotype (Schizophrenic).*

16. ────── "Mind, Unconscious Mind, and Brain."

CHAPTER 6

1. RADO, S. "The Problem of Melancholia," *International Journal of Psycho-Analysis*, Vol. IX, 1928.

2. FREUD, S. "Mourning and Melancholia," *Collected Papers*, Vol. IV. London: Hogarth Press and the Institute of Psychoanalysis, 1924. G. Gero. "The Construction of Depression," *International Journal of Psycho-Analysis*, Vol. XVII, 1936. S. Rado. "The Problem of Melancholia."

3. ABRAHAM, K. "Notes on the Psychoanalytical Investigation and Treatment of Manic-Depressive Insanity and Allied Conditions," *Selected Papers*. London: Hogarth Press, 1927. K. Abraham. "A Short Study of the Development of the Libido," *Selected Papers*.

4. *Ibid.* K. Abraham. "The First Pregenital Stage of the Libido,"

Selected Papers. London: Hogarth Press, 1927. S. Freud. "Mourning and Melancholia."

5. BLANCO, I. M. "On Introjection and the Processes of Psychic Metabolism," *International Journal of Psycho-Analysis*, Vol. XXII, 1941.

6. ABRAHAM, K. "A Short Study of the Development of the Libido."

7. WULFF, M. "Zur Psychologie der Kinderlaunen," *Imago*, Vol. XV, 1929.

8. FREUD, S. "On Narcissism: An Introduction," *Collected Papers*, Vol. IV. London: Hogarth Press and the Institute of Psychoanalysis, 1924.

9. *Ibid.*

10. SCHILDER, P. "Notes on Psychogenic Depressions and Melancholia," *Psychoanalytic Review*, Vol. XX, 1933.

11. FREUD, S. "Mourning and Melancholia." S. Freud. *The Ego and the Id*. London: Hogarth Press and the Institute of Psychoanalysis, 1927.

12. ABRAHAM, K. "A Short Study of the Development of the Libido." S. Freud. "Mourning and Melancholia."

13. FREUD, S. "Mourning and Melancholia."

14. ABRAHAM, K. "A Short Study of the Development of the Libido."

15. FREUD, S. *The Ego and the Id*.

16. ———— *Totem and Taboo*. New York: Moffat, Yard, 1918. H. Zulliger. "Beitrage zur Psychologie der Trauer- und Bestattungsgebraeuche," *Imago*, Vol. X, 1924.

17. FREUD, S. *Group Psychology and the Analysis of the Ego*. London: International Psychoanalytic Press, 1922. H. Zulliger, "Beitrage zur Psychologie der Trauer- und Bestattungsgebraeuche."

18. ZULLIGER, H. "Die Roichtschaeggeten." *Imago*, Vol. XIV, 1928.

19. FREUD, S. *The Ego and the Id*.

20. ———— "Thoughts for the Times on War and Death," *Collected Papers*, Vol. IV. London: Hogarth Press and the Institute of Psychoanalysis, 1924.

21. DEUTSCH, H. "Absence of Grief," *Psychoanalytic Quarterly*, Vol. VI, 1937.

22. ABRAHAM, K. "A Short Study of the Development of the Libido." S. Freud. *The Ego and the Id*.

23. FREUD, S. "Mourning and Melancholia."

24. *Ibid.*

25. FENICHEL, O. "Die Identifizierung," *Internationale Zeitschrift fuer Psychoanalyse*, Vol. XII, 1926.

26. DEUTSCH, H. "The Genesis of Agoraphobia," *International Journal of Psycho-Analysis*, Vol. X, 1929. *Psychoanalysis of the Neuroses*. London: Hogarth Press and the Institute of Psychoanalysis, 1933.

27. ———— *Psychoanalysis of the Neuroses*.

28. FREUD, S. "Mourning and Melancholia."
29. ABRAHAM, K. "A Short Study of the Development of the Libido."
30. Ibid.
31. WEISS, E. "Der Vergiftungswahn im Lichte der Introjektions- und Projektionsvorgaenge," Internationale Zeitschrift fuer Psychoanalyse, Vol. XII, 1926.
32. KIELHOLZ, A. "Giftmord und Vergiftungswahn," Internationale Zeitschrift fuer Psychoanalyse, Vol. XVII, 1931.
33. FREUD, S. "Humor," International Journal of Psycho-Analysis, Vol. XI, 1928.
34. RADO, S. "The Problem of Melancholia."
35. FREUD, S. The Ego and the Id.
36. BENDER, L., and P. SCHILDER. "Suicidal Preoccupations and Attempts in Children," American Journal of Orthopsychiatry, Vol. VII, 1937. S. Bernfeld. "Selbstmord," Zeitschrift fuer Psychoanalytische Paedagogik, Vol. III, 1929. S. Freud. "Einlietung und Schlusswort zur Selbstmord-Diskussion," in Ueber den Selbstmord, insbes. den Schuelerselbstmord. Wiesbaden: Bergmann, 1910. J. Friedjung, "Zur Kenntnis kindlicher Selbstmordimpule," Zeitschrift fuer Psychoanalytische Paedagogik, Vol. III, 1929. Wiener Psychoanalytische Vereinigung. "Ueber den Selbstmord, insbesondere den Schuelerselbstmord." Diskussion. Wiesbaden: 1910.
37. CLARK, L. P. "A Study of Unconscious Motivations in Suicides," New York Medical Journal, September 1922. N. D. C. Lewis. "Studies on Suicides," Psychoanalytic Review, Vol. XX, 1933, and Vol. XXI, 1934. L. Peller-Roubiczek. "Zur Kenntnis der Selbstmordhandlung," Imago, Vol. XXII, 1936. B. Warburg. "Suicide, Pregnancy and Rebirth," Psychoanalytic Quarterly, Vol. VII, 1938.
38. HENDRICK, I. "Suicide as Wish Fulfillment," Psychiatric Quarterly, Vol. XIV, 1940.
39. ZILBOORG, G. "Differential Diagnostic Types of Suicide," Archive for Neurology and Psychiatry, Vol. XXXV, 1936. G. Zilboorg. "Considerations on Suicide, with Particular Reference to that of the Young," American Journal of Orthopsychiatry, Vol. VIII, 1937.
40. FRIEDLANDER-MISCH, K. "On the Longing to Die," International Journal of Psycho-Analysis, Vol. XXI, 1940. A. Garma. "Psychologie des Selbstmordes," Imago, Vol. XXIII, 1937.
41. REICH, W. Psychischer Kontakt und vegetative Stroemung. Kopenhagen: Sexpol Verlag, 1935.
42. BROMBERG, W., and P. SCHILDER. "Death and Dying," Psychoanalytic Review, Vol. XX, 1933. W. Bromberg and P. Schilder. "Attitude of Psychoneurotics towards Death," Psychoanalytic Review, Vol. XXIII, 1936. E. H. Connell. "The Significance of the Idea of Death in the Neurotic Mind," British Journal of Medical

Psychology, Vol. IV, 1924. J. Glover. "Notes on the Psychopathology of Suicide," *International Journal of Psycho-Analysis,* Vol. III, 1922. F. Moellenhoff. "Ideas of Children about Death," *Bulletin of the Menninger Clinic,* Vol. III, 1939. H. Sachs. "Das Thema 'Tod,'" *Imago,* Vol. III, 1914. G. Zilboorg. "Suicide among Civilized and Primitive," *American Journal of Psychiatry,* Vol. XCII, 1936.

43. THORNER, H. A. "The Mode of Suicide as a Manifestation of Fantasy," *British Journal of Medical Psychology,* Vol. XVII, 1938.

44. RADO, S. "The Problem of Melancholia."

45. BRILL, A. A. "The Concept of Psychic Suicide," *International Journal of Psycho-Analysis,* Vol. XX, 1939. K. A. Menninger. "Psychoanalytic Aspects of Suicide," *International Journal of Psycho-Analysis,* Vol. XIV, 1933. K. A. Menninger. "Organic Suicide," *Bulletin of the Menninger Clinic,* Vol. I, 1937.

46. HARNIK, J. "Introjection and Projection in the Mechanism of Depression," *International Journal of Psycho-Analysis,* Vol. XIII, 1932.

47. FREUD, S. *Introductory Lectures to Psychoanalysis.* New York: Boni and Liveright, 1920.

48. ABRAHAM, K. "A Short Study of the Development of the Libido."

49. *Ibid.*

50. JACOBSON, E. "Depression, the Oedipus Complex in the Development of Depressive Mechanisms," *Psychoanalytic Quarterly,* Vol. XII, 1943.

51. FREUD, S. *The Future of an Illusion.* London: Hogarth Press, 1928.

52. NICOLINI, W. "Verbrechen aus Heimweh und ihre psychoanalytische Erklaerung," *Imago,* Vol. XXII, 1936.

53. FREUD, S. "Mourning and Melancholia."

54. ———— "On Narcissism: An Introduction."

55. ABRAHAM, K. "The Applicability of Psychoanalytic Treatment to Patients at an Advanced Age," *Selected Papers.* London: Hogarth Press, 1927. M. R. Kaufmann. "Psychoanalysis in Late-Life Depressions," *Psychoanalytic Quarterly,* Vol. VI, 1937.

56. JONES, E. "Psychoanalyitic Notes on a Case of Hypomania," *American Journal of Insanity,* 1909. P. Schilder. "Vorstudien einer Psychologie der Manie," *Zeitschrift fuer die gesamte Neurologie und Psychiatrie,* Vol. LXVIII, 1928.

57. FREUD, S. *Group Psychology and the Analysis of the Ego.*

58. FENICHEL, O. "Ueber Trophäe und Triumph," *Internationale Zeitschrift fuer Psychoanalyse,* Vol. XXIV, 1939.

59. FREUD, S. *Wit and Its Relation to the Unconscious.* New York: Moffat, Yard, 1916.

60. FENICHEL, O. "Ueber Trophäe und Triumph."

61. ABRAHAM, K. "A Short Study of the Development of the Libido." *cf. also* I. M. Blanco. "On Introjection and the Processes of Psychic Metabolism." H. W. Eddison. "The Love Object in Mania," *International Journal of Psycho-Analysis*, Vol. XV, 1934.

62. LEWIN, B. D. "Analysis and Structure of a Transient Hypomania," *Psychoanalytic Quarterly*, Vol. I, 1932. B. D. Lewin. "A Type of Neurotic Hypomanic Reaction," *Archive for Neurology and Psychiatry*, Vol. XXXVII, 1937. B. D. Lewin. "Concepts on Hypomanic and Related States," *Psychoanalytic Review*, Vol. XXVII, 1941.

63. ———— "Analysis and Structure of a Transient Hypomania."

64. FREUD, S. *Totem and Taboo.* S. Freud. *Group Psychology and the Analysis of the Ego.*

65. ———— *Group Psychology and the Analysis of the Ego.*

66. JEKELS, L. "Zur Psychologie der Komodie," *Imago,* Vol. XII, 1926.

67. FREUD, S. *Totem and Taboo.*

68. ALMASY, E. "Daten zur manischen Assoziation und Affektuebertragung," *Zeitschrift fuer Sexualwissenschaften,* Vol. XIX, 1933. H. Deutsch. "Zur Psychologie der manisch-depressiven Zustaende, insbesondere der chronischen Hypomanie," *Zeitschrift fuer Sexualwissenschaften,* Vol. XIX, 1933. S. Freud. "Mourning and Melancholia." B. D. Lewin. "Analysis and Structure of a Transient Hypomania."

69. DEUTSCH, H. "Zur Psychologie der manisch-depressiven Zustaende, insbesondere der chronischen Hypomanie."

70. FREUD, S. *Group Psychology and the Analysis of the Ego.*

71. MASSERMAN, J. H. "Psychodynamisms in Manic-Depressive Psychoses," *Psychoanalytic Review,* Vol. XXVIII, 1941.

72. DEUTSCH, H. *Zur Psychologie der weiblichen Sexualfunktionen.* Vienna: Internationaler Psychoanalytischer Verlag, 1925.

73. CHADWICK, M. *Women's Periodicity.* London: Noel Douglass, 1933.

74. ABRAHAM, K. "Notes on the Psychoanalytical Investigation and Treatment of Manic-Depressive Insanity and Allied Conditions."

75. ———— "The First Pregenital Stage of the Libido."

76. FREUD, S. "Mourning and Melancholia."

77. ABRAHAM, K. "A Short Study of the Development of the Libido."

78. RADO, S. "The Problem of Melancholia."

79. FREUD, S. *Group Psychology and the Analysis of the Ego.*

80. GERO, G. "The Construction of Depression." E. Jacobson. "Depression, the Oedipus Complex in the Development of Depressive Mechanisms." S. Lorand. "Dynamics and Therapy of Depressive States," *Psychoanalytic Review,* Vol. XXIV, 1937.

81. ABRAHAM, K. "A Short Study of the Development of the Libido."

82. *Ibid.*

CHAPTER 7

1. FREUD, S. "Mourning and Melancholia," *Collected Papers*, Vol. IV. London: Hogarth Press and the Institute of Psychoanalysis, 1924.
2. ABRAHAM, K. "The First Pregenital Stage of the Libido," *Selected Papers*. London: Hogarth Press, 1927.
3. ———— "A Short Study of the Development of the Libido," *Selected Papers*. London: Hogarth Press, 1927.
4. RADO, S. "The Problem of Melancholia," *International Journal of Psycho-Analysis*, Vol. IX, 1928.
5. FENICHEL, O. *The Psychoanalytic Theory of Neurosis*. New York: W. W. Norton, 1945.
6. WEISS, E. "Clinical Aspects of Depression," *Psychoanalytic Quarterly*, Vol. XIII, 1944.
7. FEDERN, P. "Some Variations in Ego Feeling," *International Journal of Psycho-Analysis*, Vol. VII, 1926.
8. JACOBSON, E. "The Effect of Disappointment on Ego and Superego Formation in Normal and Depressive Development," *Psychoanalytic Review*, Vol. XXXIII, 1946.
9. LEWIN, B. D. *The Psychoanalysis of Elation*. New York: W. W. Norton, 1950.
10. FENICHEL, O. "Zur Psychologie der Langeweile," *Imago*, Vol. XX, 1934.
11. GREENSON, R. R. "On Boredom," *Journal of the American Psychoanalytic Association*, Vol. I, 1953.
12. FREUD, S. *The Problem of Anxiety*. New York: W. W. Norton, 1936.
13. ERIKSON, E. H. *Childhood and Society*. New York: W. W. Norton, 1950.
14. JACOBSON, E. "The Effect of Disappointment on Ego and Superego Formations in Normal and Depressive Development."
15. HORNEY, K. *Our Inner Conflicts*. New York: W. W. Norton, 1945.
16. DEUTSCH, H. "Ueber Zufriedenheit, Glück und Ekstase," *Internationale Zeitschrift für Psychoanalyse*, Vol. XIII, 1927. H. Deutsch. "Zur Psychologie der manisch-depressiven Zustande, insbesondere der chronischen Hypomanie," *Internationale Zeitschrift für Psychonalyse*, Vol. XIX, 1933.

CHAPTER 8

1. GLOVER, E. "A Psycho-Analytic Approach to the Classification of Mental Disorders," *Journal of Mental Science*, October 1932.
2. FREUD, S. "Notes upon a Case of Obsessional Neurosis" (1909), *Collected Papers*, Vol. III. London: Institute of Psychoanalysis and Hogarth Press.

3. SCHMIDEBERG, M. "The Rôle of Psychotic Mechanisms in Cultural Development," *International Journal of Psycho-Analysis*, Vol. XII, 1931.
4. DEUTSCH, H. "Zur Psychologie der manisch-depressiven Zustände," *Zeitschrift fuer Sexualwissenschaften*, Vol. XIX, 1933.
5. GLOVER, E. "A Psycho-Analytic Approach to the Classification of Mental Disorders."
6. KLEIN, M. "Early Stages of the Oedipus Conflict," *International Journal of Psychoanalysis*, Vol. IX, 1928. M. Klein. "Personification in the Play of Children," *International Journal of Psycho-Analysis*, Vol. X, 1929.
7. ———— *The Psycho-Analysis of Children*, chap. VIII. London: Hogarth Press and Institute of Psychoanalysis, 1932.
8. RADO, S. "The Problem of Melancholia," *International Journal of Psycho-Analysis*, Vol. IX, 1928.
9. SCHMIDEBERG, M. "Psychotic Mechanisms in Cultural Development," *International Journal of Psycho-Analysis* Vol. XI, 1930.

CHAPTER 9

1. ABRAHAM, K. "Notes on the Psychoanalytical Investigation and Treatment of Manic-Depressive Insanity and Allied Conditions," *Selected Papers*. London: Hogarth Press, 1927.
2. FREUD, S. "Mourning and Melancholia," *Collected Papers*, Vol. IV. London: Hogarth Press and the Institute of Psycho-Analysis, 1924.
3. SPITZ, R. A. "Hospitalism; An Inquiry into the Genesis of Psychiatric Conditions in Early Childhood," *The Psychoanalytic Study of the Child*, Vol. I, 1945.
4. ABRAHAM, K. "Notes on the Psychoanalytical Investigation and Treatment of Manic-Depressive Insanity and Allied Conditions."
5. ———— *Ibid*. K. Abraham. "The First Pregenital Stage of the Libido," *Selected Papers*. London: Hogarth Press, 1927. K. Abraham. "A Short Study of the Development of the Libido," *Ibid*. S. Freud. "Mourning and Melancholia."
6. FENICHEL, O. *The Psychoanalytic Theory of Neurosis*. New York: W. W. Norton, 1945.
7. KLEIN, M. "Emotional Life and Ego Development of the Infant, with Special Reference to the Depressive Position," Controversial Series of the London Psychoanalytic Society, IV, *Discussion*, March 1944.
8. ———— *Ibid*. M. Klein. *The Psycho-Analysis of Children*. London: Hogarth Press and the Institute of Psycho-Analysis, 1932. M. Klein. "Mourning and Its Relation to Manic-Depressive States,"

International Journal of Psycho-Analysis, Vol. XXI, 1940. M.
Klein. "The Oedipus Complex in the Light of Early Anxieties,"
International Journal of Psycho-Analysis, Vol. XXVI, 1945.

9. RIVIERE, J. "Original Papers on the Genesis of Psychical Conflict
in Earliest Infancy," *International Journal of Psycho-Analysis,*
Vol. XVII, 1936.

10. KLEIN, M. "Emotional Life and Ego Development of the Infant."

11. RANK, O. *Das Trauma der Geburt und seine Bedeutung für die
Psychoanalyse.* Vienna: Internationale Psychoanalytischer Verlag,
1924.

12. HETZER, H. and K. M. WOLF. "Baby Tests," *Zeischrift für Psychologie,* 1928. R. A. Spitz and K. M. Wolf. "Diacritic and Co-
enesthetic Organizations," *Psychoanalytic Review,* Vol. XXXII,
April 1945.

13. BÜHLER, C. *Kindheit und Jugend.* Leipzig, 1931. H. Hetzer and
K. M. Wolf. "Baby Tests." A. T. Jersild and F. B. Holmes. "Chil-
dren's Fear," *Child Development Monographs,* 1935. M. M.
Shirley. *"The First Two Years, A Study of Twenty-Five Babies,"*
Vol. II. Minneapolis: Minnesota Press, 1933.

14. SPITZ, R. A. and K. M. WOLF. "The Smiling Response: A Contribution to the Ontogenesis of Social Relations," *General Psychology
Monographs,* XXXIV, 1, 1946.

15. SPITZ, R. A. "Hospitalism: An Inquiry into the Genesis of Psychiatric Conditions in Early Childhood."

16. FENICHEL, O. *The Psychoanalytic Theory of Neurosis,* p. 402. J.
Harnik. "Introjection and Projection in the Mechanism of Depression," *International Journal of Psycho-Analysis,* Vol. XIII,
1932.

17. ABRAHAM, K. "A Short Study of the Development of the Libido."
O. Fenichel. *The Psychoanalytic Theory of Neurosis,* p. 404.
E. Jacobson. "Depression: The Oedipus Conflict in the Develop-
ment of Depressive Mechanisms," *Psychoanalytic Quarterly,* Vol.
XII, 1943.

18. ABRAHAM, K. "A Short Study of the Development of the Libido."

CHAPTER 10

1. BOWLBY, J. "Grief and Mourning in Infancy and Early Childhood," *Psycho-Analytic Study of the Child,* Vol. XV, 1960, pp.
9–52.

2. DARWIN, C. *The Expression of the Emotions in Man and Animals.*
London: Murray, 1872.

3. SHAND, A. F. *The Foundations of Character,* 2d ed. London, Mac-
millan, 1920.

4. WALLER, W. W. *The Family, a Dynamic Interpretation*, rev. ed. New York: Dryden, 1951.
5. ELIOT, T. D. "Bereavement: Inevitable but not Insurmountable," in *Family, Marriage and Parenthood*, Becker and Hill, eds. Boston: Heath, 1955.
6. MARRIS, P. *Widows and Their Families*. London: Routledge, 1958.
7. WYNNE, L. "The Contribution of Innate Imitative Tendencies to Identification Processes."
8. BOWLBY, J. "The Nature of the Child's Tie to His Mother," *International Journal of Psycho-Analysis*, Vol. XXXIX, 1958, pp. 350–373.
9. HINDE, R. A. "Energy Models of Motivation," in *Symposia of the Society of Experimental Biology*, Vol. XIV. London: Cambridge University Press, 1960.
10. BOWLBY, J. "Separation Anxiety," *International Journal of Psycho-Analysis*, Vol. XLI, 1960, pp. 89–113. J. Bowlby, "Grief and Mourning in Infancy and Early Childhood."
11. DARWIN, C. *The Expression of the Emotions in Man and Animals*.
12. BIBRING, E. "The Mechanisms of Depression," in *Affective Disorders*, Greenacre, ed. New York: International Universities Press, 1953.
13. RADO, S. "An Anxious Mother," *International Journal of Psycho-Analysis*, Vol. XLII, 1928, pp. 219–226.
14. BOWLBY, J. "Separation Anxiety."
15. FREUD, S. "The Dynamics of the Transference," *Standard Edition*, Vol. XXII, p. 106.
16. —————— "Totem and Taboo," *Standard Edition*, Vol. XIII, p. 60.
17. —————— "A Case of Homosexuality in a Woman," *Standard Edition*, Vol. XX, pp. 162–163.
18. —————— "Mourning and Melancholia," *Standard Edition*, Vol. XIV, pp. 250 and 256.
19. LINDEMANN, E. "Symptomatology and Management of Acute Grief," *American Journal of Psychiatry*, Vol. CI, 1944, pp. 141–148.
20. MARRIS, P. *Widows and Their Families*.
21. ELIOT, T. D. "Bereavement: Inevitable but not Insurmountable."
22. DURKHEIM, E. *The Elementary Forms of the Religious Life*. London: Allen and Unwin, 1915.
23. SHAND, A. F. *The Foundations of Character*.
24. BIBRING, E. "The Mechanisms of Depression."
25. JACOBSON, E. "Normal and Pathological Moods: Their Nature and Functions," *Psychoanalytic Study of the Child*, Vol. XII, 1957, pp. 73–113.
26. FREUD, S. "Instincts and Their Vicissitudes," *Standard Edition*, Vol. XIV, p. 139.

27. HINDE, R. A., W. H. THORPE, and M. A. VINCE. "The Following Response of Young Coot and Moorhens," *Behaviour*, Vol. IX, 1956, pp. 214–242.
28. KLEIN, M. "Mourning and Its Relation to Manic-Depressive States," in *Contributions to Psycho-Analysis, 1921–45*, Klein. London: Hogarth Press, 1948.
29. ENGEL, G. "Is Grief a Disease?" *Psychomatic Medicine*, Vol. XXIII, 1961, pp. 18–22.
30. FREUD, S. "Totem and Taboo," p. 65.
31. ——— *Standard Edition*, Vol. XIV, pp. 244, 249.
32. ——— "Inhibitions, Symptoms and Anxiety," *Standard Edition*, Vol. XX, p. 172.
33. ——— "Mourning and Melancholia."
34. ——— "Inhibitions, Symptoms and Anxiety," pp. 171–172.
35. ——— *Standard Edition*, Vol. XIV, p. 240.
36. ——— "Totem and Taboo," pp. 63–65.
37. ——— *Standard Edition*, Vol. XIV, p. 244.
38. ——— *Standard Edition*, Vol. XIV, p. 269.
39. JONES, E. *Sigmund Freud: Life and Work*, Vol. II. London: Hogarth Press, 1955.
40. FREUD, S. *Standard Edition*, Vol. XIV, pp. 249–250.
41. ABRAHAM, K. "Notes on the Psycho-Analytical Investigation and Treatment of Manic-Depressive Insanity and Allied Conditions," *Selected Papers*. London: Hogarth Press, 1927.
42. ——— *Selected Papers*, p. 143.
43. ——— *Selected Papers*, p. 275.
44. ——— "A Short Study of the Development of the Libido," *Selected Papers*.
45. *Ibid.*, pp. 436–437.
46. BURLINGHAM, D. and A. FREUD. *Infants with Families*. London: Allen and Unwin, 1944.
47. KLEIN, M. "Mourning and Its Relation to Manic-Depressive States."
48. RADO, S. "The Problem of Melancholia," *International Journal of Psycho-Analysis*, Vol. IX, 1928, pp. 420–438.
49. KLEIN, M. "A Contribution to the Psychogenesis of the Manic-Depressive States," in *Contributions to Psycho-Analysis, 1921–45*, Klein. London: Hogarth Press, 1948.
50. ——— *Contributions to Psycho-Analysis, 1921–45*, p. 307.
51. ——— "Weaning," in *On the Bringing Up of Children*, Rickman, ed. London: Kegan Paul, 1936.
52. RADO, S. "The Problem of Melancholia."
53. GLOVER, E. "A Psycho-Analytic Approach to the Classification of Mental Disorders," *Journal of Mental Science*, Vol. LXXVIII, 1932.

54. BALINT, M. "New Beginning and the Paranoid and the Depressive Syndromes," in *Primary Love and Psycho-Analytic Technique*, Balint. London: Hogarth Press, 1953.

55. —— *Primary Love and Psycho-Analytic Technique*, pp. 258–259. M. Balint. "Primary Narcissism and Primary Love," *Psychoanalytic Quarterly*, Vol. XXIX, 1960, pp. 6–43.

56. JACOBSON, E. "Normal and Pathological Moods: Their Nature and Functions."

57. BIBRING, E. "The Mechanisms of Depression."

58. *Ibid.*

59. FREUD, S. *Standard Edition*, Vol. II, p. 162.

60. LINDEMANN, E. "Symptomatology and Management of Acute Grief."

61. LORENZ, K. *King Solomon's Ring*. London: Methuen, 1952.

62. —— *Man Meets Dog*. London: Methuen, 1954.

63. TANNER, J. M. and B. INHELDER. *Discussions on Child Development*, Vol. I. London: Tavistock, 1956.

64. MANN, T. *Bashan*. (English trans.) London: Collins, 1923.

65. YERKES, R. M. *Chimpanzees: A Laboratory Colony*. New Haven: Yale University Press, 1943.

66. Zedtwitz, F. X. von. "Beobachtungen in Zoologischen Garten Berlin," *Der Zoologischen Garten*, Vol. II, 1929–1930.

67. POLLOCK, G. H. "Mourning and Adaptation," *International Journal of Psycho-Analysis*, Vol. XLII, 1961, p. 341.

68. LEVY, D. M. "Animal Psychology and Its Relation to Psychiatry," in *Dynamic Psychiatry*, Alexander and Ross, eds. Chicago: University Press, 1952.

69. TINKELPAUGH, O. L. "The Self-Mutilation of a Male Macacus Rhesus Monkey," *Journal of Mammalogy*, Vol. IX, 1928, p. 293.

70. ROMANES, G. J. *Mental Evolution in Man*. London: Kegan Paul, 1888.

71. YERKES, R. M. *Chimpanzees: A Laboratory Colony*.

72. POLLOCK, G. H. "Mourning and Adaptation."

73. YERKES, R. M. *Almost Human*. New York: Century, 1925.

74. TINKELPAUGH, O. L. "The Self-Mutilation of a Male Macacus Rhesus Monkey."

75. CAIN, A. C. "The Presuperego 'Turning-inward' of Aggression," *Psychoanalytic Quarterly*, Vol. XXX, pp. 171–208.

76. DEUTSCH, H. "Absence of Grief," *Psychoanalytic Quarterly*, Vol. VI, pp. 12–22.

77. BRACKBILL, Y. "Extinction of the Smiling Response in Infants as a Function of Reinforcement Schedule," *Child Development*, Vol. XXIX, 1958, pp. 115–124.

78. RHEINGOLD, H. J., J. L. GEWIRTZ, and H. W. ROSS. "Social Condi-

tioning of Vocalizations in the Infant," *Journal of Comparative and Physiological Psychology*, Vol. LII, 1959, pp. 68–73.

79. FENICHEL, O. *The Psychoanalytic Theory of Neurosis*. New York: W. W. Norton, 1945.

80. ROBERTSON, J. Film: *A Two-Year-Old Goes to Hospital* (1952). London: Tavistock Child Development Research Unit. New York: Univ. Film Library.

81. ——— *Guide to the Film "A Two-Year-Old Goes to Hospital* (1953). London: Tavistock, 2d ed. 1958.

82. ANDERSON, C. "Aspects of Pathological Grief and Mourning," *International Journal of Psycho-Analysis*, Vol. XXX, 1949, pp. 48–55.

83. FREUD, S. *Standard Edition*, Vol. XIV, p. 255.

84. LINDEMANN, E. "Symptomatology and Management of Acute Grief."

85. BALINT, M. *Primary Love and Psycho-Analytic Technique*, pp. 248 and 264.

86. FRANK, R. L. "The Organized Adaptive Aspect of the Depression-Elation Response," in *Depression*, Hoch and Zubin, eds. New York: Grune and Stratton, 1954.

87. RITTER, C. *A Woman in the Polar Night*. New York: Dutton, 1954.

88. FREUD, S. "Mourning and Melancholia," "Inhibitions, Symptoms and Anxiety."

89. LEWIN, B. *The Psycho-Analysis of Elation*. London: Hogarth Press, 1951.

90. GOLDSTEIN, K. *The Organism*. New York: American Book Co., 1939.

91. FREUD, S. "Splitting of the Ego in the Defensive Process," *Collected Papers*, Vol. V. London: Hogarth Press and the Institue of Psychoanalysis, 1924.

92. LINDEMANN, E. "Symptomatology and Management of Acute Grief."

93. BENEDEK, T. *Insight and Personality Adjustment: A Study of the Psychological Effects of War*. New York: Ronald Press, 1946.

94. COCHRANE, A. L. "Notes on the Psychology of Prisoners of War," *British Medical Journal*, Vol. I, 1946, pp. 282–284.

95. NEWMAN, P. H. "The Prisoner-of-War Mentality: Its Effects after Repatriation," *British Medical Journal*, Vol. I, 1944, pp. 8–10.

96. CURLE, A. "Transitional Communities and Social Re-Connection," *Human Relations*, Vol. I, 1947, pp. 42–68.

97. LILLY, J. C. "Mental Effects of Reduction of Ordinary Levels of Physical Stimuli on Intact, Healthy Persons," *Psychiatric Research Reports of the American Psychiatric Association*, Vol. V, 1956, pp. 1–9.

CHAPTER 12

1. ABRAHAM, K. "Notes on the Psychoanalytic Investigation and Treatment of Manic-Depressive Insanity and Allied Conditions," *Selected Papers on Psychoanalysis.* New York: Basic Books, 1953. K. Abraham. "A Short Study of the Development of the Libido," *Ibid.*
2. GERO, G. "The Construction of Depression," *International Journal of Psycho-Analysis,* Vol. XVII, 1936, pp. 423–461.

CHAPTER 13

1. BIBRING, E. "The Mechanism of Depression," in *Affective Disorders. Psychoanalytic Contribution to Their Study,* P. Greenacre, ed. New York: International Universities Press, 1953.
2. MENDELSON, M. *Pychoanalytic Concepts of Depression.* Springfield, Ill.: Charles C. Thomas, 1960.
3. EISSLER, K. R. *The Psychiatrist and the Dying Patient.* New York: International Universities Press, 1955, p. 144.
4. BIBRING, E. "Psychoanalysis and the Dynamic Psychotherapies," *Journal of the American Psychoanalytic Association,* Vol. II, 1954, pp. 745–770.
5. BERLINER, B. "The Role of Object Relations in Moral Masochism," *Psychoanalytic Quarterly,* Vol. XXVII, 1958, pp. 38–56. M. Brenman. "On Teasing and Being Teased; and the Problem of 'Moral Masochism,'" in *The Psychoanalytic Study of the Child,* Vol. VII. New York: International Universities Press, 1952, pp. 264–285. C. Brenner. "The Masochistic Character: Genesis and Treatment," *Journal of the American Psychoanalytic Association,* Vol. VII, 1959, pp. 197–226. G. Bychowski. "Some Aspects of Masochistic Involvement," *Ibid.,* pp. 248–273. L. Eidelberg. "Technical Problems in the Analysis of Masochists," *Journal of Hillside Hospital,* Vol. VII, 1958, pp. 98–109. S. Freud. "The Economic Problem in Masochism," *Collected Papers,* Vol. II. London: Institute of Psychoanalysis and Hogarth Press, 1924, pp. 255–268. E. Menaker. "Masochism—a Defense Reaction of the Ego," *Psychoanalytic Quarterly,* Vol. XXII, 1953, pp. 205–220. E. Menaker. "The Self-Image as Defense and Resistance," *Psychoanalytic Quarterly,* Vol. XXIX, 1960, pp. 72–81.
6. LEVIN, S. "Depression in the Aged: A Study of the Salient External Factors," *Geriatrics,* Vol. XVIII, 1963.
7. FREUD, S. "Mourning and Melancholia" (1917), *Standard Edition,* Vol. XIV.
8. MENAKER, E. "The Self-Image as Defense and Resistance."
9. FREUD, S. "Mourning and Melancholia."

10. WAELDER, R. *Some Reflections on the Role and Manifestations of Narcissism in Ordinary Life and in Psychopathology.* Symposium on Narcissism, Boston Psychoanalytic Society and Institute, April 1962.

11. FREUD, S. "Notes Upon a Case of Obsessional Neurosis" (1909), *Standard Edition,* Vol. X., p. 166.

12. LEVIN, S. "Mastery of Fear in Psychoanalysis," *Psychoanalytic Quarterly,* Vol. XXXIII, 1964, pp. 375–387.

Index